6-23-06

SING SING

THE INSIDE STORY
OF A NOTORIOUS PRISON

DENIS BRIAN

Prometheus Books

59 John Glenn Drive
Amherst, New York 14228-2197

Published 2005 by Prometheus Books

Inquiries should be addressed to
Prometheus Books
59 John Glenn Drive
Amherst, New York 14228–2197
VOICE: 716–691–0133, ext. 207
FAX: 716–564–2711
WWW.PROMETHEUSBOOKS.COM

09 08 07 06 05   5 4 3 2 1

Library of Congress Cataloging-in-Publication Data

Brian, Denis.
    Sing Sing : the inside story of a notorious prison / by Denis Brian.
        p. cm.
    Includes bibliographical references and index.
    ISBN 1–59102–357–2 (hardcover : alk. paper)
    1. Sing Sing Prison—History. I. Title.

HV9475N72S562 2005
365'.9747'277—dc22

                                                                        2005020039

Printed in the United States of America on acid-free paper

To Martine, Danielle, Alex, and Emma, with love

CONTENTS

Acknowledgments   9

Introduction   11

1. Riding the Tiger (1821–1839)   15

2. Another Reign of Terror (1840–1859)   33

3. Abraham Lincoln Passes Through (1860–1887)   41

4. Thomas Edison Promotes His Rival's Electric Chair (1887–1904)   47

5. The Convict Who Trapped Himself and the Great River Disaster (1904–1914)   63

6. Warden Osborne—The Voluntary Prisoner (1913–1920)   85

7. Warden Lawes and the Rose Man of Sing Sing (1920–1929)   113

8. Murder Incorporated and the Movies (1930–1949)   145

9. The Lonely Hearts Killers and the Rosenbergs (1950–1982)   167

8   CONTENTS

10. Riots and Reforms (1980s and 1990s)   193

11. Recovering the Prison's Missing Archives   207

12. Sing Sing in the Twenty-first Century   223

     Afterword: Sing Sing Today and Tomorrow   239

     Notes   245

     Select Bibliography   255

     Index   259

ACKNOWLEDGMENTS

Many thanks to my editor, Linda Regan, for her enthusiasm, encouragement, and challenging questions.

Many thanks to my wife, Martine, for her always invaluable advice, support, and help.

INTRODUCTION

If Sing Sing can be epitomized in a sentence,
it's on a tablet in the prison's hospital.
The Latin phrase reads: *Nihil Humani Probis Alienum*—
Nothing Human Is Foreign to Us.

The story of Sing Sing, the notorious maximum-security prison on the Hudson River, encompasses much of this country's vivid and violent history. Built in 1825, the year John Quincy Adams became president, its time frame covers the Lincoln era—he drove through it twice by train, the second time in his coffin—the Civil War, New York's draft riots, and Boss Tweed's corrupt regime—a word from him and a cop killer imprisoned in Sing Sing walked free. It encompasses the adoption of the electric chair instead of the hangman's rope and Thomas Edison's cunning efforts to have it powered by the rival Westinghouse system rather than his; the era of the dreaded Murder Incorporated gangsters; two world wars; the McCarthy years; the execution of convicted atom-bomb spies, Ethel and Julius Rosenberg; and, finally, life today.

A small, walled city of some seventeen hundred men seventeen-years-old and up guarded by several hundred male and female correction officers, as guards are now called, Sing Sing has been the scene of bravery, chicanery, compassion, butchery, high drama, and low comedy.

Its inmates have made music, pulled hoaxes, contrived daring and ingenious escapes and equally ingenious failed attempts. They have set and fought fires, appeared in movies, divorced, married, and even given birth in the women's prison, which is no longer there.

Sing Sing inmates have saved and taken lives, started riots and taken hostages, made furniture, volunteered for medical experiments as human guinea pigs, gone mad, formed a union, and found God.

In 1825 its first warden, Elam Lynds, made it a torture chamber with punishment a spectator sport. A former army captain in the War of 1812, Lynds called all inmates cowards and treated them with contempt. He had prisoners flogged unconscious for simply winking or smiling. Suicide was their only sure escape and plenty of men took that route out.

Anything resembling humane treatment came slowly and reluctantly. Often, one warden's reforms were canceled by the next. For close to a century Sing Sing—the world's only prison with a railroad running through it—remained a house of horror, a monument to man's inhumanity to almost anything that breathed.

Changes came with educated and enlightened wardens. Then, for example, Thomas Mott Osborne had himself imprisoned incognito in Auburn Prison, to learn how it felt to be a prisoner, in preparation for becoming Sing Sing's warden. His successor, Lewis Lawes, saved the life of a depressed and suicidal inmate by encouraging him to transform a desolate prison yard into a wonderland—a flourishing garden with thousands of flowers, trees, a fountain, and a birdhouse.

After pets were officially tolerated, some convicts showed extraordinary tenderness in caring for rats, mice, sparrows, and every stray animal found wandering in the prison grounds.

Over time, Sing Sing held the good as well as the ghastly; brutal, corrupt, and ignorant wardens, and some of the country's most intelligent and humane. It was also home to brutal, corrupt, and mentally disturbed prisoners: among them wife-killers, husband-killers, serial killers, rapists, and a cannibal. Then there were the kind, the caring, and the innocent—some of whom were eventually freed, or at least escaped electrocution.

Murderers found themselves among unlikely cellmates, such as Truman Capote's stepfather, in for fraud; Armand Hammer's physician father, in for performing illegal abortions, and later pardoned; and Richard Whitney, former head of the New York Stock Exchange, for embezzlement.

Sing Sing's celebrity visitors have included Commodore Vanderbilt, reputed to be the richest man in the world; escape artist Harry Houdini; author Arthur Conan Doyle—who was so shocked by the conditions that he recommended burning the prison to the ground.

Tea-tycoon Thomas Lipton paid several visits; Nellie Bly went once—to her regret—to report an execution; other visitors included inspirational speaker Billy Sunday; politicians William Jennings Bryan, Jacob Javits, and Mario Cuomo; baseball great Babe Ruth; and religious leaders Rabbi Stephen Wise, Cardinal Cooke, and Mother Teresa.

Italian tenor Benjamini Gigli from the Metropolitan Opera and folk singer Joan Baez were among the hundreds over time who have entertained the prisoners.

In his youth, before his movie role as a killer who goes to the electric chair, Jimmy Cagney played baseball against Sing Sing inmates on the prison grounds—and was surprised to find some of his school-day friends facing execution among the home team.

As a profession actors seem to have been the most frequent visitors, often for location shots. Among them were Charlie Chaplin, Spencer Tracy, Charles Bronson, Red Foxx, Woody Allen, Peter Falk, Goldie Hawn, Ossie Davis, Tony Danza, James Woods, and Bruce Willis.

Television news personalities have included Dorothy Kilgallen, Geraldo Rivera, Jane Pauley, and Mike Wallace.

One authentic account of Sing Sing in its early years was by visiting French magistrate Alexis de Tocqueville, who also interviewed the first warden, Elam Lynds. Since then, others who knew it well—its wardens, guards, doctors, psychiatrists, executioners, chaplains of various faiths, would-be reformers, and the prisoners themselves—have written compelling firsthand reports of Sing Sing life and death. The most recent appeared in *Newjack: Guarding Sing Sing* by Ted Conover (Random House, 2002), an investigative reporter who spent eight months as a guard.

Soon after, in the late 1990s, after being stored away and forgotten for years, a treasure trove of official documents, photographs of some of the 606 men and eight women executed in Sing Sing's electric chair, and copies of their letters came to light. These give a poignant picture of their lives in the death house. This book makes use of all these sources.

Sing Sing has inspired scores of plays, films, TV documentaries, and novels, notably by Theodore Dreiser and by John Cheever, who got to know it from the inside by teaching inmates creative writing.

Strangely, no one has provided a detailed picture of life and death in Sing Sing, from its conception to today. My aim is to remedy that, by providing an account of its rich and tragic history by those who knew it—and know it—best.

CHAPTER ONE

RIDING THE TIGER

1821–1839

Sing Sing's first warden, Elam Lynds, never met a convict he couldn't control. Or so he claimed. "They're all cowards," he said, "Intimidated by my superior personality." Given his record, it was easy to believe. When Alexis de Tocqueville, a French magistrate and writer visiting American prisons on a fact-finding tour, arrived at Sing Sing, he was told a story that bolstered the warden's boast. An inmate had threatened to kill Lynds. On hearing about it, he ordered the man to shave him, with a potentially deadly cutthroat razor—and survived without a scratch. Lynds had then dismissed him with a scornful, "I know of your threats, but I despise you too much to believe you have the courage to kill me. Alone and unarmed I am always stronger than you."[1]

What Lynds failed to mention to the French visitor was that he reinforced his rules with a range of tortures apparently inspired by the Spanish Inquisition.

Before he took charge of Sing Sing, Lynds had been warden of Auburn Prison in upstate New York. There, on Christmas Day 1821, with state backing, he locked eighty unruly Auburn inmates in dark, damp dungeons—virtual cesspools—fed them just enough to keep them alive, and, if they complained, flogged them. For two years he kept them in these awful conditions, completely isolated from the outside world. The experiment ended on Christmas Day 1823. Having completed their prison sentences, a lucky handful among the eighty had already been released. Of the scores of others, only two convicts emerged. The rest had died or gone mad. Apparently, this was regarded as a success, enhancing Lynds's reputation as the most feared and famous warden in America.

One inspector, Rev. Lewis Dwight, head of the Boston Discipline Society, enthusiastically approved of Lynds's methods, noting that in the prison's dining room, the convicts "must not disturb their fellows by even a whisper," while eating their "wholesome and frugal meal," and that in their cells they could read the Scriptures "and then reflect in silence on the errors of their lives."[2]

A veteran of the War of 1812, during which he was promoted for bravery from private to captain, Lynds behaved as if still in battle, with inmates the enemy. And because his harsh and often hideous methods seemed to work—there were no reports of riots or escapes at Auburn, only of suicide and insanity—his "silent system" forbidding a prisoner to make any sound or gesture took hold in prisons throughout the country.

A vivid exception was Manhattan's Newgate Prison, where a quarter of the inmates were lifers. And it was debatable whether the warden or inmates ran the pestilential place. There, in groups of eight to a cell and two to a bed, several hundred of the city's most vicious and depraved criminals held temporary residence. Muggers and murderers shared their know-how, and planned joint enterprises for when they would hit the streets again. Muggers taught murderers to pull their punches in order to get repeat business, while murderers impressed on muggers the wisdom of wiping out witnesses. Some graduated ahead of time from this state-run school for scum by bribing or outwitting the guards, themselves hardly the cream of society. Being in the heart of the city, today's Greenwich Village, teeming street crowds provided natural cover for a quick and fairly easy getaway. So, Manhattan was constantly restocked with rapacious gangs, recruited and retrained in Newgate.

New Yorkers were also enduring the first devastating depression since George Washington took office. Banks failed, scores of businesses went bust, and hordes of the destitute survived by stealing. Those unable to pay their debts were treated as harshly as criminals. Mothers owing a few dollars were torn from their screaming children and chained in roach-ridden, stinking debtors' prisons along with the insane who were regarded as depraved animals that had to be punished.

Illiterates, or crooks, or illiterate crooks, often ran prisons and other public institutions, having bribed or bullied their way to the top. It was an open secret that Samuel Swartwout, chief of customs at the Port of New York, was a thief. But he kept his job, salted away a million dollars stolen from the public, and took it with him on a getaway trip to England.[3]

What Manhattan visitors and residents shared was a fear of the stop-at-nothing gangs roaming the streets in search of prey, even in daylight.

Among the more than fifty gangs, the ferocious Plug Uglies restricted membership to tall, tough Irishmen, who plugged their hats with straw and rags to make them protective helmets. Their modus operandi was often fatal: armed with bricks, clubs, and heavy, hobnailed boots, Plug Uglies battered their victims to the ground then kicked them senseless before robbing them. Another all-Irish gang of armed robbers, the Kerrogians from County Kerry, added a wry political twist to their operations by mostly mugging Englishmen.

Most formidable of all were the early-rising Daybreak Boys, who committed at least forty murders in two years. To join them a youngster needed one killing to his credit and to be willing to start work at dawn. It also helped if he lived in the huge, one-hundred-room tenement called the Old Brewery, because it established his credentials as a survivor against all odds. Almost every resident was a mugger, pickpocket, burglar, or murderer. The Irish monopolized the top floor, and escaped slaves filled the basement rooms, some with their white wives and children. Newgate, more often than not, was the crook's alma mater.

Over fifteen years, on average, someone was murdered in the Old Brewery every twenty-four hours.[4] That's 5,475 corpses! Strangers called at their peril, and, on their rare visits, the police went fifty strong.

It was hardly safer in nearby streets. Manhattan was not only under siege by the denizens of the Old Brewery, but also violent panhandlers, and especially by the proliferating street gangs recruited largely from Newgate prisoners, who had escaped or bribed their way out of prison. New Yorkers blamed the lax and corrupt warden and guards at Newgate prison for allowing inmates to escape and terrorize the city. "For Godsake do something about it!" was the public's constant cry.

One proposal was to stop escapes by replacing Newgate's warden with Elam Lynds, now practically a national hero. It would have been a popular move. Apologists for his harsh methods wildly outnumbered those who sym-

Fig. 1. Elam Lynds, Sing Sing's first and most brutal warden. He terrorized the inmates and frequently had them flogged. (Library of Congress)

pathized with his victims. Lynds's admirers had only to mention the recent Manhattan murder of a five-year-old girl stabbed to death for the penny she had begged from a passerby—to justify Lynds's treatment of such criminals as depraved animals.

Pressured into action, officials bought the more radical idea of destroying Newgate Prison and transporting its inmates en masse to some distant spot well away from the city. That, of course, meant providing another huge building to cage them—if it could be done on the cheap. After all, the depression was felt throughout the country.

Although there was plenty of open land available above Fourteenth Street, then the northern border of the city, it was considered too close. So they began searching farther afield, even beyond Manhattan Island.

New Yorkers were reassured when they learned that the fearsome Lynds of Auburn Prison was to supervise the prison's construction, and would become the first warden of what became known worldwide as Sing Sing. The clincher had been his promise to cut costs by using slave labor—a workforce of Auburn convicts with construction experience and unquestionably under his control. His terrible legacy remained for almost a century, long after he had left the scene.

Following his advice to look for a place where the inmates could earn their keep by quarrying stones, a committee considered a spot near the villages of Sparta and Sing Sing. It was thirty-four miles up river on the Hudson's east bank. West Point was another sixteen miles north on the opposite bank. Formerly named Mount Pleasant, Sing Sing consisted of 130 unspoiled isolated acres of rocks and trees with a clear, wide view of the river and of spectacular sunsets—an ideal spot for a palace, a picnic, or a prison. That's where it was decided to locate the new penitentiary. Soon after, the New York Legislature appropriated $20,100 to buy the site. And Lynds hired architect John Carpenter to design the building, using Auburn's north wing as a model.

Now forty-one and eager to live up to his reputation, Lynds hired canal boats to move one hundred convict-laborers, first east along the Erie Canal to Troy, then in two steamships south down the Hudson River—almost three hundred miles.

Armed with whips and loaded guns, thirty guards escorted the prisoners. As the convicts were chained together, escape seemed impossible, especially as guards had shoot-to-kill orders if any escape artist tried to jump overboard. And there was little chance of them conspiring to escape together. Even a whisper meant a fierce flogging, because Lynds demanded absolute silence from the prisoners. An involuntary wink, or twitch, was also considered an offense. During the three-week journey, guards gave offending prisoners one thousand lashes on their bare backs and sponged the open wounds with salt water.

On May 14, 1825, the mute, dispirited men disembarked from the steamers at Sing Sing and, still in chains, climbed the rocky bank to a level spot where they were ordered to build a temporary shelter for the night. At first light next morning, in smaller chained groups, they set to work on a barracks, a cookhouse, a blacksmith shop, and a carpentry shop. Then, wielding pickaxes and shovels, they worked throughout the summer and fall to clear and level the sloping, rock-strewn ground. Stung by horseflies and mosquitoes—not perfect for a picnic or palace, after all—taunted and spattered by seagulls, subdued into fearful silence by the guards, day after day they labored from dawn to dark.

Elam (male spelled backward) Lynds surpassed expectations. He not only kept his promise of free labor, but spent next to nothing on material, constructing the prison's foundation from rock, cinders, and rusty scrap iron; and the building itself from local limestone.

When winter came and the daylight hours shrank, the warden decided that as they worked shorter hours, the convicts needed less sustenance, so he slashed their food rations. The state, however, provided the same amount of food throughout the year. Lynds sold the surplus and pocketed the proceeds.

After three years, by May 1828, only two of six projected floors had been completed. Still, there were four hundred cells; enough to take all Newgate's male prisoners. And they began to arrive in batches. Though there were not yet any facilities for women at Sing Sing, the agitation to empty Newgate was so feverish that women inmates were scattered to other prisons throughout the state.

Lynds greeted each group of arriving Newgate men as if they were diseased and dirty, which many were: he made them bathe, had their hair clipped close to the skull—the ancient mark of a slave—though this was more to discourage head lice than to humiliate, and had their clothes burned. Each prisoner was given a similar suit, alike even in its poor fit, with an arresting pattern of alternate dark and light horizontal stripes. The stripes served as a security measure: should a prisoner escape, except after dark or in a thick fog, he would be clearly visible and a good target for the gun-toting guards.

Cleaned, clipped, and uniformed, the prisoners had their first encounter with Warden Lynds, who, having examined their records sent to him from Newgate, ordered his guards to flog the worst offenders—a taste of things to come.

At their first traumatic meeting with the warden, the new inmates learned what Lynds meant by his "silent system." Forbidden to communicate in writing or by exchanging winks or nods, they must never laugh, motion to each other, sing, whistle, dance, run, or jump. An inmate with an uncontrollable facial tic could expect the same punishment as a defiant rebel—the cat (cat-o'-nine tails), a whip made of nine leather strips with metal tips that scratched and tore the flesh to an agonizing bloody mess and was sometimes fatal. The inmates would never hear from relatives or friends and would be literally buried from the world. Lynds promised them a living death, and kept his word.

The prisoners were led to their cells by guards who stressed that failure to keep their mouths shut or to lower their eyes in the presence of others meant certain pain. And to make sure that they got the message, the guards took the men past the whipping post.

Their cells were even more alike than the prisoners' uniforms and contained, at least to start, identical equipment: a pinewood bunk, two blankets, two tin cups, a spoon, a comb, a towel, a bucket, and a Bible. The iron doors shut with the same emphatic clang. To stifle any spark of individuality that might threaten his control, Lynds also decreed that inmates must never cross the prison yard alone, but line up together and face the same direction, in single-line squads. All except the man at the front had to look directly over the shoulder of the one ahead. Then they shuffled off in lockstep, as it was called, a grotesque imitation of a dejected chorus line. By outlawing every conceivable carefree or spontaneous noise and movement, Lynds enforced on inmates a zombielike existence. To some, shuffling in a single line across the yard, lowering their eyes as a guard glanced their way, hearing the recurring cries of seagulls must have seemed to be surrogates for their own suppressed feelings, and the occasional bird droppings landing on a particularly unpopular guard, a heaven-sent response.

By contrast the inmates' old prison, Newgate, had been a blast, with constant visitors, guards on the take, the occasional riot to break the monotony, and a daily beer bribe for good behavior. Lynds gave no beer and got good behavior with the whip, though he never got absolute silence. Despite his rules, the prison was a cacophony of noises, starting with a loud gong to signal the start of the workday and punctuated, while there was light, by explosions of blasting rock, and the chatter and thud of pickax and hammer.

Unlike Newgate where almost anything went, with eight or more felons crowded into one cell, in this new prison each inmate remained isolated in a cell of his own. This put an end to criminal think tanks, conspiratorial get-togethers, and brainstorming sessions on escape tactics. Each cloned cell was the size of an average fresh-dug grave, and almost as escape-proof: seven-

STATE PRISONERS.

Fig. 2. Prisoners were made to walk in lockstep, and in absolute silence, like a chorus of zombies. (Library of Congress)

feet long, six-feet-seven-inches high, and three-feet-three-inches wide. Any hope of communication between cells other than by telepathy was stymied by a foot-thick stone wall separating all prisoners, precluding tapped messages or spy holes. A laborsaving pulley invented by an inmate moved a 150-foot bar across the cell tops and enabled a guard to open or close fifty cells at a time.

Inevitably a prisoner was caught whispering or gesturing to another, to be followed by his animal shrieks as the cat clawed his back and sent him into convulsions. After thirty or so lashes, with pauses for the guard to rest between blows or to let a partner take over, the victim's screams would slowly diminish to nothing. He felt less pain, at least for the moment, because the cat had dulled or destroyed his nerve endings. Between them, the guards kept at it, pacing themselves so that the fiftieth crack of the whip did almost as much damage as the first. By then, for all the effect it seemed to be having, they might as well have been flogging a corpse—and sometimes they were.

Dead or unconscious, the prisoner remained upright, hands above his head and chained by his wrists to an iron bar overhead. To check if he was alive, the guards dipped a sponge into a bucket of salt water and squeezed it into his raw wounds. All but the corpses, or those who had fainted, responded with gasps of pain. If the prisoner had survived, the flogging continued.

Harsh with prisoners, Lynds indulged his guards, letting them decide how often and how severely they punished inmates. And they went wild. During the first three weeks of his regime, several convicts were beaten unconscious and one was almost flogged to death. Guards were not restricted to the cat. They could resort to a range of other punishments approved by Lynds: the paddle, the cold-water cure, the Chinese water cure, the coolers, the cage, the crucifix, and the ball and chain.

The paddle, made of leather, resembled a canoe paddle. A prisoner to be paddled was strung up by his thumbs from a rope and pulley in the ceiling and his feet strapped to the floor. Then a guard would apply the paddle vigorously. The first blow usually winded the prisoner and the last—about the fifteenth—knocked him unconscious, his bare back one massive bruise.

The cold-water cure, also known as "the shower bath," began when the prisoner was seated and trapped in what looked like medieval stocks, unable to move hands, feet, or head. Cold, often icy water was poured over him until he almost drowned. This "cure" had a lasting effect, causing chronic ill health and at times driving victims mad.

The Chinese water cure saved water, being applied to the victim's skull a drop at a time, from a metal container. Although it drowned no one, it left some insane.

The coolers were eighteen dark, damp cells that stank like sewers, and were fully occupied the year-round by convicts and cockroaches. The steady starvation diet was bread and water. Inmates invariably emerged deathly ill, insane, or carried out as corpses.

The cage, a heavy iron collar lined with spikes bent inward and upward, was padlocked around a prisoner's neck so that the slightest head movement caused intense pain.

The crucifix required the prisoner to stretch out his arms sideways, as if to be crucified. Then a long iron bar was lowered onto his neck and shoulders, and his wrists were chained to each end of it. He was locked in that position to endure the permanent burden of the iron bar until a guard decided to free him.

The ball and chain ensured that great effort would be needed each time a prisoner moved from one spot to another. A massive iron ball was attached

Fig. 3.
The cold-water cure in which the victim was almost drowned. (New York State Archives)

by a chain to an iron girdle around the man's waist, and more weights were added at the guard's discretion.

The only fearless opposition to Warden Lynds was the prison's one-man reform unit, its young, ascetic chaplain, Garrish Barrett, who asked the warden to relax the rules of silence to allow him to teach illiterate convicts to read. Lynds refused. Barrett persisted. Finally, the warden said that even if he approved, there were no books or classrooms available. Barrett replied

Fig. 4. "The Bishop's Mitre."
(Library of Congress)

that they could use the Bibles they already had, and he could teach the men through the gratings of their cell doors. The hitherto inflexible warden unexpectedly capitulated.

In 1829 the chaplain recorded his triumph in a diary: By February he had taught one prisoner to identify four letters in the first verse of Genesis. A month later, Barrett wrote of the same student: "Read correctly the first chapter of Genesis."[5]

The chaplain's greatest success was with an illiterate inmate who, after eighteen weeks of almost daily lessons, had learned 1,605 verses of the Bible by heart! Barrett even persuaded Lynds to allow some prisoners a recreation break and to receive religious instruction. But as the chaplain urged more compassion, and the warden favored less, they frequently clashed. Before the year was out, to avoid further challenges to his authority, Lynds fired the chaplain.

By 1830 the massive main cellblock, almost five hundred-feet long and about thirty-six-feet high, was finished. The prison had twelve hundred individual back-to-back cells in six tiers that were reached by narrow walkways. It had taken five years to build, but like the granite from which it was made, looked as though it would last forever. While inspecting the place, a prison commissioner raved as if touring a cathedral and called it a noble structure. Another commissioner with him rated it the world's best prison. Strolling together on the grounds, they noted how convenient it was for convicts condemned to hard labor to have rocks they could crush, literally underfoot.

Before the year was out, the convict laborers had added a detached two-story building to serve a threefold purpose, as a kitchen and a hospital, as well as a chapel seating nine hundred. Then, at the north end of the twenty-acre yard, they began to construct workshops. And on the river front, for ships expected to transport goods to and from the prison, they built a six-hundred-foot wharf.

Not all who worked on it saw the prison finished. A handful took off for the hills or the nearby Hudson River, risking sudden death from bullets or slower death by drowning. So few got away that, under the circumstances, their escape was not regarded as a blot on Lynds's record. Survivors were told that they were there to stay, having built their own cells as well as those occupied by the hundreds transferred from Newgate. It was never in doubt that Lynds would remain as the first warden and put his stamp on it. He had already demonstrated his control over Auburn convicts and the more recent horde from Manhattan. And it didn't hurt that he offered to run the prison at little cost to the public, on convict labor. He intended to sell products made by inmates in the prison workshops, as well as the still plentiful stone, which was specially suitable for massive Gothic government buildings.

Two young Frenchmen, twenty-six-year-old Alexis de Tocqueville, an assistant magistrate of Versailles law court (later France's foreign minister), and his friend, publicist Charles de Beaumont, would soon see for themselves if Sing Sing was the world's greatest prison. They had decided to travel to the United States to discover if France had anything to learn from Americans about how to treat criminals. Failing to persuade their government to fund the trip, they borrowed the money from their families.

They shared the ship across the Atlantic with the crew of 18, 163 other passengers, a cow, and a donkey. Both worked on improving their somewhat shaky English by chatting with any man or woman they could find among the Swiss, French, Cuban, American, and, of course, British passengers, who spoke English. To prepare for their imminent investigations, they had read a book on the history of America, and spent much of their time onboard translating into French an English book on American prisons.

Their cabin gave them a foretaste of the claustrophobic nature of a Sing Sing prison cell. It was so narrow that they had to dress outside in the corridor.

The *New York Evening Post* of May 11, 1831, predicted that the American authorities would cooperate with them: "Two magistrates, Mssrs. De Beaumont and de Tonqueville [*sic*] have arrived in the ship *Havre*, sent by order of the Ministry of the Interior, to examine the various prisons in our country, and make a report on their return to France. The French government have it in contemplation to improve their Penitentiary system, and take this means of obtaining all proper information. In our country, we have no doubt that every facility will be extended to the gentlemen who have arrived."[6]

On May 28, 1831, de Tocqueville wrote to Abbe Lesueur: "We are going tomorrow to Sing-Sing, a village ten leagues from New York and situated on the North River. We shall stay there a week to study the discipline of a vast penitentiary recently built there. What we have seen up to now suffices to prove to us that prisons attract general attention here and that in several respects they are much better than those of France. We are delighted to go to Sing-Sing. It is impossible to imagine anything more beautiful than the North of Hudson River. The great width of the stream, the admirable richness of the north bank and the steep mountains which border its eastern margins make it one of the most admirable sights in the world."[7] His first sight of the prison was a fearful contrast. As de Tocqueville's biographer reported: "The place was bathed in heat and an unnatural silence, and there was an unmistakable undercurrent of terror in the silence. Mingling with the handful of keepers and watching the inmates at work, the French commissioners themselves became afraid."[8]

His partner, Beaumont, was surprised, as he wrote to his mother, that nine hundred inmates were all around the unfinished cellblock, unrestrained by chains and all engaged in hard labor, and yet, despite the absence of a wall (a few guards were stationed around the perimeter), "they labour assiduously at the hardest tasks. Nothing is rarer than an [escape]. That appears so unbelievable that one sees the fact a long time without being able to explain it."[9]

De Tocqueville's diary entry for May 30, 1831, reads: "We have seen 250 prisoners working under a shed cutting stone. These men, subjected to a very special surveillance, had all committed acts of violence indicating a dangerous character. Each . . . had a stone cutter's ax. Three unarmed guards walked up and down in the shed. Their eyes were in continuous agitation." After a week of visiting the prison, de Tocqueville also explained why he would not recommend the Sing Sing system:

> The penitentiary system such as is established at Sing-Sing seems to me dangerous to apply. This is the reason: beyond question the discipline at Sing Sing is infinitely better than anything comparable one can see in France. Its effects are:
>   1st. The health of the prisoners.
>   2nd. Their extreme concentration on work.
>   3rd. The revenue the State gets from their work.
>   4th. Perhaps the moral reform of a certain number. [Lynds would later dispute this.]

> How are these effects produced? By the complete silence which isolates the prisoners from one another, and the continual work which occupies their physical and moral faculties. How is a sufficient degree of silence and work obtained? By the power of inflicting corporal punishment given arbitrarily to all guards.

The prisoners are free; they are armed (working tools), have no chains and are kept in by no walls. An act of simultaneous determination on their part would infallibly set them at liberty. The preservation of discipline is the only tie that holds them. Every moment the guard tells himself that his life depends on the care with which he prevents plots, maintains assiduous work, and also avoids exasperating by unjust treatment an irascible character whose sudden influence might lead all the rest to follow him. Therefore he will be severe and just, and he will be so not from a sense of duty or fear, but from self-interest.

So then it is by putting themselves in the midst of danger, by braving it face to face, that the Americans seem to me to have succeeded in conquering it. And it is in that that I find their example dangerous to follow. As long as the machinery is in good order, the discipline prevailing in their prisons will be a thousand times better than that of any of Europe. But there cannot be a half-revolt there. So the system at Sing-Sing seems in some sense like a steamship which the Americans use so much. Nothing is more comfortable, and, in a word, perfect in the ordinary run of things. But if some bit of the apparatus goes out of order, the boat, the passengers and the cargo fly into the air."[10]

On the evening of the team's second visit to Sing Sing, de Tocqueville again recorded his impressions:

We saw 250 prisoners working in a shed cutting stone. These men, put under quite special supervision, had all committed acts of violence marking them as characters particularly to be feared. Each had to left and right a stonecutter's hatchet. Three unarmed guards walked about the shed. Their eyes were ever restless. The same day, 30th May 1831, in a quarry we saw several hundred prisoners working the stone under a burning sun, (on one of the hottest days of the year) they seemed to be working as energetically as workmen paid for the job.

Mr. Prince, Minister at Sing-Sing [the new chaplain, Barrett's replacement] and master of a boarding-school at the same place, told us that, all considered, he looked on the prison guards as men exposed to great danger, and felt that experience to date of the obedience of prisoners was too recent to be absolutely decisive. He compared the director of the establishment to a man who had tamed a tiger which, one day or another, might eat him up. Mr. Prince seemed to me an intelligent man and in a position to have an opinion. He did not believe in any great moral reform effected by the Sing-Sing system. . . . But no one can know anything about it, as authentic statistics are missing."[11]

During their nine-day stay at an inn near Sing Sing, the visitors were taken by Chaplain Prince to a cell where de Tocqueville recalled meeting a poor Negro who had learned to read in prison, and who recited by heart two pages from the Bible without making the slightest mistake.

One unnamed informant confirmed the story of Lynds risking being shaved by a convict—a professional barber before his incarceration—who had threatened to kill him the first chance he got.

Lynds took the Frenchmen on a nighttime tour of the cells, and they left with a much grimmer impression of the prison. "It was a tomb of the living dead," they reported. "We could not realize that in this building were 950 human beings. . . . A faint glow from a lantern held by an inspector in the upper galleries moved slowly back and forth in the ghastly darkness. As it passed each narrow cell door we saw, in our imagination, the gateway to a sepulcher instead. The watchman wore woolen moccasins over his shoes to deaden even the faint scrape of his shoes on the gallery floor. There was no sound."[12]

Afterward the two men interviewed Lynds for hours as he stressed the necessity of breaking a prisoner's spirit, after which, he said, the most dangerous situation becomes safe. He had not only shown them the prison and its docile inmates but a glimpse of his own megalomania. Sheer personality alone, he emphasized, turned dangerous criminals into harmless zombies. He also reiterated his conviction that all dishonest men were cowards. In their subsequent report, the two Frenchmen concluded ominously: "One cannot see the prison of Sing Sing and the system of labour which is there established without being struck by astonishment and fear. Although the discipline is perfect, one feels that it rests on a fragile foundation. The safety of the keepers is constantly menaced. In the presence of such dangers, avoided with such skill but with difficulty, it seems to us impossible not to fear some sort of catastrophe in the future."[13]

That same year, 1831, a British House of Commons committee sent William Crawford across the Atlantic to see if Britain's penologists had anything to learn from their American cousins. He disapproved of a system that allowed a prison guard to be arresting officer, judge, jury, and disciplinarian. In Crawford's view, Sing Sing guards had what amounted to a free hand in using the cat; in short, a license to kill. But in one respect he rated New York's Sing Sing as superior to a Pennsylvania prison where eighty convicts were shut up for months in claustrophobic cells and never once allowed out. The Englishman also preferred Sing Sing to a Maine prison where convicts were kept in deep underground pits covered with two-foot-square trapdoors.

Neither British nor American guards knew how to distinguish the mentally disturbed from the clever fakers. Some Sing Sing guards suspected that prisoner Theodore Whiting was slightly insane, but made no allowances and when he repeatedly broke the rules he repeatedly got the cat. Had he thrown what appeared to be an epileptic fit, they would have tested him by dousing him with alcohol and setting him alight. If the flames stopped the fit, he was judged to be faking. Guards gave themselves the benefit of the doubt, however, and flogged Whiting for every infraction. After one lengthy session, most of which he suffered in silence, he was sponged with the customary salt water. It didn't even raise a whimper. It wasn't stoicism, however. Whiting was dead.

Reformers led a public outcry, charging that Whiting had been tortured to death. It had an effect on "the drummers," as they were known, who were instructed to flog only the most blatant rule breakers. Outraged guards predicted anarchy, riots, and bloodshed. They were wrong. As the average daily tally of lashes dropped from a thousand to two hundred, so did the number of punishable offenses fall from one hundred thirty a month to fifty.

Lynds had promised to run the place without milking taxpayers, so he had to make the prison self-supporting. To this end, convicts made, repaired, and washed the clothes and bedding of all inmates; regularly kept their hair clipped to the skull; cooked and served meals; handed out a weekly change of underwear; and, when the occasion arose, buried fellow convicts in coffins made by prison carpenters. All but the seriously sick had to work from dawn to dusk—ten hours forty minutes in the summer—their output assured by the ever-present guards. On Sundays inmates were locked in their unlit, unheated, unsanitary cells for twenty-four hours.

The old, weak, and docile made boots and coffins; and what inmates didn't need was sold to outside tradesmen. The young, strong, and those on hard time worked in the blacksmith shop, or were sent to the hills overlooking the prison to blast loose huge blocks of granite, which would be used for buildings. The men teamed up in pairs for this risky and exhausting work, laboriously battering a hole in a rock with a heavy seven-foot-long drill. When the hole was large enough for a wad of explosive, one inmate would insert and ignite the charge, then rush to join his partner under cover. Several were killed in such explosions—some suspected of making death their way of escape—and scores were injured.

Massive memorials to this forced labor are scattered throughout several states, because the prison's granite blocks sold to contractors were used to construct Auburn's City Hall and Hall of Records, Troy's courthouse, New Haven's State House, Rhode Island's Fort Adams, and even a place of worship,

Grace Church on Manhattan's Broadway. And somewhere in Mexico are the rusted remains of an iron steam boiler made in the prison's blacksmith shop.

It may seem bizarre that this prison where inmates were forbidden to sing became known as Sing Sing. It has no musical connotations, though, being the name of a nearby village, itself derived from a local "Sin Sinck" Indian tribe, itself a variation of "Ossine Ossine," meaning "stone upon stone."

Now with some eight hundred convicts under his absolute control, Warden Lynds was determined to make his grip on the inmates a twenty-four-hour hammerlock. He ordered frequent nighttime forays into the cellblock. Then, to catch the prisoners unawares, the guards wore woolen moccasins and walked barefoot or on tiptoe as they prowled the walkways to enforce the rule of perpetual silence. Sometimes Lynds joined the hunt and many a prisoner, murmuring in a dream or nightmare, was jolted awake to a real nightmare. There stood the warden, towering over them, about to slash away with his metal-tipped whip.

When female convicts began to arrive, a women's prison was built, to separate the sexes, overlooking the other buildings. As if to cater to their religious sensibilities, it resembled a Greek temple with massive marble pillars. But, because the architect forgot to design a kitchen, all meals had to be carried by male prisoners from their kitchen, which made mingling of the sexes inevitable.

The matron, two female assistants, and an internal police force were expected to enforce a no-talking rule for the women, too. Still, one inspector reported "a continual hum of conversation."

It didn't stop at talk. Several inmates became pregnant and gave birth in a cramped, unventilated "delivery room."[14] An inspector once found eight women and five babies there. Many of the babies died.

Women who broke the rules were gagged, their hair was cut off, and they were half-starved. Some were manacled in handcuffs and chains. The most serious offenders got the cat or were suspended by their wrists with their toes barely touching the ground. As visitors were forbidden, no one from the outside world could protest these horrors except the businessmen who were now virtually in charge. They tolerated the system that assured them cheap labor. And most inspectors, being part of the establishment, tempered their criticism. The plight of women prisoners was never raised in the press or pulpit. The prospect of relief seemed as unlikely as a prisoner breaking from his lockstep shuffle to race across the yard.

The first glimmer of hope came with the arrival of prison inspector John Edmonds. As a five-year-old he and other boys had tormented a cat before stoning it to death. Although he expected to be punished, he told his mother what he had done. But, instead of beating him, she spoke movingly about cruelty to animals. It turned him around. From then on if he came across an animal in distress, he acted on his mother's plea to be humane. So, as a man, when someone tried to prejudice him against Sing Sing prisoners by calling them "animals," it had the opposite effect, arousing his compassion.

His report on conditions there swung the pendulum toward reforms that allowed inmates twice-yearly visits by relatives and a hearing before they were punished. The chief guard would listen to both an accusing guard and the prisoner before deciding what punishment, if any, was justified. Instead of being flogged for the slightest infraction, inmates faced a sliding scale of penalties. For minor offenses guards had the choice of depriving the offender of food, bedding, showers, books, tobacco, or a change of clothing.

Despite these reforms, about a dozen women prisoners went berserk in 1843, smashing anything breakable and fighting the guards with such ferocity that reinforcements had to be called to quell the riot. But these women had less to complain about than inmate John Murray, who, because of his fierce temper and independent spirit, was picked on by guards and often flogged when others were to blame. It was more than likely he would not survive his fifteen-year sentence for robbery.

Other convicts helped Murray escape by nailing him shut in a case meant for boots, then trundling it to the dock among cases of prison-produced goods to be shipped to Manhattan markets. Because there was no This Side Up sign, Murray stood on his head for half an hour before being loaded on the ship, still head down. Placed near a red-hot stove he was almost roasted alive but saved just in time by a sailor who moved the box away and on its side to use as a seat.

When Lynds sounded the alarm, guards locked all other prisoners in their cells then scurried into the nearby woods to flush Murray out. Meanwhile, he had saved himself from suffocation by making holes in the case with a gimlet smuggled in his pants, and was approaching Manhattan and freedom.

However, one savvy guard suspected he was on the ship and hurried by road to Manhattan to meet it when it docked. Once on board, he noticed air-holes in a case from Sing Sing, opened it, and found Murray. He was in a pitiful state, so crippled from his cramped position that he couldn't stand, and his voice was just a hoarse whisper.

Back in Sing Sing the spirit of Inspector Edmonds prevailed: Murray's ordeal was considered almost punishment enough, so he escaped the cat. But he still had the warden to contend with. Lynds put him on a near-starvation diet.

Not that the other prisoners had it much better. Lynds gave them cheaper meat than had been contracted for, and shared the savings with his suppliers. He further enriched himself by selling a hefty part of the convicts' food to local farmers for pig swill. He let several escapes go unreported, but kept the men on the books and pocketed the money for their rations. Lynds also profited by accepting bribes from moneyed inmates for double rations.

Inspector Edmonds's report of these crimes sparked a hearing before the state legislature, where former army officer Col. Levi Barr testified against Lynds. Barr had spent three years in Sing Sing before he was declared innocent of the crime for which he'd been incarcerated. Prison meals were so inadequate, he said, that he had "gladly eaten the roots of shrubs and trees that I dug up from the ground in which I labored. I saw no exception among individuals around me. Some told me they ate the clay they worked on. It at least filled their stomachs."[15]

One of Sing Sing's assistant keepers dared to report: "There is evidence so abundant to establish the fact of the Captain being an inebriate, a tyrant, abusive to the Assistant Keepers, oppressive and contradictory in his order, of his having cursed both the Board of Inspectors and his Excellency the Governor, and also of his having appropriated the property of the State for his own use."[16]

Testimony in his favor by corrupt prison officials got Lynds off the hook, but not for long. He had originally endeared himself to the public by promising to make Sing Sing self-supporting. The shocking news in 1845, that it cost taxpayers $30,000 a year, caused a public outcry that forced him to resign. Yells of delight at his departure were soon stifled, because, after three very temporary wardens, his replacement, Hiram P. Rowell, showed that he could be just as sadistic a son of a bitch as Lynds.

CHAPTER TWO

ANOTHER REIGN OF TERROR

1840–1859

Stripped to the waist, glistening with sweat, John Murray, the convict who had tried to escape in a box, worked at the prison forge. Through the heat haze he saw guards approaching, armed with guns and lead-weighted canes. He froze for a moment like a trapped animal. Then, wielding a six-foot red-hot iron bar, he knocked out the first man, crippled the second, and panicked the rest. Several shots fired by the guards missed him. Keeping the survivors at bay, he bellowed curses and taunted them to come and get him or shoot him. But they held their fire, and one of them ordered a group of convicts to overpower the crazed inmate.

When they had subdued Murray by a combined attack, he was hung from his wrists, flogged senseless, and thrown into his cell. He could expect the cat again as soon as feeling returned to his bloody back. It would have been quicker to hang him then and there. But this torture by installments sometimes proved just as fatal and more painful.

Chaplain John Luckey was in Murray's cell when he recovered consciousness. Hiram P. Rowell, the new warden, had made one major concession—revoking Lynds's rule of perpetual silence. He still forbade prisoners from addressing one another, but he let the chaplain talk with them more frequently in their cells after their silent workdays.

The chaplain asked Murray why he had taken on such desperate odds and the wounded convict replied: "The new keeper don't understand me as you do, and will never hear any explanation or defense: so, if there is anything wrong or amiss in the shop it is charged to me. And I am instantly punished for it, and the punishment is increased if I deny it. So, when I saw the keeper making towards me, I became frantic, and felt that I had rather die than live. A speedy death from a pistol or loaded cane is preferable to being tortured to death by the Cat, as was my only prospect under the circumstances."[1]

The chaplain believed Murray but wondered if the others in the shop would back him up if questioned by the prison inspectors. "I have no doubt about it," Murray replied. "And I'll pray for you, wicked as I am, as long as I live, if you bring this to pass."

Chaplain Luckey first got to John Edmonds, the kindhearted inspector, and convinced him that Murray's story was probably true. Edmonds immediately ordered the second flogging postponed until the inspectors had made a thorough investigation. When other inmates confirmed Murray's version of the fight, the second flogging was canceled. "Ever after," said the chaplain, "Jim Murray showed his gratitude by a uniform course of obedience and integrity."[2]

Within a year Murray was almost flourishing as he worked in a blacksmith shop on a hill four hundred yards from the main building, where he made and repaired iron tools, collected broken tools from other inmates, and returned them in good shape. The guard who locked him up for the night told the chaplain that now Murray did his job with such dignity that the other prisoners tolerated his claim to be "boss" of the shop. And in time no one objected when he fenced in a patch of land near his workplace, where he raised chickens.

Shortly before Christmas 1845, Murray called Luckey to his cell and the chaplain took notes of their conversation: "John [Murray] says he wants to be baptized; that he is a different man from what he was; had no father, when he was young, to watch over and care for him; says that Keeper K's wife knew him well for years; had frequently in his boyhood to sleep among the hogs, and by this hard usage was led nearly to destruction; met with his present change, which he thinks was spiritual, on the 15th of last November; feels no rising of bad temper since he made up his mind to be useful."[3]

Skeptical of Murray's motives and wary of his "natural impulsiveness and self-conceit," the chaplain declined to baptize him immediately, wanting to see if his change of heart was genuine and permanent.

The following spring the chaplain was shown a letter that Murray had addressed to his "Dar Brother [sic]," in which he expressed his hope for a pardon in order to devote the rest of his life "to him Blessed be his name and his suns name with the devine spirit," and would make good use of his freedom by going to Africa as a "Mishenary [sic]." Apparently the chaplain did not take the letter at face value. He felt that his caution had been justified and that Murray's purported conversion was merely a trick to get out—just another less painful escape attempt.

Chaplain Luckey left Sing Sing soon after to run a small Manhattan chapel at Five Points, though he kept in touch with Murray by mail. Six years later, New York governor Washington Hunt pardoned Murray after he'd served eleven years of his fifteen-year sentence. Instead of Africa, Murray headed for Luckey's chapel where he insisted on preaching a sermon against the evils of strong drink. But he was so vehement and excited that he was almost incoherent.

Luckey was now convinced of Murray's honest intentions. And although he tried to persuade him that preaching was not his forte, Murray would not be discouraged. When the minister last heard from him, the ex-con said he no longer planned to do his missionary work in Africa but was off to California, where, presumably, Californians were more in need of it.

In 1846 a group of public-spirited citizens persuaded the state to allow tobacco to prisoners addicted to smoking. Inmates were also rewarded for good behavior by visits from relatives as often as twice a year. And keepers were no longer free to inflict instant punishment at will. They had to report the alleged offense to Warden Rowell who then decided on a punishment to fit the "crime." He had ten choices: (1) privation of food, (2) privation of bedding, (3) privation of books, (4) privation of tobacco, (5) change of work, (6) no change of clothes, (7) solitary confinement, with or without light, (8) change of rations, (9) the cold-water cure, which almost suffocated the victim, and (10) the cat.

While checking on inmates' records to see if they were persistent troublemakers, a guard encountered one with no record of any crime, sentence, or punishment, yet he had been in Sing Sing for several years. It was assumed that he was in for the free food and board, and the "volunteer inmate" was discharged.

A glimmer of hope came for inmates in 1847, when the cat was abolished for a three-year trial period. Guards immediately warned that mayhem would result—but they were wrong. Convicts did not riot, made fewer escapes, and even increased production in the various workshops. Other reforms mandated by the state legislature included providing a Bible for each cell and religious worship on Sundays. And inspectors were required to visit Sing Sing at least four times annually and to stop giving jobs to relatives. The warden was instructed to keep a daily account of all prisoner complaints about punishment, unjust treatment, and inadequate or rotten food.

The chaplain now had to manage the prison library to make sure that no convicts got hold of "improper" books; to visit inmates in their cells to devote an hour each week and the afternoon of each Sunday to religious and moral instruction; to visit sick inmates in the hospital; and to hire instructors to teach English to inmates who might benefit from it.

The prison doctor had to inspect the food given to the inmates for its quality and condition and to prescribe a diet for the sick.

Finally, at the suggestion of the Correctional Association of New York, the warden was ordered to stop permitting anyone to visit the prison to gawk at the prisoners after paying him and the guards an entrance fee.

Four years later New Yorkers elected a new political party with a get-tough-on-crime platform. They appointed a new warden, Munson J. Lockwood, who canceled all reforms, destroyed the library, and restored the cat. He justified the crackdown as a result of a surprise search of cells, which turned up the following contraband: a knife, hammer, cane, chisel, maps, scissors, gloves, bottle of alcohol, chest of drawers, writing desk, box of rubbish, sewing implements, looking glass, paintings, collection of lice and bedbugs, onions, tobacco, and matches. Also found were books: *Burglar's Companion, History of Buccaneers, The Murderer, French Grammar, Dictionary, Lady of Refinement, Lives of Females, Treatise on Surveying, Latin Grammar, Domestic Medicines*, and *A Comic Book*. In one cell a guard found enough provisions to last for a week and in another, a box containing meat, files, soap, nails, and bread.

Convicts who had smuggled in the contraband by guile, bribery, or sleight of hand, paid for their prowess with the cat. No offender escaped it regardless of his mental state.

From such ever-present misery two prisoners attempted to escape.

The first, a twenty-year-old orphan, convicted of burglary for a second time, had been sentenced to life imprisonment in Sing Sing. He had been there three months in the summer of 1853 when he decided to leave. He made himself a water-tight coat with a hood and pockets, the material lifted from the tailoring shop, and fixed a small pane of thick glass to the front of the hood. He attached, to each side of the hood, a tube made of a gummy substance with "a hollow decoy duck at the end of each tube." Then he hid this primitive diving suit near the Hudson River. When he decided that the time was right, about two hours before the end of the workday, he recovered the suit, put it on, and walked to the river's edge. There he placed a heavy stone in each pocket, tightened the sleeves and waist of the coat, and, crouching low, waded into the water. About two hundred yards from shore, he released the tubes and the attached duck decoys, which followed on the current a few feet behind him. He then sank under the surface and, breathing through the hollow tubes and ducks, began to walk under water toward a village a mile and a half to the north.

He had only waded a few steps when an armed prison guard spotted the floating ducks, and in the half-light mistook them for the real things being carried away on the current. They were easy targets, and if he hadn't been on duty, he admitted later, he would have shot them because he very much wanted them for his breakfast.

Fortunately he was no longer thinking of breakfast when the young convict got into trouble. One tube burst, water poured into the hood, and the would-be escaper quickly surfaced. He discarded his gear and swam for about a half mile to Brandreth's pill factory, out of sight of Sing Sing. When he reached the shore, he rid himself of his prison garb and walked naked to the factory. He persuaded a worker there to give him two dollars as well as a shirt and pants, by saying that someone had stolen his clothes and money while he was swimming. He had no trouble reaching his brother's home in Manhattan, but was immediately told to beat it, as this would be the first place the cops would look for him. He agreed to lie low in the country for a few weeks. But he missed the excitement of the city and the better opportunities to exercise his craft and soon returned. Three days later the police grabbed him and returned him to Sing Sing for the rest of his life.

Another prisoner followed the same escape route, though instead of an elaborate diving suit he used wood shavings and a raft. He had noticed with great interest how piles of wood shavings from the carpentry shop habitually dumped at the river's edge sometimes drifted into the water and were carried away by the tide. Wishing to emulate them, it spurred him to make a raft by lashing two watertight casks together, covered himself with wood shavings, and launched himself into the Hudson. If guards happened to glance his way all they saw was another pile of wood shavings on the move. They eventually found the makeshift raft, but never found him. He either drowned or got clean away.

Soon after the second escape the newly appointed warden, C. A. Batterman, lived up to his ominous name by maintaining Warden Lockwood's reign of terror. He conceded that the guards had been right after all: pain and intimidation were the most effective ways to keep control, and even the occasional killing. One such killing occurred in the winter of 1855 when a guard shot an inmate to death, in his words, because the prisoner was disobedient and menacing—and for the morale of the other prisoners. Batterman must have chuckled at this blatant hypocrisy. As if the staff gave a damn about the prisoners' morale! A later, humane Sing Sing warden, Lewis Lawes, was incredulous that Batterman could justify killing a prisoner to impress or intimidate the others.

The rule of silence still prevailed even at meals when the men sat at narrow tables placed against the walls, their backs to the center of the dining hall where guards stood watching them. The only communication was a simple sign language. If a prisoner wanted more bread, he raised one finger; more soup, two fingers; extra potatoes, three fingers.

No warden lasted long. Between 1825 and 1855, ten came and went. Batterman lasted only fifteen months, from January 1855 to May 1856. But he made the most of it and was long remembered for introducing an agonizing new instrument of torture—the skull-crushing iron cap, in which the prisoner's head was squeezed like a nut being cracked.

Even such a fearful punishment failed to intimidate Edward McGrath, a small, angry Irishman doing four years for grand larceny. Before the year was out he started a riot in the metal foundry by accusing guard Adam Bird of reporting him and his mates for smuggling coffee, tea, sugar, and rum into the workplace. Bird denied it, but McGrath called him a liar, smashed him in the face, and yelled out for support. Ten other enraged convicts joined the fight, taking turns attacking the guard until he fell to the ground badly bruised and bleeding—and at their mercy. As he lay there, McGrath yelled through a window to inmates in the nearby brass and file shops, "The war has commenced! Come in!" Before they could respond to his rallying cry, guard Abram Van Wart rushed to Bird's rescue, probably saving his life. Assisted by two prisoners curiously named Freeman and Foe, he carried Bird from the war zone to safety.

When Warden William Beardsley replaced Batterman in 1856, his record of inflicting punishment was hardly better than those of previous wardens. During his first year, 501 punishments were inflicted on a prison population of 963. Beardsley even stepped up punishments in his second year, claiming that a spirit of insubordination required 794 punishments for 983 convicts.

But Beardsley did make inmates' lives a little easier: putting lights in the cells to let them read until nine at night, and installing steam heat in the chapel, mess halls, hospital, and main prison building, which meant less frostbite, pneumonia, and bronchitis in the winter.

Nevertheless, Sing Sing remained a grim, desolate, and dangerous place. Scores died over the years in riots and fires, in explosions and other accidents, and by authorized torture. Epidemics of cholera, smallpox, and other killer diseases carried off even more. The prisoners had little resistance on a near-starvation diet that included just two eggs a year. Any brave or desperate soul creeping into the kitchen for more was likely to be severely punished for his impudence.

The inmates' diet left those who survived the epidemics weak, dispirited, or fighting mad. The political party in power in New York State insisted on having its own man, however unsuitable, to head the prison. Their ignorance and inexperience partly explains the five wardens in eleven years. But nothing was done to change the system.

Almost every day a prisoner or two tried to escape. Some succeeded by killing themselves. Those who got away or finished their time were welcomed by the street gangs still plaguing Manhattan.

CHAPTER THREE

ABRAHAM LINCOLN PASSES THROUGH

1860–1887

By 1860 the convict population had swollen to over twelve hundred. As there were only 1,072 cells, some prisoners had to share their cramped cells for the first time in Sing Sing's history. Two hundred of them doubled up: a situation which the prison doctor warned was "unwholesome and demoralizing."[1]

Prison morale plummeted. In the following year 706 punishments were inflicted, including solitary confinement, the yoke, ball and chain, iron caps, and the dreaded cold-water treatment.

Reformers like Chaplain John Luckey opposed torture of any kind, believing that much more depended on the sound judgment and humane feelings of the disciplinarian than upon the instrument of punishment he used. He maintained that the only cruel men to enter prison should be convicts, never guards. Others suggested building a separate prison for inmates convicted of minor crimes, banishing the degrading uniform and lockstep, and rewarding good behavior by shortening the sentences. But no one with the authority to make such changes was listening.

Abraham Lincoln inadvertently paid a fleeting visit to Sing Sing in 1861. A railroad ran through the prison grounds. No wall separating it from the prison had yet been built, even though it was a tempting escape route. When Lincoln traveled by train from Springfield, Illinois, for his presidential inauguration in Washington DC on February 19, 1861, he briefly passed through Sing Sing itself. Forewarned, guards and prisoners stopped work to salute the presidential train.

Fig. 5. On arriving at Sing Sing in the 1860s, prisoners dressed in striped uniforms. (Library of Congress)

Prison conditions got progressively worse. In 1863, although there were considerably fewer inmates—890—1,213 punishments were handed out.

Even so, the inmates were safer in Sing Sing in the summer of 1863 than on the streets of Manhattan, where savage, armed mobs protesting the draft terrorized the city. Incensed by an escape clause for the rich that let them buy their way out of the draft for $300, the rioters almost started another civil war of poor versus rich. They set station houses ablaze; smashed windows; looted stores; hanged several black men from trees; drowned five in the Hudson and East rivers; burned down an orphanage for black children—who escaped out the back; and drove off police and firemen, with knives, crowbars, bricks, and bullets.

Many rioters saw the blacks as the cause of the Civil War as well as their rivals for jobs. The mobs were eagerly joined by local gangs, the Plug Uglies and the Dead Rabbits, as well as visitors—the Blood Tubs from Baltimore and the Schuylkill Rangers from Philadelphia.

Five battle-hardened Union army regiments, armed with field guns and howitzers, rushed to the rescue of the outnumbered police and firemen and after several days of fighting put down the riot. Estimates of fatal casualties ranged from a hundred to two thousand. Several policemen and some sixty soldiers were killed and three hundred wounded. Most rioters who had been arrested were soon released and as few as nineteen were sent to Sing Sing.

These doubtless were among the enraged Sing Sing prisoners who, soon after their arrival in 1863, began an uprising that the guards couldn't control. The warden sent an SOS to the governor who ordered a hundred soldiers, fifty policemen, and thirty extra guards to the prison. Punishment was swift and terrible: 551 of 796 convicts were subjected to various means of torture over the next twelve months, some repeatedly.

Inmates rioted en masse in 1869, protesting the various tortures. Many of them and one guard were killed. Soon after, cold-water baths were abolished. Two years later, New York's legislature decided on a daring experiment, abolishing all corporal punishment in state prisons except for the dreaded solitary confinement known as "the dark cell." Sing Sing Warden E. M. Russell noted an immediate improvement, confirmed by an inspector, who concluded that "the general discipline of the several prisons is good, if not better than might be expected under existing conditions."[2]

Hardliners who warned that going easy on inmates would encourage

Fig. 6. Prisoners working in the Sing Sing quarry in the 1870s. (Courtesy Ossining Historical Society)

crime both inside and outside prison were refuted by statistics. In fact, the inmate population decreased so rapidly that soon every prisoner had his own cell again—which did not make it a holiday camp. Prisoners still tried to escape almost daily and suicides were frequent. The men were still worked hard as unpaid contract laborers from dawn to dusk, except on weekends, when they were locked in their cells. The profit from their work went into contractors' pockets and the money contractors paid to hire them went to New York State.

No reform lasted for long. In 1873 Gaylord B. Hubbell was reappointed warden, having previously been in charge of Sing Sing for two years. He was quickly disillusioned, saying: "Ten years ago I was warden of this prison. I then considered it a failure and yet, compared with it now, it was a model of perfection. The system of labor has degenerated, the convicts have grown saucy and lazy, officers and convicts mingle on a complete social basis, buildings are in a terrible condition of decay, some have even been torn down for supplies."[3]

Hubbell's solution was to defy the reforms instituted by the state and revert to the days of torture for the 1,163 "saucy and lazy men" under his complete control. In the first year of his new regime ninety-four were capped, ninety-eight locked in solitary confinement, and seventy-two strung up by their thumbs with their toes barely reaching the ground.

For a quarter of a century wardens had agitated to have a wall built around the prison. Finally, one was completed in 1877, when Warden B. S. W. Clark was in charge. Made of bricks, many by local brick makers, it was twelve feet tall with guard posts at intervals from which armed guards had a bird's-eye view of the place.

The pleas of reformers weren't always ignored. When the prison doctor protested that the dark cells were inhumane, he got action. A well-ventilated building was constructed for solitary confinement in 1897 with ten cells, each with its own water supply and water closet.

Despite the wall, eventually the public got an insider's view of life in Sing Sing from an ex-convict who had served three prison terms there between 1874 and 1883. During the Lexow investigation which looked into police corruption and found plenty, pickpocket George Appo testified that: "I was at work only three days when the paid instructor of the contractor put a dozen shirts on my table. 'You will have to do these shirts today.' He said, 'And see that you do them perfect or I'll know the reason why.' I told him I would do my best. I finished two shirts, but unfortunately while on the third shirt, I had to go and get a hot iron. Before using it I dipped it in water to cool off. Then I started to iron the sleeve of the shirt and it accidentally scorched it. I reported the accident to the citizen [civilian] instructor. He went to the keeper and told him I willfully burned the shirt. The keeper said to me: 'Get your hat and coat.' I did so. He and the instructor took me to the guard room to the Principal Keeper [head guard] and reported me to him as deliberately burning shirts." When Appo said it was an accident, the head guard replied: "Well, we'll make you more careful after this. Take off your clothes." Because Appo didn't respond at once, two guards grabbed him, one by the throat, tore off his coat, shirt, and pants, knocked out several front teeth, handcuffed his hands behind his back, and beat him unconscious with a wooden paddle.

As he came to, lying on the ground, he heard the doctor say, "He's all right now." The head guard then asked Appo, "Do you think you can go back and do your work all right now?" To which he replied, "You punished me for nothing and the next time I'm brought here you will punish me for something." Appo then took the shirts he hadn't ironed to the stove and threw them in the flames. He was again brought before the head guard who ordered him to be beaten a second time. But the doctor said it was too dangerous and, instead, Appo was put in solitary confinement.

"I lay there for fourteen days," Appo testified, "on two ounces of bread and a gill [a quarter pint] of water every twenty-four hours. When I was taken from the dark cell, I was carried to the hospital injured for life."[4]

First imprisoned in 1874, Appo returned to his life of crime and by 1883 had served three terms in prison, during which there had been seven wardens. Each time, he reported, "The discipline was just as severe and brutal and the food and everything in general unfit for the lowest animal life. In fact, there was an epidemic among the prisoners caused by rotten and filthy meat and other foodstuffs they had to eat, and during my first two terms I never saw or knew of a place to bathe after a hard day's work in the Stove Foundry."[5]

Some fifty years after Lynds had enforced the silent system it was still in operation. And Appo described how it led to the death of Ginger Thompson, who was serving a five-year sentence in the plumbing shop. Thompson was telling the convict who worked beside him how to complete a piece of work. Warden Tierney caught him talking, rushed over and poked him in the neck with a stick. Thompson, who was holding a hammer, explained that he had to instruct the other man. "Shut up!" said Tierney, again prodding him with the stick. He ordered Thompson to put down his hammer and not to give him any back talk. When the convict stepped away, Tierney drew his gun and shot him dead.

According to Appo, nothing was said to Tierney, who claimed self-

Fig. 7. Warden Charles Davis examines the morning mail in the prison's library-post office. (Library of Congress)

defense. "Thompson had no relatives or even a good friend in the outside world to take an interest in his case. He was only twenty-seven years of age at the time. . . . The prison authorities nailed his body in a pine box and buried him up the hill . . . without even a prayer from the so-called chaplain."[6]

There was a happier ending for Appo. Two men connected with the Lexow investigation took an interest in him and found him a job. And sixteen years after his last prison term he wrote a book about his life in Sing Sing.

For twenty years, from 1860 to 1880, Sing Sing had thirteen wardens. Not one lasted longer than three years and most only made it for a year. However, Warden Augustus A. Brush, first appointed in 1880, lasted a remarkable seven years and seemed to have almost all 1,522 inmates under control by 1884. That year only eight were given solitary confinement, perhaps because more and more of the inmates were nonviolent white-collar criminals.

One, Ferdinand Ward, had been US president Ulysses S. Grant's financial partner. Ward was starting to serve a ten-year term for massive fraud, swindling customers out of sixteen million dollars. (Because of good behavior, he served six and a half.) Grant, robbed blind by Ward, was exonerated.

Having invested all his assets in the bank Ward had run, Grant, now dying of cancer, was financially ruined. To support his family, he made a sustained, agonizing effort to complete his memoirs. The book earned five hundred thousand dollars, to more than recoup the family fortune.

CHAPTER FOUR

THOMAS EDISON PROMOTES HIS RIVAL'S ELECTRIC CHAIR

1887–1904

Since the 1880s convicts had been allowed to receive a letter and a visitor each month and a package every two months. Lamps previously forbidden were given to those able to read, so that they could read in their cells after dark. But a well-meaning attempt by labor unions to improve Sing Sing's conditions backfired. The unions protested that the inmates were slave labor, controlled by outside contractors who also undercut the work of law-abiding union members outside the prison. The unions prevailed, and in 1888 contract labor ended.

The result was an immediate disaster. With no work the hundreds of inmates were locked in their cells day and night with nothing to do except perhaps plan escapes or mayhem. This was quickly remedied. The prison was made almost self-supporting, and without the use of middlemen, by supplying New York State with such goods as highway signs made by the convicts for which they were paid a few cents a day.

Reformers never stopped trying to make changes that would give inmates hope. They succeeded in passing a law in 1889 to give judges and prosecutors the option of choosing an indeterminate sentence for those found guilty of various crimes, a sentence that could be reduced for good behavior. Bu the authorities were slow to adopt the law and in 1891 Sing Sing warden W. R. Brown reported that two years after the law took effect, "not one convict received at this prison has been so sentenced."[1]

Inmates were isolated from the outside world until the end of the nineteenth century, after which visitors other than relatives entered Sing Sing to teach, preach, entertain, or satisfy their curiosity. One unlikely visitor was Cornelius "Commodore" Vanderbilt, reputedly the world's richest man, whose fortune surpassed the entire US Treasury. Because of these visitors, word leaked out about botched executions. One story told of a condemned man who tried to beat the rope by cutting his throat. A doctor sewed him up and nursed him until he was fit to be hanged. But the hangman miscalculated and, because the wound had not healed, ripped the prisoner's head from his shoulders.

Responding to press and public pressure, New York State governor David Hill agreed that the gallows was a relic of the Dark Ages and appointed a three-man commission to investigate a less barbaric way of taking life. For years executions in the United States had been a spectator sport with standing room only, the overflow hanging out of windows or climbing poles for a clear view.

One of the most gruesome executions took place in 1825 when a South Carolina man convicted of rape and murder was chained to a stake, dowsed with turpentine, and burned alive. In their report the commission members rejected the wisdom of the past when men and women were thrown to wild animals, fired from canons, boiled, burned, or buried alive, or had holes bored in their bodies that were filled with oil and set alight. They also turned thumbs down on the contemporary French method, the guillotine, as too bloody, and shooting as too unpredictable. Doctors, especially, were uneasy about using hypodermic needles as instruments of death.

The impetus to use electricity came from an unlikely source, Alfred Southwick, a Buffalo, New York, dentist not unacquainted with pain. As early as July 1887 he had witnessed an experiment by the Society for the Prevention of Cruelty to Animals, when several stray dogs were electrocuted for the purpose of euthanasia. It did not occur to him to use the same method on humans until one night when he saw a drunk stumble into a live electric wire and die instantly with no sign of fear or suffering. After that Southwick launched a campaign to promote electric shock as more humane than the hangman's rope. (Mild electric shocks had been used to punish Ohio State Penitentiary prisoners while they sat in three inches of water.)

This idea caught not only the public's imagination but that of the great inventor Thomas Edison. Though opposed to capital punishment, his motive was probably profit, and he had his own Machiavellian reason for supporting the crusading dentist. Anxious to have his DC (direct current) accepted nationally for power and lighting, instead of rival George Westinghouse's AC

Fig. 8. One proposal for electrocuting condemned inmates was to stand them on a metal plate in an "Electric Closet," with electrodes attached to their heads. (New York Medico-Legal Society journal, 1888)

(alternating current), he used scare tactics, aiming to expose Westinghouse's system as far more dangerous than his. What better way to demonstrate its suitability for snuffing out the lives of condemned killers—and so, by implication, its unsuitability for domestic and industrial use? When electrician Harold Brown offered to demonstrate with scientific exactitude that alternating was more deadly than direct current, Edison gave him his blessing and the use of his New Jersey laboratory.

Brown paid youngsters twenty cents for each stray cat or dog they brought to the West Orange lab, then, when some fifty animals were delivered, he called in the press. Watched by reporters and safely insulated, Brown enticed a dog onto a tin sheet, took hold of a wire hanging from the ceiling and carrying 1,200 volts of Edison's direct current, and applied it to the dog. The animal seemed paralyzed but withstood the current for ninety seconds before collapsing. A second dog, zapped with 1,400 volts of direct current, appeared invigorated by the charge and trotted off cheerfully. Switching to a mere 300 volts of Westinghouse's alternating current, the electrician quickly killed the remaining animals.

To advance his campaign, Brown also gave a public demonstration at Columbia University's School of Mines on June 30, 1888. Edison's man, Arthur Kennelly, assisted Brown and, strangely, so did Dr. Frederick

Fig. 9. Another rejected method of executing prisoners was to seat them in what looked like a dentist's chair with a footrest. (New York Medico-Legal Society journal 1888)

Peterson from a Poughkeepsie, New York, mental asylum, where he had pioneered electro shock treatment on patients.

A caged seventy-six-pound dog was brought into the room, a front and hind leg wired for current. One reporter called the animal "mild," another, "a large mongrel Newfoundland with a vicious eye and ready tooth."[2] The ready tooth had recently made contact with both attendants, but their pain was nothing compared with what the dog was to endure.

Many witnesses walked out of the torture chamber, as Brown gradually increased the direct current from 300 to 1,000 volts. One man pleaded with Brown to put the animal out of its misery, another called it "heartrending," and a third said that it made Spanish bullfighting seem a normal and decent spectacle. Brown assured those who stayed that the dog "will have less trouble when we try the alternating current."[3] He was right: 300 volts instantly put the animal out of its misery. But it was not the victory Brown had anticipated.

Critics said that the experiment was flawed because the dog had been weakened by direct current. Brown's answer was to electrocute more dogs. To meet the concerns of the Society for the Prevention of Cruelty to Animals, he hired the chief physician of the NYC Health Department to supervise the experiments.

Fig. 10. This picture of the chosen electric chair also shows the seats that resemble church pews—for the witnesses. (New York State Library)

Some were still not convinced that what killed animals would also kill larger humans. So the experimenters had a 12-pound calf and a 1,230-pound horse delivered to Edison's lab on December 5, 1888. They were both destroyed with thirty-second shocks of alternating current, apparently as painlessly as the smaller creatures. If that didn't convince doubters, Brown and Kennelly offered to electrocute an elephant. But New York State was already convinced.

On New Year's Day 1889, its legislature agreed to kill death-row inmates with Westinghouse's alternating current, applying no less than 300 volts for from fifteen to thirty seconds while the condemned prisoner sat in a chair, rather than have him lie on a table.

William Kemmler, a poor semiliterate laborer who had axed his mistress to death, was the first convict to go to the electric chair at New York's Auburn Prison on August 6, 1890, while four Sing Sing inmates were also scheduled to die by electric shock—all on the same day—the following July. Despite his poverty Kemmler had a first-rate lawyer, Bourke Cockran, who asked Edison how he could confidently testify as an expert that 1,000 volts of alternating current would bring instant death. How did he know? Had Edison ever killed a man with electricity? And how could Edison be sure that the man's body would not be mutilated? Edison conceded only that five or six minutes of current might mummify the body.

Cochran lost the first round, so he appealed to the US Supreme Court. Meanwhile, Kemmler awaited his fate in solitary confinement, where he learned to read and write his name. By the time the Court made its decision Kemmler could read the ruling—that electrocution did not violate the constitutional ban on cruel and unusual punishment. Warden Charles F. Durston was to put their opinion to an awful test on August 6, 1890.

But Durston wasn't ready. He had been so surprised by the Court's quick decision that workmen kept Kemmler awake the night before his execution finishing the death chamber. They were still at it when shortly after a bright summer dawn, a well-built man with a black beard, dressed as if going to a formal dinner party, was brought in and introduced by the warden to those who would soon watch him die, among them dentist Alfred Southwick, the enthusiastic advocate of electrocution; Dr. Spitka, the attending physician; Dr. Carlos McDonald, president of the State Lunacy Commission; Chaplain Yates, and two reporters.

Kemmler nodded slightly and said, "The newspapers have been saying a lot of things about me which were not so. I wish you all the luck in this world. I believe I am going to a good place."[4] Then Kemmler sat among them—

almost like another witness—until it was time for him to move to the electric chair.

Except for a faint "good-bye" to the warden, Kemmler's last words were to pacify Deputy Sheriff Joseph Veiling, who trembled as he strapped him in the chair. "Don't get excited, Joe," he said. "I want you to stay right through this thing. Don't let them experiment on me more than they ought to."[5] Unfortunately, Kemmler was in the hands of a nervous, unrehearsed executioner using cheap, secondhand equipment from Brazil. His first mistake was to forget to wet the sponges under the electrodes attached to Kemmler's skull.

To compound the problems, the executioner was to throw the switch in another room some distance from the death chamber, guided only by the warden's signal: the words "Good-bye, William."

When he got the first signal, he sent a weak current into Kemmler, then shut it off. Guards who began to unstrap Kemmler, believing him dead, found he was still alive—blood pulsing from a wound where his index fingernail had dug deeply into his thumb. "Good God, he's still alive!" someone yelled, and Kemmler was quickly strapped back in. Officials held fraught, whispered conversations. The equipment was frantically checked and a panicky voice

Fig. 11. An artist's impression of how William Kemmler, the first man to go to the electric chair, in 1890, was literally burned alive. (*Police Gazette*, 1890)

ordered the executioner to try again. This time he overcompensated, releasing such a massive and sustained charge that Kemmler began to burn alive. Smoke rose from his head and his clothing caught fire, and as the current fluctuated his burning body several times slumped and then jerked upright. District Attorney George Quinby hurried out holding his hand over his mouth and nose. A newspaperman fainted. The power was cut off and the shaken witnesses silently filed out.

Kemmler's body was left in the chair until it was cool enough for the guards to handle. By then rigor mortis had set in and his corpse was rigid in a sitting position.

After the autopsy, the examining physician reported that parts of Kemmler's body had been charred black, and declared that the law should be repealed and electrocution banned. A *New York World* reporter wrote a first-hand account of the execution headlined: "A Roasting of Human Flesh in Prison—Strong Men Sickened and Turned from the Sight."[6] The *New York Times* called it an awful spectacle and "a sacrifice to the whims and theories" of a coterie of cranks and politicians."[7] The *London Times* suggested a more effective method would have been to hit him with an ax.

As might be expected, the official version of the execution by Dr. McDonald painted an almost rosy glow to the gory scene. Kemmler, he wrote, had wished the world good luck before meeting sudden and painless death. And he compared Kemmler's movements after he had been pronounced dead with those sometimes exhibited by decapitated animals. Edison did not deny that mistakes were made but stuck to his opinion that correctly applied it was the quickest and least painful method of execution.

But word of Kemmler's fate had reached four men in the Sing Sing death cells awaiting their turn. The prison's new warden, W. R. Brown, formerly a Newburgh, New York, postmaster, was a political appointee. He exacerbated their fears by hiring Warden Durston from Auburn as technical advisor, an incredible choice considering how he had botched Kemmler's execution. Fearing the worst, Brown determined to keep the press out of the death house when the four murderers were executed.

This infuriated a *New York Times* reporter who ridiculed Warden Brown as an idiot who behaved as if Sing Sing was his private fiefdom, mocking him as an insolent despot in a top hat, a cigar clenched between his teeth, and a yellow flower in his buttonhole.

Meanwhile, reporters gave sympathetic coverage to the four condemned men. They told how Shibuya Jugiro, a Japanese, had seemed about to convert to Catholicism but, as a priest put it, remained a heathen. Harris Smiler, the only Protestant and a member of the Salvation Army, had read a hundred religious books in the previous months and, as his execution approached, became entirely absorbed in the Bible. James Slocum, a baseball player, confided to his Catholic chaplain that he was not afraid to die, but prayed that it would not be as horrible as Kemmler's execution. Joseph Wood, a black man, liked by the guards as sensible and good-natured, clung to the slim hope that his lawyer would save him, but was ready for the worst.

All finished their last breakfast of steak, eggs, and coffee. All asked for dinner to be rare roast beef, and cleared their plates. When Warden Brown looked in on their last night alive, they said they had as much reading matter and as many cigars as they could manage. There was nothing else they wanted.

Brown stuck to his decision to keep the executions secret from the press but, to placate persistent reporters, he arranged for a series of colored flags to be flown from the staff of the prison's cupola visible from outside the prison grounds, to indicate the time when each man died. Smiler's death would be announced by a blue flag, Slocum's, white; Wood's, black; and Jugiro's, red.

It was a safe bet that Sing Sing prisoners would have calmly looked on had the four men been hanged, some might even have relished the sight. They had done so in other prisons where inmates had been encouraged to watch executions in the vain hope of intimidating them. But electrocution was a different matter. Now they felt that fellow convicts were to be tortured to death, burned by hellfire, mutilated. Hadn't that happened to the poor simpleton at Auburn? Sing Sing seethed with resentment and was flooded with rumors, among them that prisoners planned a mass attack on the death house to destroy the electric chair. So, the warden armed his guards and put them on special alert.

The four prisoners were awakened before dawn on July 6, 1890, a hot, humid morning, and prepared for death—shaved, shorn, and their clothes cut to make room for electrodes.

Meanwhile, on a road outside the prison entrance reporters had already joined a curious crowd of thousands, but armed guards ordered them farther away, threatening to shoot anyone who crossed a certain line. When reporters protested that they were entitled to stay on public property, guards set a pack of snarling and barking dogs on them. Suddenly a gun was fired from Peekskill camp—audible ten miles up the river—as if announcing the start of the execution ceremony.

Moments later, at 4:41 AM, a white flag appeared on the staff, signaling Slocum's death. Thirty minutes later, at 5:12, a blue flag replaced it. Twenty-six and a half minutes later, at 5:38, a black flag appeared for Wood, followed twenty-six and a half minutes later by Jugiro's red flag. Judging by the signals, everything had gone without a hitch. In fact, through inefficiency or spite, Brown had given the wrong order for the four men's deaths. Smiler went first, not Slocum.

Years later, using prison records, Lewis Lawes, a great Sing Sing warden, explained what really happened. Two of the men had died without a word. Slocum began to pray but had not finished saying "Lord have mercy on my soul" when the electric current was switched on and the final word was inaudible or never uttered. The fourth and final man, Jugiro, according to the raised red flag, had died just twenty-six minutes after Wood. Instead, at that time, he was putting up a fierce fight in his cell. Guards then debated whether to sedate him or call for reinforcements to overpower him and carry him to the chair. But head guard Connaughton, called in to help, knew exactly what to do. When he said, "Come on, Jugiro. You wouldn't want to join your ancestors like a coward, would you?" Jugiro stopped fighting and walked, head held high, to his death.[8] His resistance had gained him an extra twelve and a half minutes of life.

Smiler's wife claimed his body. The other three were put in pine boxes and packed in quicklime. Fellow inmates dug their graves on state property opposite the north wall. There were no religious services. Six months later, Sing Sing stopped the flag-raising signal because rubbernecking passersby outside the prison caused massive traffic jams.

Death by electrocution was still an uncertain business. Several men were alive after they'd been put through it—even after they'd been pronounced dead. So, to make sure, autopsies immediately after executions became mandatory. No one survived those.

To avoid that certain fate, two condemned men, Thomas Pallister and Frank Roehl, escaped from the death house during a rainstorm on the night of April 20, 1893. Pallister was to have been executed for killing a policeman, Roehl for killing an old Civil War veteran. Roehl had a hair-trigger temper and during his trial, when Assistant DA McIntyre asked if he was in fact married to the woman he called his wife, Roehl grabbed the attorney by the throat and it took several court officials to loosen his grip.

On the night of their escape from adjoining cells, Roehl pretended to have a headache and asked guard John Hulse for a cup of coffee. When, instead of handing him the drink through the bars, the guard opened the door, Roehl blew red pepper in his eyes and backed him against the bars of Pallister's cell. Pallister pinned the guard's arms while Roehl took his cap, shoes, and gun, and locked him in the cell. Then he unlocked the cells of Carlyle W. Harris, a medical student who had poisoned his wife, and two other murderers. But Pallister was the only one willing to join him. Roehl and Pallister locked the cells of those who declined to escape with them, waited for relief guard John Murphy to arrive, took his gun, and locked him in with Hulse.

Having helped to build the death house while serving a previous sentence, Pallister knew the layout. He led the way through a ceiling skylight and made a hole in the roof with a poker and shovel taken from the stove used to heat the cells. They then climbed the twelve-foot iron fence, which was unguarded after prisoners were locked in their cells at night, and headed for the Hudson River. The bodies of the two men washed ashore a few days later, one with a bullet in him. The other had drowned. It was assumed that

Fig. 12. A double row of inmates about to march in lockstep.
(Library of Congress)

they had quarreled in the boat they had stolen and that one had fatally shot the other with the guard's pistol and thrown him overboard. The killer was believed to have been run down by a passing craft.

Carlyle Harris, who had refused the chance of freedom, later explained why. He had previously threatened to kill himself and so had been under a twenty-four-hour guard. The constant surveillance had unnerved him and he promised, if the guards were removed, not to commit suicide. Warden Charles F. Durston had taken him at his word. Because the warden had trusted him, Harris explained, he, as a man of principle, felt honor-bound not to try to escape.

William Taylor, who had murdered a fellow prisoner, was another who had decided to stay put, though due to die three months later on July 27, 1893. His execution, like Kemmler's, would prove a fiasco. The executioner, Edwin Davis, a professional electrician, was a small wiry man with piercing eyes and a drooping mustache. His hobby was beekeeping. Davis had patented electrodes which he used at executions and eventually sold to New York State for $10,000, agreeing to teach two other electricians the tricks of the trade. He showed them how to attach two sponges to a large piece of beef to ensure that the electric current was working properly, then threw the electrified beef into a furnace, much to the regret of hungry convicts who worked around the death house.

For Taylor's execution, the warden agreed to communicate with Davis by ringing a bell. The first time he would ring it fifteen minutes before the condemned man was due to walk from his cell. Then Davis would start the generator. At the second bell ringing, he would throw the switch, sending the current to the execution chamber. At the third, he'd increase the current. At the fourth, he would reduce the current. Finally, at the fifth ringing, he would switch off the current.

All went well until the third bell, when the increased current hit Taylor with such force that his legs stiffened and shot forward, tearing away the front of the chair to which his ankles were strapped. The current was switched off, guards placed a heavy box under the chair to support his feet, and then Davis tried to kill him again. After Davis finally switched off the electricity, the doctor put his stethoscope to Taylor's chest and reported that he was still breathing. When the warden called for more electricity, Davis threw the switch, but nothing happened. He rushed to the warden to say that the generator had burned out. Guards unstrapped Taylor and carried him to a cot where the doctor injected him with a drug to prevent pain should he regain consciousness.

Meanwhile, Davis frantically supervised electricians who were stringing electrical cables over the prison wall from the city's power plant to the death house. That completed, the warden ordered the execution to resume. Pointless, said the doctor. Taylor had died while the wires were being fixed. But the warden insisted that the guards strap the corpse into the chair and be subjected to thirty seconds of electricity. Asked how it went Davis replied that the poor fellow took it like a man and didn't say a word!

In the late 1880s guards found a prisoner, A. Schiller, dead in his cell. He had been serving a life sentence for forgery and was almost blind. They were surprised to find seven pins in his body. Close examination, presumably with a powerful magnifying glass, showed that The Lord's Prayer—254 letters—had been engraved on the head of each pin. The twenty-five-year task had cost him his eyesight. When the one flawless copy was exhibited at the Chicago World's Fair in 1893, someone stole it. It reappeared in a San Francisco store in the late 1930s and is now in Ripley's Believe It or Not! Museum in St. Augustine, Florida.[9]

The poor and desperate were not the only ones to find themselves in Sing Sing's death house. A prosperous physician, Robert Buchanan, occupied one of the eighteen cells in 1895. He was the widower of Anne Sutherland, a former madam of a New Jersey brothel. She had taken her share of the profits—$50,000—when she chose early retirement. The brothel proved to be a healthier environment than her husband's home. Their honeymoon was hardly over when Dr. Buchanan confided to friends that Anne had become dangerously ill and, soon after, that she had died. In fact he had fatally poisoned her, cleverly disguising the effect of morphine poisoning, pinpoint pupils, by applying a few drops of belladonna that restored them to a more normal state.

After killing her, Buchanan scurried north to Nova Scotia, Canada, taking the bulk of Anne's $50,000 golden handshake with him. Her friends wondered how close proximity to a healer had so rapidly changed a healthy woman into a dead one and demanded an autopsy, which justified their doubts. In 1895 Dr. Buchanan paid for his crime in Sing Sing's ever-ready electric chair.

Though prison guards were not notably softhearted or sensitive, many dreaded the death watch over condemned men and did it with reluctance. Guard William Hopper was given an especially stressful assignment in the winter of 1896. He was put on the death watch of William Caesar who was awaiting execution for murdering a woman during a quarrel. Caesar had heart disease, and shortly before his scheduled execution beat the chair by dying of a heart attack. Head guard Connaughton, who had pacified the Japanese prisoner, Jugiro, apparently had become mentally unbalanced by his job. He confirmed for himself that Caesar was dead, but warned Hopper, "He may be putting something over on us. You better stay with the fellow all night. He might come to life, and if there's no one to watch him he might just wander out of prison." The idea horrified Hopper, who yelled, "I came here to watch live men, not dead men! Give the job to someone else!"[10] And he quit.

In 1899 the chair claimed its first female victim, Martha Plant, a wildly jealous woman who had tortured her stepdaughter to death, first blinding her with acid, then strangling her. She had then attacked her husband with an ax. Martha appealed for clemency to Gov. Theodore Roosevelt, former NYC police chief and future US president. Finding no reason to reduce her sentence he sent her to the chair.

Joseph Pulitzer assigned his ace woman reporter Kate Swan to cover the execution for the *World*. She persuaded Warden Omar V. Sage to let her interview the executioner, who vowed that he would never kill a woman—a promise he soon broke. Swan reported that Mrs. Plant went to her death bravely and instantaneously. Another paper reported that she had been tortured to death and died in agony.

The silent system was still in effect. On rare occasions prisoners were permitted to speak when a guard questioned them or during the even more infrequent occasions when they were entertained—the talent provided by the inmates themselves—as Amos O. Squire, an enthusiastic and idealistic young doctor discovered on his visit to the prison on New Year's Day 1900.

Living in the nearby village known as Sing Sing, now Ossining, Squire had been invited to the show by a friend, the prison's chief physician. As he recalled, after entering "the bleak, grey precincts of the prison," he found that the performances were rather crass and uninspired, but were "gratefully received by the subdued and furtive convict audience." In the middle of the show, staged in the chapel, the prison's doctor was called away on an emergency in the village. Afterward, the prisoners were marched off in lockstep back to their cells, leaving Squire alone in the chapel. A guard then interrogated him as if he was either a prisoner trying to break out or had illegally broken in. The authorities finally contacted the chief physician. Distracted by his emergency case, he had forgotten about Squire and gone home. But Squire was not free to leave until the doctor returned to the prison late that night and personally identified him.

The experience made the young doctor curious to know more about what went on in the prison, to learn "in what way convicts differ from law-abiding citizens, physiologically and psychologically," and if they were entirely responsible for their criminal behavior or if there were extenuating circumstances.[11] He told this to his forgetful friend, the prison's chief physician, who was amused and pleased because he was about to take a leave of absence abroad and offered Squire the job as his temporary replacement. Squire jumped at the chance and stayed on as a consultant when the chief physician returned.

Reformers prevailed at the turn of the century despite the strong resistance of those who insisted that prison was to punish. On August 9, 1900, Superintendent of Prisons C. V. Collins abolished the degrading lockstep, "that sluggish, shuffling gait that affected (the prisoner's) mentality and his view on life. Its abolition put new spirit in the hearts of the prisoners. They could walk like men."[12]

Then Superintendent Collins let in the light. Sing Sing's cellblock had always been a damp, gloomy, and depressing place, its windows mere slits in the thick walls. In 1902 Collins had installed twenty huge windows, 31 feet high and 5½ feet wide, which, on good days, flooded the place with sunshine.

Because of massive immigration to the United States, by the early 1900s over 40 percent of the prison population was foreign-born. Many couldn't speak English, so that misunderstandings between them and the guards were inevitable. However, they had another good incentive to learn the language, besides avoiding punishment due to misunderstanding. Warden Addison Johnson, in charge since May 1899, announced the first parole system available to those who had played by the rules. It took effect in 1902, when 133 of 288 applicants were freed on parole.

Two years later, when striped uniforms were abolished, prisoners were noticeably more cheerful even though, as they undertook their various tasks, their every move was still supervised, regulated, and, if necessary, punished.

CHAPTER FIVE

THE CONVICT WHO TRAPPED HIMSELF AND THE GREAT RIVER DISASTER

1904–1914

When Sing Sing decided on a separate wing for the electric chair and eighteen death cells, Warden Addison Johnson chose convict Tom Tobin, a trained stonemason, to design the place and to oversee its construction. Made of stone and steel, it was a small replica of the main cellblock, with slightly bigger cells.

Under cover of this work, Tobin was able to burrow his way to a sewer leading to the Hudson River and freedom. During his eighteen months at large he murdered someone. He was caught and returned to Sing Sing where he learned that his tunnel had been discovered and sealed.

Trapped in the escape-proof death house that he had helped construct, he moaned that he had built his own tomb. Having fooled the guards once before, Tobin thought he could do it again. In a frenzied effort to survive, he feigned madness, racing around his cell chasing imaginary rats. The guards fell for it, reporting that Tobin had gone crazy. But a state-appointed commission concluded that he was simply trying to escape the chair. He was electrocuted on March 1, 1904, his last words a prayer his mother had taught him as a child.

The last roughly forty-foot walk taken by Tobin and other condemned prisoners from their cells to the electric chair became known in gallows-humor tradition as the dance hall, because guards played requested phonograph music there on execution eves and through the long final night of a prisoner's life. The next day it was customary for the warden, state officials, a few invited guests, and a handful of journalists to sit on the pewlike seats and witness the grisly ceremony a few feet from them—usually in grim silence, except for the whir of the ceiling fan in summer, and clergyman, priest, or rabbi intoning prayers.

Three months after Tobin's execution, an unprecedented disaster occurred that brought sixty-one-year-old ship's captain William Van Schaick to Sing Sing, facing a ten-year sentence. Crippled and blind in one eye from the fire aboard his ship, he had been found guilty of criminal negligence that cost the lives of over a thousand of his passengers on the *General Slocum*. Hundreds of those under his care who drowned or burned to death were children on a Sunday outing heading for their annual Lutheran Church picnic on Long Island.

On that bright sunny morning of June 4, 1904, the three-decked paddle wheeler set off along New York City's East River with thirteen hundred passengers when, to the horror of watchers ashore, it burst into flames. The fresh paint on the ship concealed the fact that it was a death trap. It had not been inspected for years, the crew had never had a fire drill, the fire hose was all but useless, the life preservers had disintegrated with age, and the lifeboats were inaccessible. Of the injured survivors, dozens later committed suicide while others ended their lives in mental asylums, their minds unhinged by the horrifying ordeal.

Van Schaik was paroled after three years and six months in Sing Sing and President William H. Taft pardoned him on December 19, 1912.

Alabama-born Florence Maybrick was an unlikely visitor to Sing Sing during the captain's incarceration there. Although she was a convicted murderess and had spent many years in an English prison for fatally poisoning her husband, she had been shocked by her tour of Sing Sing in December 1906. Now an active proponent of prison reform, she told a Young Mens' Club audience at Dr. Parkhurst's Church in Madison Square that one could write one's name on Sing Sing prison's moist walls. "I claim for all men," she continued, "human rights, the right to sunshine, to ordinary decencies, to labor. But at Sing Sing, strong men are shut up in cells, six feet by three, without ventilation, sanitary provisions, or water. [And the system condemns] thousands of men to absolute idleness and [educates] the prisoners in habits of idleness, so that they are absolutely unable to hold a steady job, if they can get one, after their release."[1]

After eight years as Sing Sing's warden, Addison Johnson was succeeded in July 1907 by Jesse D. Frost. That same month a former prisoner who had just been released from Sing Sing charged that the guards were

Fig. 13. William Van Schaick, captain of a New York paddle steamer, *General Slocum*, was found criminally responsible for the deaths by fire or drowning of more than a thousand passengers when his ship caught fire in New York's East River. He was sentenced to Sing Sing for ten years. (Courtesy Wikipedia Free Encyclopedia)

brutal, that the poor inmates were neglected, and some were allowed to cook in their cells. In response, C. V. Collins, the state superintendent of prisons, said that he had twice investigated conditions at Sing Sing. As a result, he said, Rabbi S. Braverman had been dismissed after he confessed to smuggling opium into the prison and selling it to inmates. Three guards were also fired for helping to smuggle money to prisoners from friends and relatives. However, Collins called most complaints unjustified, though he admitted, with a smile, that about a hundred convicts had tried to carry out "light housekeeping" by connecting the electric lights in their cells to bent tin plates. All these improvised electric stoves, he said, had been confiscated.

Former warden Johnson told a reporter, "I know all about the inspiration of those charges. Only a few days ago we released a prisoner who said he was a 'journalist,' and had just concluded an eight-year sentence for grand larceny. He had been very refractory and we had found it necessary to discipline him a number of times. Before he left he told one or two prisoners that he would make me sit up and take notice. He also said he would 'get even' by getting published in a New York paper a story that would cause a sensation."[2]

On taking over from Johnson, Warden Frost made a puzzling statement. "I do not owe my appointment to political influence," he said. "I was recommended for the place by prominent Democrats in Brooklyn."[3] A few days later he supervised the electrocution of a black man, William Nelson.

By 1909, in just two years the inmate population had grown by 350 to 1,855. To accommodate the huge overflow, Frost converted the Protestant chapel into a dormitory for some two hundred men. Because the chapel had been the only suitable place for a minstrel or vaudeville show, this meant no Christmas entertainment. On Christmas morning, Father C. V. Mahony celebrated high mass for Catholics who then joined the other prisoners in their cells for the rest of the day. Frost tried to make it up to them by providing a dinner of chicken fricassee, mashed potatoes, mashed turnips, bread and butter, hot tea, biscuits, cocoa with milk and sugar, mince pie, cookies, oranges, and two cigars apiece.

A commission charged with trying to solve Sing Sing's overcrowding had recommended building a new prison at Bear Mountain. Work had been underway there for two years when J. Pierpoint Morgan, Mrs. Edward H. Harriman, Rockefeller family members, and other plutocratic opponents of the new site bought the surrounding land and gave it to the state for a park— on condition that none of it should be used for a prison. They got what they paid for. Rather than have a prison surrounded by a public park, the state capitulated and construction for the new prison was abandoned.

The morning of July 28, 1909, a few weeks after Frost took charge, was a normal weekday. Inmates were working around the yards and in the shops, and armed guards were patrolling the grounds and manning the watchtowers on either side of the north gate. It was so hot that the warden ordered a wagon driver to go to the icehouse outside the prison walls and bring back a load of ice. As the gate opened to let the wagon through, twelve inmates made a run for it. Guards on the north wall opened fire with their rifles, the bullets kicking up the dust so close to the men on the run that eight turned back and gave up. The warden then ordered the gate closed, work to stop, and the remaining 1,832 prisoners inside to be hurried to their cells.

One of the four at large braved the bullets and ran for some three hundred yards before falling exhausted. A second was found hiding in the icehouse. A third gave up after a few minutes of flight. The fourth leaped aboard a freight train speeding through the prison grounds. Warden Frost sent a wire ordering the freight train to be stopped and several guards commandeered a passenger train going in the same direction. The freight stopped just north of Scarborough and when guards on the passenger train were dropped off near the freight train they began a careful search. Their quarry escaped them by ducking and dodging under and between the cars, then making a break for it, running north along the tracks. But a squad of guards, rifles at the ready, were waiting for him.

Frost was pleased to announce that three fugitives had been captured after fifteen minutes and the fourth after an hour. Not one got away.

However, twenty-nine-year-old convict William Green would soon embarrass Frost by making one of the most daring escapes in Sing Sing's history. Before his conviction for highway robbery, "Big Bill" Green was already known to the police as desperate and dangerous. Fellow prisoners regarded him as the toughest among them although he was under five feet eight and overweight at 249 pounds. His strength had been appreciated in the laundry where he worked during the day wringing the clothes dry—and of course, exercising his muscles. At night, because of overcrowding, he was one of 195 convicts sleeping on cots in long rows on the second floor of the three-story building previously used as the Protestant chapel.

The windows of this dormitory had heavy iron bars sunk into the stone frames. At one end of the room, a guard used what had been the chapel's altar as a platform from which, seated at a desk, he watched the inmates. A second guard paced in rubber-soled shoes between the rows of cots and frequently checked the adjoining washroom, hardly bigger than a closet, which also had a barred window.

On October 6, 1910, after dinner in the mess hall on the ground floor, Green was among the 195 inmates who climbed the one flight to the dormitory. There, he undressed, put his clothes in a bundle at the foot of his cot, and apparently went to sleep. Most lights were extinguished except for six dim bulbs which allowed the guards on duty to detect any attempt to leave the room or cause trouble.

There were only two guards armed with wooden clubs to control almost two hundred prisoners. One, Edward Foley, kept watch from his desk on the former altar while the other, Ferneau Drum, silently crept in rubber-soled shoes among the sleeping inmates throughout the night.

Shortly after midnight, when a howling wind and rainstorm hit the area, Green left his cot and went to the washroom. Two inmates followed him. Moments later Green came out and whispered to Drum, "There's a sick man in there."[4] He then led the way back into the washroom.

As Drum entered the room the swing door closed on him and Green felled him with a powerful punch to the side of his head, grabbed the guard's club, and battered him senseless. Guards no longer carried firearms, except in the watchtowers, for fear that the inmates would overpower them and steal them, as some had done in the past. The noise of the attack having been muffled by the raging storm, Green returned to the dormitory and walked toward the other guard. Not knowing what was going on, Foley had just stepped down from the platform to enquire about Drum when Green hurled himself on the guard, knocking him to the ground and smashing him against a sharp corner of the altar steps.

Awakened by the noise, other inmates watched silently, many standing with blankets clutched around them but making no attempt to help or hurt either of the men. Green quickly put a choke hold on the guard, stuffed a handkerchief in his mouth and secured it behind his ears, and then carried Foley like a child to his own cot. There he tore his sheet into strips and tied Foley to the cot. Still conscious, the guard watched helplessly as Green took a saw from under his mattress and returned to the washroom.

Despite the storm, Foley could hear Green sawing through one of the window's 1¼-inch iron bars. The window was six feet above the floor, so it is assumed that he stood on the backs or shoulders of the other two inmates as he made a horizontal cut. After about twenty minutes he severed the bar and, using his exceptional strength, wrenched it aside to make a ten-inch gap.

Green returned to the dormitory, calling out, "Any one who wants to get out can follow me."[5] Then he dressed and retrieved a long rope from under his mattress which he or a confederate had stolen from the prison's shipping department. Before leaving, he took $40 from Foley's pocket, then went to the altar platform and tore out the telephone wires to the warden's office.

Four inmates accepted the offer to escape with him. And their photos and descriptions were later distributed nationwide. They were: Isadore Blum, twenty, and 5 feet 2½ inches, serving a ten-year term for grand larceny; Joseph White, twenty-two, and 5 feet 6½ inches, serving ten years for robbery (White had a large irregular scar in the center of his forehead and a scar under his right eye); Walter Branigan, twenty-three, 5 feet 9 inches, still facing several more years of his fourteen-year sentence for assault and blackmail; and a convict named Boyland.

Green led the way to freedom, tying one end of the rope to the bar and squeezing through the ten-inch-wide space. When on trial for highway robbery, his defense had been that it would prove impossible for a man of his bulk to squeeze through a fourteen-inch-wide alleyway in which the crime had been committed! One by one, under cover of the pitch blackness and raging rainstorm, the five men climbed down the rope to the ground twenty feet below.

It was at least an hour before a convict warned Warden Frost of the escape. As he and several guards rushed to the dormitory, they saw a rope dangling from the second-floor window. To their surprise, when they entered the room every convict was lying on his cot, many with blankets pulled up over their heads—perhaps so they could say they saw nothing. Guard Foley was still tied to Green's cot with the gag in his mouth. Guard Drum crawled from the washroom, semiconscious and blinded by his own blood.

By the time the prison's steam whistle wailed out the escape warning, the five men had climbed over the river wall, swum the three miles across the Hudson to the village of Rockland on the Palisades, and separated.

Boyland was captured after three months, on January 6, 1911. Joseph White crossed the Atlantic by steamship to Liverpool where he got a cold reception from the local underworld and barely made a living. And he was homesick. So he returned to the United States where he worked as a waiter in Chicago. Not the most suitable work for a convict on the lam with distinctive facial scars and whose photo had been displayed across the nation. While eating at the restaurant, a detective recognized White and took him into custody. By February 1911, after four months of freedom, he was back in Sing Sing.

"Big Bill" Green, Walter Branigan, and Isadore Blum remained at large.

There was another dramatic escape on January 26, 1911, by three members of the prison band, one a murderer. During a rehearsal they used their cornets to batter two guards unconscious, then rushed from the building and disappeared into the cold, foggy night.

Band practice was a regular weekly event. Every Thursday evening at 6:30, sixteen prisoners were released from their cells to make music in the auditorium of the administration building. On the evening of January 26, guard Wilfred Webster escorted them there and remained, sitting near the locked door, listening to the music. When guard Alexander McGinley knocked on the door, Webster opened it and the two stood talking in the open doorway. As they spoke, three members of the band sprang from their chairs and, using their musical instruments as weapons, battered the guards unconscious and then ran into the foggy prison yard.

Another convict musician ran after them, yelling, "Help! They've killed the keepers! There they go!"[6] Guard James Woodley, armed with a revolver, heard him and fired five bullets at the dim figures racing past. Soon the yard was full of armed guards. Some followed the inmate who had raised the alarm back to the administration building, where the other convicts had made no attempt to escape. The wounded guards were carried to the warden's office where they recovered consciousness, and survived.

Every three minutes the shrill blast of the prison steam whistle brought off-duty guards flocking back to the prison to help in the hunt. Warden Frost told thirty of them to search the prison grounds, some the riverbank, and others to patrol the roads around the prison. He also telephoned the police in nearby towns and villages as well as in New York City with descriptions of the fugitives.

William Bush was serving a life sentence for killing the woman he had lived with; Charles McGinn, a burglar, in for five years, would have been eligible for parole in eight months; and Ralph Taylor, known as "The Silk Hat Burglar," had been given a twenty-one-year term for robbing seashore homes on Long Island Sound. When first arrested, Taylor had posed as a yachtsman and claimed that a companion in crime had hypnotized him into committing the robberies so that he did not realize he was doing anything wrong.

Until their escape, the three men had impeccable prison records. Taylor worked in the knitting shop where he may have obtained the tools to make two stilettos. McGinn had worked in the print shop. Bush worked in the wash house and as assistant librarian, taking books from the library to inmates in their cells.

The guard's five wild shots having missed them, the fugitives climbed an iron fence and reached the frozen Hudson. Taylor tied the rope around his waist and led the way on the ice, with McGill holding the other end of the rope, prepared to pull Taylor out if the ice broke under him. Bush brought up the rear. They stayed close to the shore until about halfway to the Ossining railroad station where they tried to return to the mainland. As they clambered up the steep, muddy bank in the thick fog, they lost touch with each other. Afraid that the pursuing guards were close by, Taylor dared not call out to try to locate the others. So he pressed on alone, sinking up to his knees in mud as he climbed a steep hillside and then headed for the Connecticut border.

Stumbling and staggering for hours through the cold fog, even though he kept the sound of the prison's warning whistle behind him to make sure he was heading north, he found that he had often walked in circles. Cold, hungry, dizzy, and nearly exhausted, he reached the village of Bedford Hills, fourteen miles north of Sing Sing.

Told of the escape, Eugene Fee, Bedford Hills' police chief, had sent his six-man police force on horseback to find the fugitives—a hopeless quest because of the thick fog.

On the afternoon of the second day, when the fog was lifting, Fee and a railroad man, F. R. Brigge, drove by car north of the village. They had gone about a mile and a half on Old Church Road, when in a depression at the road-side they glimpsed a man of average size who, despite the cold, was without a hat or coat. Moving closer, Fee took in the man's closely cropped hair and grey pants spattered with mud to the waist, and knew he had his man.

With a shout, Fee leaped from the car, followed by Brigge. Taylor ran for it, but the two quickly caught up with him. He turned, brandishing a stiletto. But they jumped him before he could use it and wrestled him to the ground. He continued to fight and tried to stab them, until Fee drew his revolver and held it at the fugitive's head.

Searching him, they found under his shirt a second prison-made stiletto, a fifteen-foot length of rope, and in one pocket a map of the country between Ossining and the Connecticut border. In the other pocket was a prescription for a morphine-based drug, which he said was to help him sleep when he finally reached a safe haven.

Weak from hunger, Taylor was taken in handcuffs to Bedford Hills' warm police station where he got coffee and sandwiches—his first food in twenty-four hours. Meanwhile, Police Chief Fee telephoned Sing Sing's Warden Frost to take Taylor back to his cell. One certain additional punishment Taylor now faced was to have four years and three months added to his sentence.

There was no thought of ending band practice—the band was a twenty-year tradition. Prisoners were very proud of their musicians who gave them concerts in the prison yard on the Fourth of July and other national holidays. To prevent similar future escapes, it was proposed that two guards attend future band practices—which might explain why escapes were inevitable. After all, two guards had been present during this latest escape!

Frost commanded Sing Sing for just five more months when, in July 1911, John S. Kennedy became his replacement.

No warden, and certainly not Kennedy, proved more daring and enterprising as a crime fighter than Dr. Amos O. Squire, the man destined to become Sing Sing's chief physician. He had already briefly served as a substitute doctor and later as a consultant at the prison.

When Kennedy took over, Dr. Squire was employed as Westchester County coroner. But he had expanded his growing job description by appointing himself the leader of a pack hunting down a woman's savage killer and his five accomplices.

On November 9 of that year, Mrs. Mary Hall was found lying in a pool of blood on the floor of her farmhouse near Croton Dam. She had been gagged with her own apron and slashed fifteen times with a stiletto plunged and twisted in her body. Her femoral artery severed, she had bled to death in minutes. The room was ransacked: bureau drawers left open and an empty jewel case, clothing, and other articles scattered on the floor.

When told of the killing, Dr. Squire was in his Ossining office. He immediately called District Attorney Lee Parsons Davis to join him at the farmhouse. Volunteer posses were already searching the nearby woods and Squire was afraid people were so scared that some innocent victim would be caught and lynched before the actual killer or killers were found. Then someone discovered a pile of workmen's clothing about fifteen hundred yards from the scene of the crime, identified as belonging to a group of Italian immigrants seen the previous day at Croton Road railroad station.

Sitting under a tree in the farmyard, Squire ordered every Italian within a radius of five miles of the farmhouse without a solid alibi to be brought to him (what today would be deplored as racial profiling). Within two hours, thirty Italians appeared before him. Adopting a new role, as magistrate, he dismissed four men and had twenty-six suspects sent to White Plains jail.

Back in his office he persuaded the district attorney to join him in the investigation while keeping the local police in the dark. Instead of seeking police cooperation, they hired a Manhattan detective who agreed, for $10 a day, to follow their instructions in every detail. Which meant that he didn't shave next morning. He dressed in old clothes, rumpled his hair, and, armed with a stiletto and a revolver, set off for Westchester. Reaching Ketchawan Bridge, near Croton Lake, he hid under it. And waited.

By this time Squire knew the details of the killing. A Miss Anna Griffin, tax collector for the local school district, had been downstairs in the farmhouse where she lived when several men invaded the place. One held Anna at gunpoint, told her to lie down and threatened to kill her if she disobeyed. As she lay on the floor she heard Mary Hall's screams coming from the second floor. After Anna handed over her pocketbook containing $15 and a bag of coins from the sale of milk and eggs, the men told her they wanted the

$3,000 they believed was in the house. They made her crawl to the safe and open it. Rather than $3,000, there was only $65—school funds—which she gave them. After the men left, Anna dashed up to Mary Hall's bedroom and found her tortured body.

Taking no one into their confidence, County Coroner Squire and District Attorney David had a chauffeur drive them, a county detective, and Anna Griffin, the crime-scene witness, toward Ketchawan Bridge. They misled the county detective into believing that they were merely going to interview another witness. In fact they were heading for the spot where the undercover detective, following their instructions, was hiding.

Squire planned to reach the hidden man first, claim that he was a suspect—he was certainly dressed for the part—and to appear to arrest him. Then Squire would put him in a cell with a real suspect, hoping that the undercover detective would get him to talk.

But the plan began to go awry. Just before reaching the bridge, Squire told the chauffeur to stop the car. But then he jumped out too soon, lost his footing, fell to the ground, and rolled off the highway. By the time Squire got to his feet, the county detective had already reached the disguised Manhattan detective and begun to beat him up. "Here, here!" Squire yelled. "None of that! You'll only damage our case by such tactics."[7] But the county detective was sure that the disreputable-looking character armed with a pistol and stiletto was the killer. "This is the bird we want, all right," he cried out. "You can tell he's a murderer by looking at him."[8]

For a moment Squire feared that their man would renege on the deal, but he proved to be a good sport as well as a convincing actor, glaring at them, as Squire recalled, "with a vicious, sullen expression—and contrived to look as guilty as a dog."[9] When he was locked in a White Plains jail cell with one of the real suspects, Squire and the DA took the sheriff into their confidence and he agreed to go along with their plan.

Before long the undercover detective's cellmate was sympathizing with him and ridiculing the authorities for imprisoning an innocent man. "You were not there," said the suspect to the detective. "You had nothing to do with it!" Then he gave his own self-serving account of the killing, even naming six others involved in the crime. Five were already in custody. When questioned, they guessed one of the gang had squealed and were eager to give their version of the event.

The five in custody—Santa Zanza, Angelo Guista, Vincenzo Ciornu, Felipe DeMarco, and Lorenzo Cali, all from Brooklyn—had been working on the Croton dam. When they bought milk and eggs from the nearby Griffin farmhouse they saw a safe there, which according to rumor held $3,000 that Anna Griffin had inherited from her father. Knowing there were only women in the house in the daytime, they decided to terrorize them and steal the money. While others threatened and robbed Anna downstairs, two of them went upstairs to rob Mary Hall. She gave them the small amount of cash she had, but they thought she was holding out on them and went berserk. When she screamed, they tore off her apron and gagged her with it, and, as one held her down, the other stabbed her repeatedly. Within a month of the crime all five were sentenced to death.

Soon after, the sixth man, Salvatore Demarco, was reported to be hiding in Brooklyn. Coroner Squire and two sheriffs went there and pulled him out from under a bed. They were just in time. He'd already booked his passage home to Italy. When he persistently denied being involved in the Griffin farm crime, Squire got a court order to allow the five held in Sing Sing to confront him. The mere sight of the prison seemed to break his nerve. Finally, after all five had identified him, he confessed. DeMarco led them to a field where he had thrown his revolver and to a stone wall where he had stashed the stolen money.

Zanza, who eventually admitted he had fatally stabbed Mary Hall, was executed a month before the others. On the day when the rest were electrocuted, two other condemned men also went to the chair—seven in one day—a New York State record.

Present as a witness, Coroner Squire recalled it as a ghastly occasion he never forgot. "Awaiting their turn in the condemned cells, the four who had never seen Mrs. Hall, the murdered woman, howled and screamed. All of us in the execution chamber—witnesses and officials—could hear them as could those who went first. The shrieking and wailing I heard that day is indescribable. I'm sure that all the witnesses in the room were indeed sorry they were there."[10]

Making a fast buck also seemed the aim of friends and relatives of the dead men, who claimed their electrocuted bodies and exhibited them in Brooklyn for a small admission fee—but not for long. Health officials visited the exhibition and ordered immediate burial.

The new warden, John S. Kennedy, in charge since July 1911, witnessed the seven executions along with Squire. Soon after, he fired John T. Powers, who for fifteen years had been the prison's Superintendent of Industries. Kennedy accused Powers of using inmates for his personal benefit, buying unnecessary articles and machinery, neglecting his duties and being frequently absent, and stiffing the government for his own private or business trips throughout the United States and Europe.

Months later Kennedy himself was on the firing line. George Blake, sent by the governor to investigate prison conditions, called Kennedy a brutal, wasteful, corrupt warden who let paying visitors meet convicts alone in a room next to his office.

Incensed, Kennedy demanded a grand jury to exonerate him. "I never accepted a dollar of graft in my life," he told a reporter. "Since I have been in charge here . . . I have yet to get one penny that was not honestly mine." He denied wasting money on food. Questioned about allowing paying visitors to be alone with prisoners, he replied: "No such incident ever happened." Kennedy did concede that the place was overcrowded with twelve hundred cells for 1,598 prisoners, which meant some shared a cell.

When he took charge, Kennedy said, "We had the problem to contend with of keeping apart old offenders or separating A men, first offenders, from the B and C men, both in the workshops and confinement. When I came here the B and C men were kept in confinement generally twenty hours of every day, and they did no work. Now I have changed that by putting the second offenders to making clothing in a special shop, and provided for the third class of prisoners in a rope-braiding shop for making mats."[11]

Warden Kennedy got his wish and doubtless wished he hadn't. A Westchester grand jury investigated Sing Sing and though, surprisingly there was no mention of drug traffic, they came up with a devastating indictment. Here it is in brief:

The Cells

The eighty-year-old cells are unfit for the housing of animals, much less human beings. They caused chronic rheumatism, and sometimes fatal heart disease and many inmates (in for from one to twenty years) leave the prison permanently crippled. The confinement of an average human being in a cell . . . is terrific punishment and if it does not lead to the contraction of some disease it results in an impairment of the nervous system.

The Toilets

Inmates are locked in their cells each with a bucket containing their excreta from 5:30 PM until next morning. And on weekends and holidays for twenty-one hours at a time. The bucket's "presence there in such restricted space and with the defective ventilation (especially in hot weather) is offensive and unsanitary, and when the cell is occupied by two persons these conditions are intensified. Drinking water is placed in a bucket which stands in the cell for hours at a time, and is therefore subject to contamination."

Vermin

The cell block is infested with disease-carrying vermin which it is impossible to eradicate. Vermin swarm in every corner of the cells, and on the bedding and bedclothes.

Two Men to a Cell

Sing Sing has 1,200 cells. Between 1911 and 1913 at any one time there were between 1,500 and 2,000 prisoners. A makeshift dormitory takes care of 135 inmates. But the rest of the overflow has to double up. The warden and head guard select those men. And frequently put inmates who are "repugnant and dangerous to each other" in the same cell despite their protests. No prison physician examines the men forced to share cells, consequently physically or mentally diseased prisoners are frequently "coupled with clean bodied, clean minded, and clean mannered men." Often men with advanced tuberculosis or syphilis are housed with men in perfect health. "Young boys are condemned to room with habitual criminals and creatures who made a practice of sodomy; no effort being made to prevent the doubling up of a hardened or habitual criminal with a first offender. . . . Immoral practices obtain among many of the inmates"

The Beds

The gas-piping frame of the prison bunk is hinged to the wall and the mattress made of vegetable fiber. When two share a cell the bunks are stacked one above the other. Their beds are two-feet wide but less than six-feet long, so that "an unusually tall man is uncomfortably placed, unless he has the good fortune to be transferred to the dormitory."

The Dormitory

This former chapel has been converted to sleeping quarters but "the bed space is grossly inadequate, the ventilation is insufficient, the close contact of the prisoners is demoralizing. Immorality abounds, disease is fostered, criminal propensities cultivated and inculcated."

The Cooler

The cooler is the dreaded solitary-confinement for breaking a prison rule. The accused faces the punishment board of three: the warden, principal guard, and physician, who decide on his fate. If found guilty, he is locked into one of two padded cells or one of the eight dungeons, all airless and pitch-black, for up to ten days or longer. Although required by statute, no doctor examines him to see if he is fit enough to survive the ordeal. In the daytime, the mattress is taken away and the inmate can rest only on the stone floor or his bucket. Once every twenty-four hours he gets a slice of bread and eight ounces (three-quarters of a glass) of water, when a man weighing 150 pounds requires fifty ounces of water daily. "This situation is as deplorable and pitiful as any we have found. So desperate is their condition that they have been known to drink their own urine, as well as the disinfectant placed in the cell buckets. This condition exists today, under the present administration, and is approved by the present Warden (Kennedy)." At night, no doctor is available to treat those suffering from various illnesses, wounds, hysteria, or imminent insanity. As a result some are driven insane, others attempt suicide.

The Hospital

Insane patients and those with contagious diseases share the same room and sleep in bug-infested cots. The head physician lives outside the prison grounds. Should a prisoner become ill during the night he is taken to the hospital but has to wait until the following morning for treatment.

The Kitchen

Odors from an unsanitary toilet in the prison kitchen intermingle with the food being cooked and the germs contaminate the food. Cut meat remains in buckets for several hours a few feet from the toilet, which has no vent pipe. The kitchen has a wooden floor under which is a cesspool from which water had been drained.

The Bath House

Half the showers don't work and sometimes as many as twelve prisoners, the diseased and the healthy, crowd under one shower. The steamy conditions allow perverts "thus screened from observation to practice acts of sexual degeneracy."

The Laundry

When, after they shower, inmates are handed their laundered underclothes they are usually damp. "The change from a hot steam bath to the damp clothing and the subsequent exposure in winter to the icy winds from the Hudson, render the prisoner susceptible to rheumatism and pulmonary troubles."[12]

The grand jury recommended abandoning Sing Sing and constructing, instead, a new state prison on a fertile and well-located site of up to fifteen hundred acres, and, by implication, recommended the firing of Warden Kennedy. He was fired that same month, and James M. Clancy moved into this house of horror.

Clancy quickly put down a mutiny and an attempted mass escape. A hundred and twenty of the ringleaders were transferred to Auburn Prison. Then Clancy gave those who remained a break. Instead of continuing to lock them up for the weekend, he let them out to "enjoy," as he put it, "the freedom of the prison" for the whole of Columbus Day.[13] However, they weren't allowed to move around, but had to stand or sit in groups, mute as cattle, and honor-bound not to cause trouble. Just in case, each group had guard escorts. Still, Clancy believed it was appreciated by the prisoners and improved discipline.

He had only been in charge for four months when a *New York Times* editorial recalled that the state had been trying to abolish Sing Sing since 1906. Why? Because

> the whole system under which this institution is conducted, for the reform of those undergoing for the first time a felon's sentence, is pernicious. The principle . . . is that of confinement, not of reform. Confinement breeds disease. As a disease-breeder Sing Sing has a record almost unequaled in the history of contemporary prisons. The physical infection is a sign, also, of lasting moral infection. The prisoners are not reformed. They are merely penalized, and in the worst way. The State Prison Association has asked Gov. Glynn to discount the pleas made for the renovation of the old prison and to expedite the plans for doing away with it altogether by building a prison industrial farm . . . that could be run in the interest of really reforming the prisoners. Such reformatories are bound to be healthful, since they require work in the fields, and not a life within dark walls. New Jersey has bought 1,000 acres for such a farm, Pennsylvania, 500 acres for its central prison, the district of Columbia is building a house of correction on 1,000 acres and Ohio is looking about for a farm site with broad acreage to replace the old State penitentiary at Columbia. In the Western States the prisoners are being transferred to the roads and fields, and cell blocks with their high prison walls are being abandoned. It is time we had more prisons like that at Great Meadow, where the inmates are locked in their cells only while asleep.[14]

Clancy was still in charge on May 30, 1914, when author Arthur Conan Doyle arrived. Of all the distinguished visitors to date, none was more interested or adept in criminology than Conan Doyle, creator of Sherlock Holmes.

He had also solved real-life crimes that baffled Scotland Yard. A man of curious contradictions, he happily harpooned whales in the Arctic while publicly deploring the killing of egrets to make feather hats for the likes of the queen of Denmark. He claimed to talk with the dead and confidently described life in heaven as if he were a heavenly travel agent.

In search of hell, perhaps, he toured Sing Sing, where Warden Clancy locked him in a cell for a few minutes. He also sat in the cane-bottomed electric chair, "with a good many sinister wires dangling round it," while puffing at his pipe, and suffered only slightly from the tight helmet squeezed over his head. This was a simulation of electrocution offered to VIPs short of pulling the switch. He quipped to the warden that it was a restful respite from reporters and described his stint in the chair as quite comfortable. But he expressed what were surely his true feelings when a *New York Times* reporter asked him how he would improve the prison. "Burn it down!" he replied.

> The buildings are absolutely antiquated and it is nothing less than a disgrace for a State so great and wealthy as New York to have a prison which is a hundred years behind the times. I am a medical man and naturally I was interested in the sanitary conditions . . . and I saw enough.
>
> When I say this I want to be understood as referring only to the mechanical side. Warden Clancy is a very remarkable man. It would be a great pity if for any political reason or through any change of influence he should be taken away. He has a big brain and a big heart, and is deeply interested in humanitarian measures for the prisoners. The way he has made the place work with insufficient means is extraordinary. I'd rather have a bad machine with Clancy at the head of it than a good one under an unsympathetic disciplinarian.
>
> As a medical man I took a great interest in the appearance of the men I saw, and it seemed to me that probably a third . . . were defective—men whose cases called for medical treatment or care in an asylum. Perhaps another third were young men who ought never to have been put in with hardened criminals, and the last third were the men for whom such places as Sing Sing have to exist.[15]

By chance, the day he arrived the inmates were enjoying one of their yearly treats, listening to a music hall troupe from Manhattan. "Poor devils," he wrote in his memoirs, "all the forced, vulgar gaiety of the songs and antics of half-clad women must have provoked a terrible reaction in their minds! Many of them had, I observed, abnormalities of cranium or of features which made it clear that they were not wholly responsible for their actions. There was a good sprinkling of coloured men among them. Here and there I noticed an intelligent and even good face. One wondered how they got there. . . . I had a long talk with the Governor, who seemed in himself a humane man, but terribly hampered by the awful building which he had to administer."[16]

Despite Conan Doyle's approval, Clancy was not retained long enough to repeat his Columbus Day experiment. Although Thomas McCormick, a former plumber who replaced him, did nothing to improve the plumbing, he went one better than Clancy. Believing that confinement within prison walls was punishment enough, he let inmates roam the prison yard on Saturday afternoons, and all day on Sundays. Guards warned him that they would be in mortal danger because the prisoners couldn't be trusted.

As was often the case, they were wrong. At first, inmates and guards eyed each other warily, but there was no violence. And there was less trouble on Mondays, when many had previously been sullen and angry after being locked up for the weekend. It encouraged McCormick to allow baseball on the recreation field and to let inmates establish a form of self-government known as the Golden Rule Brotherhood.

But McCormick's idea of brotherhood was too partial and broad-minded. He was dismissed after a reporter blew the whistle on him for giving special privileges to a wealthy inmate, David Sullivan, a former president of the Union Bank of Brooklyn, which he had wrecked through trading in worthless securities. Sentenced to hard labor, what Sullivan did was neither hard nor laborious: he did some bookkeeping in prison and acted as the warden's chauffeur, even driving him outside the prison grounds on several pleasure trips. Sometimes he even chauffeured the warden's wife and daughters without a guard along. When challenged, McCormick said that he was training Sullivan to work as a chauffeur after he left prison. He admitted that many of the eighteen hundred inmates could have driven the car, but that he wanted a gentleman as his chauffeur. Someone also suggested that McCormick had allowed prostitutes to visit favored inmates in their cells, which he vigorously denied.

Referring to the exposé, Dr. Katharine Davis, Commissioner of Corrections of New York, told a meeting of the State Federation of Women's Clubs that "One is apt to question this Warden's common sense. I know nothing against this Warden who has done so extraordinary a thing. I don't know whether he knows anything about psychology, though I understand he is a plumber by trade. Too often the Warden is appointed to pay him for political service, irrespective of his fitness, but I am glad to say we are slowly getting away from that sort of thing."[17]

Now that he was no longer warden, James Clancy brought a much more sensational charge about prison conditions. He claimed that a political ring made it possible to smuggle drugs, whiskey, and other contraband goods into Sing Sing. State Superintendent of Prisons John B. Riley fired back, asking why Clancy had never complained about political influence when he was in charge. Riley conceded that some guards probably smuggled drugs into the prison. But he pointed out that Clancy "was authorized to employ detectives and a considerable sum of money was paid in an effort to discover the guilty men. Nothing, however, was accomplished. Mr. Clancy never reported to me the seizure of whisky, cocaine, heroine, morphine and opium landed from a boat which left the dock hastily upon his appearance, as he said in an interview with him. I think he ought to tell what disposition was made of it. If there is or was a ring, Mr. Clancy after a year's experience should be able to give names of those composing it."[18]

Clancy responded three days later, testifying at a hearing before the State Prison Committee at 54 William Street in Albany. Then he denied claiming to know of a well-organized political ring in control of drug traffic at Sing Sing. He admitted that although the extent of drug traffic in the prison was appalling, sanitary conditions were worse: that the rampant tuberculosis, pneumonia, and rheumatism were more dangerous to the health of the inmates than the smuggled drugs. How the drugs got in, he said, despite the most rigid searches, was almost uncanny. One way was by boats on the Hudson, from which the drugs were unloaded and buried in spots where the guards knew where to dig them up. Others came hidden in pencils, fountain pens, the heels of shoes, in embossed postcards, and in handkerchiefs. Some guards made big profits as drug smugglers. Other prison employees, said Clancy, were paid to smuggle out letters to drug dealers with instructions on how to deliver the drugs.

Clancy revealed that "Superintendent of Prisons Riley has the sworn testimony of forty prisoners, giving the names of keepers with whom they did business. A certain lawyer who came to the prison to confer with a client, a man convicted of arson, carried away big packages of mail containing pleas for drugs. . . . We know that the lawyer and his client split the profits which they made in the drug traffic."[19] The lawyer had since been exposed and faced charges before the Bar Association for his part in the traffic.

Clancy doubted that the drug traffic could be eliminated, but might be reduced by isolating known addicts. Surprisingly he didn't criticize the crooked guards, saying instead that because of their poor pay—sixty-six dollars a month—one could hardly blame them for indulging in drug trafficking, where profit was up to 1,000 percent.

He gave the board a list of what he called high-class prisoners who might talk about the prison's drug traffic, if they could do so anonymously. Some had already helped him to fight the traffickers, at a cost. Because of their cooperation they were marked men—in danger of being killed on the prison grounds—and had to be kept in protective custody.

Clancy also warned that the prison foundry was in a dangerous condition and would collapse if not soon rebuilt. He recommended that a boot and shoe shop currently producing two hundred pairs of shoes daily should be expanded, as well as tinware, mat, and wagon production. He suggested eliminating the knitting shop because the women prisoners, who learned to knit in prison, found when they left that it didn't pay a living wage.

As for their pay while in prison, the ex-warden thought that the useful, well-behaved prisoner should be paid more than the lazy, troublesome one. (They both got the same one-and-a-half cents a day.) Or that the better worker should be rewarded by having his sentence commuted.

Clancy's final plea was to improve the sanitary conditions. He said that when he rubbed his hands over the first-tier walls, seven feet above water level, they were damp and that the odor was terrible. He didn't mention that his predecessor, as a plumber, could at least have done something about it. Perhaps, in time he might have, but McCormick was fired after only a few months and George S. Weed, an attorney, filled in until a permanent warden was appointed.

The silent rule had been abandoned for some time. Inmates were now occasionally allowed to talk to each other, as well as to express themselves in their own magazine. But were Clancy's stories of drugs, disease, and despair reflected in its features, written, edited, and printed by the prisoners themselves? Its title, *The Star of Hope*, suggested otherwise. The *New York Times* got hold of a copy and gave it a rave review.

In an editorial headed "Journalism behind Stone Walls," the writer expressed surprise "that this production of jailbirds . . . is superior to at least half the papers in the United States, not only in typographical appearance, but in the quality of English used in both its editorial and news columns. . . . The treatment shows an intelligence and thoughtfulness little to be expected from criminals, especially now that there is a common inclination to explain criminality as the result of defectiveness. Of defectiveness, none is revealed in *The Star of Hope*, at least to the inexpert observer, and strangest peculiarity of all, its editors and contributors seem to be, not a morose or resentful lot, inveighing against hostile society, but cheerful and hopeful. They are well up, too, in modern penology, and keenly appreciative of the alleviations which it is making in their lot."[20]

Among those alleviations was a Thanksgiving Day vaudeville show by the White Rats in the prison chapel. The performers gave a second performance to accommodate the overflow audience. Afterward, monitored by members of the Golden Rule Brotherhood—an organization of fellow convicts —the men played handball and baseball in the prison yard until sunset, then sat down to a turkey dinner, with a cigar apiece.

It hardly pacified the large group of convicts who staged a bloody riot on November 29. Some were doubtless members of the cocaine ring that Warden Weed had recently uncovered. He put down the riot and transferred 129 of the mutineers to upstate Auburn just in time to hand over the reins to the incoming warden, Thomas Mott Osborne, former mayor of Auburn and chairman of the Prison Reform Commission.

Osborne would be Sing Sing's most controversial warden, a man whose extraordinary positive influence is still felt in the prison community. Yet what a price he paid. No warden was to endure more attempts to destroy him than Osborne.

CHAPTER SIX

WARDEN OSBORNE— THE VOLUNTARY PRISONER

1913–1920

efore assuming command of Sing Sing, widower Thomas Mott Osborne, a wealthy businessman and father of four sons, got the go-ahead from New York State's superintendent of prisons and Warden C. F. Rattigan to live undercover for a week as an inmate in Auburn Prison, to learn for himself what it was like. Then he changed his mind.

Believing that inmates would penetrate his disguise and take him for an informer—which might have been fatal—he decided to come clean beforehand. Speaking to fourteen hundred of them crowded into the prison chapel on a Sunday in September 1913, he explained his plan. After a long introduction in which he touched on statistics, psychology, foreign travel, and foreign languages, he got to the point: "By permission of the authorities and with your help, I am coming here to learn what I can at first hand . . . to live your life, to be housed, clothed, fed, treated in all respects like one of you. . . . I am not so foolish as to think that I can see it from exactly your point of view. Manifestly a man cannot be a real prisoner when he may at any moment let down the bars and walk out. . . . (Many of the books written about you) are based upon the false and cruel assumption that the prisoner is not a human being like the rest of us, but a strange sort of animal called a 'criminal'—wholly different in his instincts, feelings and actions from the rest of mankind. I am curious to find out, therefore, whether I am right; whether our Prison System is as unintelligent as I think it is . . . whether, guided by sympathy and experience, we cannot find something far better to

Fig. 14. Thomas Mott Osborne (front row, sixth from the right in a white jacket) with inmates at Auburn Prison where he volunteered to become a temporary inmate as an experiment in empathy. (Courtesy Special Collections, Syracuse University Library)

take its place; as I believe we can. I want to see for myself exactly what your life is like, not as viewed from the outside looking in, but from the inside looking out. . . . In the meantime, help me to learn the truth."[1]

One inmate there later wrote: "The men could not realize what was actually meant by this at first; and as they grasped the idea it sort of staggered them and some thought, myself among others, 'What's the matter? What manner of man is this?'"[2] And they began to applaud with increasing enthusiasm.

On his arrival to begin the risky experiment on September 29, he was addressed by the guards as "Brown" and told to strip, then ordered into a bath—the warm water drawn by a black prisoner. After drying himself with a towel he was handed his all-new prison garb: underwear, a cotton shirt with narrow blue and white stripes, a suit of rough gray cloth, a cap of the same material, a pair of socks, and a pair of very thick, heavy shoes. Unlike other inmates he was allowed to keep and wear his wedding ring, but all the rest of his belongings were wrapped up and removed for safekeeping. He was also permitted to shave himself. The chaplain showed him a list of books he might borrow, but all those he wanted were unavailable, so he was given a Bible. When a doctor examined him and found nothing catching, a guard led him to his cell. As the door was double-locked behind him, he recalled the agonizing moment as a child when he had accidentally locked himself in a closet.

For the next week Osborne, known officially as Thomas Brown, no. 33,333x, wore a prison uniform, worked in the basket shop—for one-and-a-half cents a day—sweated on a road gang with pick and shovel, and marched to and from his cell 35, second tier north, north wing. At dinner a guard reprimanded him for turning around, saying that the rule still enforced during meals was eyes front, and absolute silence (although they were able to talk at other times).

As he had requested, Osborne mixed with the most dangerous bunch of prisoners known as the Idle Company.

Most of his communication with them was during his fourteen hours in solitary confinement, living on bread and a quarter of a pint of water, and having to sleep on the cell floor on which, he was told, an inmate had recently committed suicide. While there he listened to desperate men in nearby cells tell the heartbreaking stories of their mistreatment, as well as how they were attempting to make the best of it. "I must confess," he later wrote, "that, on the whole, more intelligent, instructive, and entertaining conversation it has seldom been my lot to enjoy."[3] Yet the week's experience enraged and traumatized him and he resolved, when he took over Sing Sing, to treat prisoners humanely and with respect.

One Sunday, now back in civilian clothes, he again stood before fourteen hundred mute prisoners in the chapel and told them how he had "lived among you, shared your food, gone to the same cells at night, and in the morning looked out at the piece of God's sunlight through the same iron bars. Believe me, I shall never forget you. In my sleep at night as well as in my waking hours, I shall hear in imagination the tramp of your feet in the yard, and see the lines of gray marching up and down."[4]

Their applause was followed soon after by letters from many of the inmates in which they showed that he had earned their affection and trust, addressing him as "Dear Tom," "Dear Pal," "Dear Brother." And often, "Dear Father."[5] A typical letter read: "You have done more good in the past few days than any other man or woman interested in Prison Reform. You was not ashamed to make yourself one of us . . . you lived as we live, ate what we ate, and felt the iron hand of discipline. You came among us as man to man and I heartily thank you for it. When you stood in the chapel last Sunday, and talked to us like a father with tears in your eyes and hardly able to speak, I prayed as I never prayed before, and asked God to care for you and watch over you in your coming struggle to better conditions here."[6]

After his voluntary imprisonment, Osborne listed his conclusions:

1. Prisoners are human beings, for the most part remarkably like the rest of us.
2. They can be clubbed into submission—with occasional outbreaks; but they cannot be reformed by that process.
3. Neither can they be reformed by bribery in the shape of privileges, special favors or tolerant treatment.
4. They will not respond to sentimentality; they do not like gush.
5. They appreciate a "square deal"—when they get one.
6. There are not many of them mental defectives; on the contrary, the majority are embarrassingly clever.
7. All these facts must be taken into consideration if we want prisons which will protect society. Unless they are taken into consideration, our correctional institutions will continue to be what they have been in the past—costly schools of crime—monuments of wasted effort, of misguided service. It is now time that a system is formulated resting upon the genuine psychology of the prisoner.[7]

He came away convinced that "every man in this place hates and detests the system under which he lives . . . even when he gets along without friction. He hates it because he knows [that] it tends to crush slowly but irresistibly the good in himself."[8]

Many guards while appearing to be noncommittal had ridiculed Osborne and considered him naïve and his "experiment" futile.

He was sorry for them and understood why, despite all precautions, they could be "reached." They were underpaid and overworked. He knew of one who augmented his low pay by about $100 a month as a dope dealer, buying three dollars' worth of opium from an out-of-town druggist, and selling it through a convict go-between for $10 a throw. He discovered that "nearly every keeper had his own special line of graft. One keeper dealt in 'crooked letters only' and if you wanted to smuggle out a letter, he would take it out for twenty-five cents."[9] Another dealt in tea.

"Much as I pity the prisoners," Osborne wrote, "I think that spiritually their position is far preferable to that of their guards [who] are placed in an impossible position; for they are not to blame for the System under which their finer qualities have so few chances of being exercised. . . . I should not like to be understood as asserting that all keepers are brutal, or even a majority of them." Then, with a touch of mockery, he added: "I hope and believe that by far the greater number of the officers serving in our prisons are naturally honorable and kindly men, but so were the slave-owners before the Civil War."[10]

The *New Republic* gave a fair account of Osborne's views: He "came out refusing to deny the existence of evil in the natures of the prisoners but believing that there is no such thing as a criminal class, believing that each convict is a different human problem, that brutality engenders brutality, and that the old system denies humanity not only cruelly but against common sense."[11]

One of Osborne's remedies was to treat every inmate fairly and to reward those who meant to go straight and "to lift himself above the level of the pervert and the degenerate."[12]

Many newspapers ridiculed Osborne's experiment, calling it variously the freakish, foolish, bizarre, and quixotic work of a dilettante. The *Bridgeport Standard* scoffed that it was "not necessary to wallow in a mud hole to know how pigs feel." The *New York Times* judged it to be "well-intentioned but ill advised." A rare exception, the *New York Tribune*, called it a "noteworthy humanitarian experiment."[13]

The eighth Sing Sing warden in ten years, the Harvard-educated Osborne was an enormous improvement over the slew of inept or corrupt wardens who preceded him, and the antithesis of Sing Sing's first sadistic warden, Elam Lynds. A former newspaper publisher and manufacturer, and a friend of Franklin Delano Roosevelt's, Osborne had been Auburn's mayor before his appointment as chairman of the State Commission on Prison Reform. A sensitive, humane, innovative man of literary and artistic tastes, his enthusiasm for amateur dramatics and his political ambitions explain why he occasionally appeared disguised in public.

As August Heckscher, a fellow Auburn resident, explained, Osborne's intent was to hear or overhear the uncensored opinion of townspeople on how he was doing as mayor: "The story about Thomas Mott Osborne was that he used to dress up—we always had lots of amateur dramatics in Auburn—in various disguises and go down into all the dives and taverns of the town to hear what they were saying about his administration and to get the real feeling and sense of the people."[14] For much the same reasons, Osborne had assumed the role of a convict.

Early in the morning of November 30, 1914, the tall, handsome, and ebullient new warden formally took charge of the prison. Knowing that he was a staunch Democrat, the Republican governor of New York State, Charles Whitman, a former state prosecutor, had promised him a free hand and to keep politics out of the Prison Department, a promise that proved impossible to keep.

The previous year, a Westchester County grand jury had made a devastating indictment of Sing Sing, where, it reported, "Immoral practices [occur] among many of the inmates; acts of perversion are taken for granted; sodomy is rife." Osborne said that he deplored "the moral perverts" and believed that they should be segregated from the general population "until science has determined the wisest method of treatment for them."[15]

On his first morning in Sing Sing, Osborne walked to the mess hall alone and watched the prisoners march in for breakfast of hash, a glance at which turned his stomach. Then he went to his apartment on the prison grounds overlooking the death house. There an inmate, formerly the chef at a prominent Manhattan hotel, prepared his somewhat more appetizing breakfast. Not only the prisoners' food, but the filth everywhere—even in the hospital's operating room and nurses' dormitory—disgusted him.

And he was dismayed by the listlessness of students in a school for illiterates. That evening Osborne invited the president and five committee members of the Golden Rule Brotherhood (the group that gave the prisoners some privileges) to his office, and told them that being new to the job he would rely on them for suggestions and advice. Next day's *New York Times* reported with a smirk: "The first day was a great success in every way. There were no incendiary fires, no riots, and no strikes—all marks of coming or going of wardens in the past."[16]

In the following days, guards were astonished to see Osborne, alone and unarmed, chatting freely with convicts in the yard.

Previously, convicts had been forbidden to approach within fifteen feet of the warden, who had always carried a loaded revolver on his rounds. After a week the bewildered head guard, who had been employed in Sing Sing for almost a quarter of a century, told Osborne the "remarkable news" that "there isn't a single man under punishment! In all my experience at Sing Sing I have never known such a condition. I don't believe it's happened before since the prison was built, certainly not in my time."[17]

One Sunday, at a mass meeting of prisoners in the chapel, the executive committee of the Golden Rule Brotherhood—which gave them a measure of self-government—formally presented Osborne with fifteen reforms they wanted put into effect. He accepted thirteen of them.

The most radical reforms he okayed were: prisoners could have visitors on Sundays and holidays, buy postage stamps and write necessary letters to those not on the official correspondence list, keep their lights on for a half hour longer to give more time for reading, and watch movies on Sunday afternoons. Sick and handicapped prisoners would get first consideration in being placed in the more comfortable dormitory that housed the prison over-flow, and, whenever possible, an inmate would get a cell to himself, instead of having to double up. Only two requests were denied: removal of the screens separating prisoners and their visitors in the visiting room, and for inmates to get the Sunday papers.

One of the thirteen reforms he approved had actually been suggested by Osborne: a prisoners' court in which fellow inmates would be the judges. The committee suggested that this should apply only to minor infractions, but Osborne decided to try all cases in the chapel each afternoon before five judges—all inmates. The accused might represent himself or employ a "counsel" of his choosing. Both accused and accuser could call witnesses and take testimony, and the court was open to all who wished to attend. This meant that if an inmate tried to murder a guard, fellow inmates, not Osborne, would judge him. However, the warden reserved for the accused the right to appeal the verdict, and for himself the right to appeal or to overturn the court's decision. It would then be heard by the warden's court consisting of Osborne, the head guard, and the prison doctor.

In return for Osborne's reforms, he told the inmates that he expected them to treat each other and prison officials with courtesy, and to keep them-selves and the prison clean.

During the first month, December, with the new rules in force, thirty-four inmates appeared before this court of their peers. Twenty-eight were found guilty. Three were judged not guilty and three cases were dismissed. Compared with the past, the punishment was mild—being suspended from the brotherhood for various periods. But it was amazingly effective. Now there were practically no violent crimes in Sing Sing and few cases of insubordination. Especially appealing to the prisoners was Osborne's order that none of the punishments were to be recorded, so that on his release a convict would have a clean record.

Later, an ex-prisoner told a meeting in New York why the new system worked: "Take the mess hall at Sing Sing. Under the old system they had forty guards along the walls at mealtime. If any fight broke out in the middle of the hall none of the prisoners would try to stop it—it was the business of the guards to do that, and to arrest the fighters. But it was very dangerous business for the guards to go into the midst of prisoners in the mess hall; for there was lots of crockery handy and we each had our favorite guard! Now, under the League . . . if there should be a fight the men around would stop it, for it would be bad for them—it would endanger League privileges. The Sergeant-at-Arms and the deputies would go right in—because they are prisoners like the rest. They can handle any such trouble without starting a riot; but the guards can't."[18]

On Christmas Day inmates were entertained in the chapel by Owen Brady and Alice Brady, making her debut as the star in a new play. The title alone, *Sinners*, delighted the audience. Its producer, William Brady, offered a $100 prize for the best review of the play. The winner donated the money to the Golden Rule Brotherhood. It would have taken the reviewer twenty-two years to earn the same amount from his prison-shop pay of two-and-a-half cents a day.

Osborne's humane attitude had a remarkable effect on one of the toughest prisoners in Sing Sing: Canada Blackie, a dark-eyed, black-haired, square-jawed man, who left Canada after his mother's death and joined the circus, then worked as a cowboy, before he turned to crime. He killed a watchman in a bank robbery, and was given a life sentence. After a clean record for seven years in Clinton Prison, he became a troublemaker and spent much of his time in solitary. Despite his reputation he was able to get material to make a gun and ammunition which he used to wound a guard during a failed escape attempt.

For that, writes Osborne, he received ten additional years, "and spent the next year and eight months in the 'dark cells' without bed or blankets, sleeping on the frigid stone floor. He kept time by reciting poetry and playing solitary games, such as throwing and retrieving buttons he tore from his clothes. When he was finally brought out, Blackie was blind in one eye and coughing from tuberculosis. For three years after that he remained in solitary confinement [though] in a lighted cell. . . . Yet somehow he managed to have dynamite smuggled into the prison and hidden for him in the main yard. But he was caught once more and transferred to Auburn, where he was placed in solitary again."[19]

Preparing for another escape attempt, after his transfer to Sing Sing, Canada Blackie made a key that could open his cell door. But then he handed it and a knife to Osborne, telling him that he had given up his new escape plan. As a reward, Osborne allowed him to walk outside the solitary area where, Blackie later wrote: "Instead of the prison pallor and haunted look which once predominated, I now notice smiling eyes, and that clean look which exhilarating exercise in the pure air always brings to a face."[20] Blackie also saw, to his delight, a ring of men watching something in the yard, which turned out to be a group of Italian prisoners dancing.

Author Scott Christianson wrote: "As an idol to the other convicts, Blackie's strong support of Osborne and the Mutual Welfare League proved invaluable. Consequently, as he lay dying of tuberculosis, Blackie was granted executive clemency and moved to a bed in the warden's house. . . . Two convicts were brought over to nurse him till the end. Blackie told the chaplain: 'As a friend, you are welcome; but I hope you don't think, after what I've been and after all I've done, that I'm going to try and sneak into Heaven through a back door!'" He died on March 20, 1915, a man Osborne called "one of the many thousands of martyrs of the brutal old prison system."[21]

Osborne believed that if he could control the most dangerous and rebellious inmates—he was warned that a group of them worked together—other inmates might follow their lead. So he told this group that on their marches to and from the mess hall he was replacing escorting guards with members of the brotherhood. The next day he complimented them on their marching, and added: "I have heard that your company is the worst behaved in Sing Sing; but there has been no trouble yet, and I don't expect any. But as I wish to make certain there will not be any, I am [also] going to take all your guards out of the shop [where the group worked]; for, of course, if there is no one to make trouble for you, there won't be any trouble."[22]

After gasping with astonishment, the men roared with laughter, and then cheered. It was his turn to be astonished the next day when a delegate from the group asked to retain one guard, whom they liked, to help maintain order and increase production in the shop. Osborne agreed. Soon afterward guards were removed from all the workshops with the exception of those who were needed to handle production problems. And most of those guards wore civilian clothes.

A major problem Osborne faced was the drug trade in prison. Three-quarters of New York State's inmates were in Sing Sing, and many had brought their drug habits with them, using ingenious modes of delivery. The dope came concealed in their clothing, "nailed under the truck which brought freight from the railroad; hidden under the coal barge . . . thrown over the wall . . . concealed in books, magazines, postcards, and letters; it came fastened by surgeon's plaster to the soles of feet. . . . The chief difficulty arose from the fact that some of the authorities themselves [as in Auburn] were engaged in the traffic."[23]

Osborne, who had asked inmates to help him eliminate the prison's drug traffic, was told how some of them had gone about it. They had confronted a "crooked screw" known to peddle liquor and drugs, found a bottle of whiskey on him, smashed the bottle, warned him, and then let him go.

When, soon after, a guard reported that Sing Sing was drug-free, except for small amounts that new arrivals might have smuggled in, Osborne was pleased but skeptical. However, he had newcomers searched more thoroughly—and successfully. Several addicted inmates even checked themselves into the hospital for a cure. Osborne was almost persuaded that the prison *was* drug-free when an addicted inmate said that he couldn't get any dope, and if he couldn't, then no one could.

His radical reforms appealed to many guards, because, as the brotherhood had taken over some of their duties, the warden was able to reduce their work hours. Instead of the two-shifts of fourteen hours each, the guards now worked three eight-hour shifts.

Among other changes that Osborne proposed was to rename the Golden Rule Brotherhood the Mutual Welfare League, with "Do Good, Make Good" as its motto. He also wanted to increase the league's executive committee from five to nine members, and to extend voting rights to all inmates in good standing, including the illiterates. His ideas were overwhelmingly approved. In return for their cooperation, he allowed prisoners to speak to each other at mealtimes, to organize a prison orchestra, and to spend an hour after work at exercise or recreation. But the recreation had its limits: he stopped the earlier practice of supplying prostitutes to moneyed inmates.

Because Osborne opposed capital punishment and was sickened at the thought of the electric chair, he sat up all night in the death house with men condemned to die the next day, but never actually witnessed an execution.

In February 1915, he supervised the predeath rituals for the execution of three men, Robert Kane, Vincenzo Campenelli, and Oscar Vogt, who had murdered a woman. In April he allowed Bishop Greer to conduct a service in the death house, during which the bishop's daughter sang. The following month, evangelist Billy Sunday, a former professional baseball player, gave the convicts a pep talk with religious overtones and theatrical gestures.

During the summer of 1915, one prisoner attempted suicide and another rescued a man and woman from a capsized boat on the Hudson River. One prisoner escaped and was recaptured. Another got away, and Osborne blamed the guards. He allowed convict Peter Cullen to marry Julia Sullivan in a prison ceremony, and okayed the request of another inmate to raise a goat on the prison grounds.

One high-profile prisoner awaiting execution in July 1915 was Charles Becker, a New York City police lieutenant twice found guilty of using a hit man to murder gambler Herman Rosenthal.

Becker was known to New York crime reporters as the city's most corrupt cop, who took bribes from petty criminals as soon as he put on the uniform. Promoted to lieutenant in 1910, he expanded his operations to brothels, nightclubs, and gambling casinos, demanding a 25 percent cut of their profits. In 1912, according to investigators, casino owner Herman Rosenthal refused to pay Becker protection money. Becker responded by raiding, looting, and destroying Rosenthal's casino. Rosenthal reported the crime to

Fig. 15. Police lieutenant Charles Becker, reviled as "The Killer Cop," with his wife, Helen, who vainly pleaded for his life. He was executed in 1915. Osborne thought he was innocent. (Library of Congress)

the New York DA, who was hell-bent on wiping out police corruption. Becker's next move was to hire hit man Big Jack Zelig to eliminate his accuser. Zelig did the job but the getaway car was traced to him. He named Becker as the client who'd ordered the killing.

Osborne had considered the handsome, six-feet-four-inch policeman capable of murder, judging by a hardness about his eyes and mouth. Becker admitted to less lethal crimes, such as graft, but swore that he had not killed Rosenthal. The more Osborne spoke with him, the more he believed that the criminals who had testified against Becker had done so to save themselves.

He was convinced of this when a Sing Sing prisoner named Murphy told him that, while awaiting trial, he had overheard men planning faked testimony to incriminate Becker. Murphy explained that he had come forward because he didn't want an innocent man's blood on his hands. However, Gov. Charles Whitman refused to hear the new evidence. But the day before the execution Murphy again approached Osborne and, sobbing hysterically, handed over a written plea that read: "I know positively, absolutely, that he is an innocent man. I overheard the plot of the real murderers who are now sacrificing Becker to save their worthless lives. If he goes to the chair I can never forgive myself for concealing what I knew for three years, but I could not believe he would be doomed."[24]

Governor Whitman could have commuted his sentence to life, but Whitman was the former state prosecutor who put Becker in the death cell in the first place. This was a unique situation in the nation's history. When it was suggested that the lieutenant governor should review the case, the governor refused to allow it.

Becker's wife, Helen, was his last hope. She arrived at Sing Sing the night before his scheduled execution, to plead for his life. She had tried to contact Governor Whitman in Albany, but no one knew where he was. After frantic efforts to find him, she finally reached him by phone at a Poughkeepsie hotel. But his answer was an emphatic no.

That night, Osborne joined Becker in his death cell lit by one light bulb, sat beside him on his cot, and stayed until almost dawn, at which time Father Curry entered. Becker told the priest that he was in no way responsible for the gambler's death.

Reporters flocked to the prison on the morning of July 30, 1915, the date for the police lieutenant's electrocution. Osborne had made Sing Sing much more accessible to the press, as representatives of the public, in line with his belief that "many, if not most of the iniquities which characterized the old prison system followed from its secrecy and seclusion."[25]

Fig. 16. The cartoon shows Osborne as Sing Sing's new warden, having changed the motto ALL HOPE ABANDON YE WHO ENTER HERE to HOPE YE WHO ENTER HERE. (*Puck* magazine 1915)

From "Puck," 1914, 1915 — Now the "Comic Weekly Puck."

THE CHALLENGE

Dressed in black, Becker's last words were, "Into thy hands O Lord, I commend my spirit!" And he died with a sheet of paper across his breast on which was scrawled: "You killed an innocent man." It took three jolts of electricity and eight minutes to kill him. He may have been innocent. Many guards believed that he was the innocent victim of a conspiracy, but no exonerating evidence has surfaced since his execution.

Becker had been an almost model prisoner. An inmate who gave Osborne more trouble than anyone in the death cells was a former crooked Manhattan banker, Williams Cummins, in for larceny. He bitterly resented the warden's sweeping reforms. Before Osborne's arrival, Cummins lived as if he owned the place, which wasn't far from the truth. He had the title of record clerk and spent his days in an unbarred room with a desk where he had transacted private business through his agent, who was allowed to visit him at any time. So were his wife and daughters. He wore custom-made prison clothes and, unlike any other prisoner, white shirts with neckties. He had never slept in a cell, bedding down in the nurses' dormitory.

At first Osborne had tolerated this favored treatment, except for putting the banker behind bars at night and making his business agent apply for the customary visitors' permits. It wasn't long before he discovered that Cummins was the prison's dictator. As president of the Golden Rule Brotherhood, he had gained control of the organization by promising other prisoners jobs in his bank when he and they got out. And he had disenfranchised almost half the prisoners he couldn't control by restricting brotherhood membership to inmates who read, wrote, and spoke English.

Osborne had first antagonized Cummins by replacing the brotherhood with the more democratic Mutual Welfare League, which gave all inmates the vote. But what drove Cummins to destroy Osborne was his refusal to join senators, governors, and judges in urging Governor Martin H. Glynn to grant the ex-banker executive clemency. Although the rules did not allow Osborne to sign such a petition, Cummins expected Osborne to break them in order to set him free.

Meanwhile, Cummins was secretly corresponding with members of the state legislature and other power brokers, asking them to bend the prison rules to his advantage. When Osborne discovered it, he had Cummins and his cronies transferred to Great Meadow Prison.

Soon afterward, Osborne got a tip that the embittered group under Cummins's control was slandering him, and he sent a private detective to Great Meadow Prison to investigate. There the detective introduced himself to Warden Homer as a writer who had heard rumors of discontent at Sing Sing, and was just after the facts. Homer complained to him that Osborne was overloading his Great Meadow Prison with Sing Sing rejects, and introduced him to one of them: none other than Osborne's bête noire, Cummins. In the warden's presence, the former banker accused Osborne of being "a visionary" guilty of favoritism, double crossing, dealing with rats, and of letting "rats get the better of him. He wanted me to be his rat, but I wouldn't, so he shipped me up here."[26]

In fact, according to Osborne, Cummins had once offered to spy for him—an offer he'd rejected.

Before the private detective left, Cummins dropped a bombshell: "Sing Sing is a hotbed of sodomy," he told him. "Osborne himself is a pervert and spends much of his time with the younger boys."[27]

Word of the charges was leaked to the *Brooklyn Times*. The paper was pleased to learn "that Governor Whitman intends to investigate the noisome scandal at Sing Sing Prison, which is being openly paraded under the guise of humanitarian and criminologist reform."[28] And the paper called for Osborne's ouster.

In October 1915, a Dr. Rudolph Diedling, hired by those out to discredit Osborne, interrogated the warden, and a stenographer recorded their conversation.

When Diedling expressed an interest in the activities of a young Sing Sing convict, James Harvey, Osborne said that Harvey claimed to have sold himself to twenty-one inmates, all of whom had denied it, until Osborne had promised them confidentiality. Then, all but three admitted that it was true. Osborne kept his promise not to name them, but told Diedling that he had deprived those concerned of all privileges, put them under special surveillance, and assigned them to digging a sewer.

Diedling, a self-proclaimed expert on penology, believed that the only way to reform an inmate was "to hit him on the nut with an ax," and that Osborne's methods were idiotic.[29]

After speaking with Osborne, he questioned nine of Sing Sing's community of 1,618, among them guards Osborne had fired, prisoners with a grudge, mental defectives, and degenerates. Next stop was Great Meadow Prison, where Cummins, the ex-banker, told Diedling that Osborne had surrendered control of Sing Sing to roughnecks, that sodomy was rampant, and that prison cell doors were often left unlocked for prisoners to get together. In a subsequent report, Diedling called for a grand jury investigation of Osborne and recommended firing him.

Although Osborne invited a Westchester County grand jury to visit Sing Sing to see things for itself, the invitation was declined. However, in December, a Kings County grand jury made the trip on its own initiative, visited every department, interviewing inmates, shop foremen, and guards. It endorsed Osborne's reforms, and was impressed with the morale of the men.

Nevertheless, the Westchester County grand jurors decided to investigate Osborne themselves. From the very start, it was clear that there was a conspiracy to discredit Osborne at all costs. Among other things, he was accused of selling a calf for fourteen dollars, and pocketing the money; of luring women who were visiting the prison into his apartment, and then insulting them.

An inmate known as Fat Alger testified that he had drunk claret on the warden's porch and stayed in his bedroom until three in the morning. Osborne's other accusers included a man awaiting trial for attempting to rape a child crippled with infantile paralysis, and who had been convicted of a similar crime. He swore that he had seen improper relations between Osborne and an inmate known as Jack the Dropper. After the rapist had testified against the warden, he went on trial himself, was found guilty, and was sentenced to a mere sixty days in jail.

A young inmate, Paul Vogel, testified that one night a guard had escorted him from his cell to Osborne's bedroom, where the warden made improper advances. Yet, that same night, Osborne was, in fact, out of the prison and many miles away, giving a talk in Germantown, Pennsylvania.

The Westchester grand jurors had heard enough. Three days after Christmas 1915, they indicted the warden for perjury and neglect of duty. The six counts included violating prison rules, and causing a general breakdown of discipline and morale. And, finally, of committing "various unlawful acts with inmates of Sing Sing Prison over whom he had supervision and control."[30]

Osborne quickly hit back:

> Because I have run Sing Sing with business honesty and efficiency I have made myself hated by the corrupt political element that have long utilized the prison for their own foul purpose. Because I have reduced vice and disorder to a minimum within the prison, I have incurred the hatred of the few prisoners who had long enjoyed special privileges at the expense of their fellows. Because I have served the state to the best of my ability, the very machinery of law intended for the protection of society has been prostituted from its high purpose to serve the vilest end by means equally vile.
>
> This is not a personal fight. It belongs to every citizen in the State of New York. It is not one innocent man alone that has been indicted. The attack is directed against every honest office holder in the state, every other believer in decency in private life, every other believer in fair dealing between man and man, every other man who has endeavored to make his faith in God a living principle of action. I have no fear of the result. No jury will be blind enough, no court unfair enough, to carry this conspiracy to ultimate success. The real question is: What do the people of New York State propose to do about it?[31]

When Osborne told the prisoners in the mess hall about the indictment, they listened in stunned silence, then, when he said he would fight it, they cheered. Aside from the clique determined to destroy him they were overwhelmingly in his corner. So were the guards.

They proved it with this letter to Governor Whitman: "Owing to the fact that the impression has gone abroad that the guards and other employees of the institution are unfavorably disposed to the new order of things installed here by our Warden, Hon. Thomas Mott Osborne, and further, that we are resentful toward him and deplore the lack of discipline now alleged to [occur] because of his placing the same, as is slanderously said, in the hands of vicious inmates, we feel it our duty to protest these statements, to repudiate them indignantly, and to state most emphatically that never in the history of this prison have such cordial and kindly relations been established and maintained between the Warden, the inmates and ourselves."[32] It was signed by the head guard, the superintendent of industries, eight foremen, eleven men on the office staff, and ninety-nine of the one hundred Sing Sing guards.

On December 31, 1915, Osborne began to work on his defense, while his friend George Kirchwey, former dean of Columbia University's School of Law, took over as acting warden.

A few days later, Prison Superintendent Riley ordered Kirchwey to reinstate the prison officials Osborne had fired. He refused. Then Riley sent Kirchwey a list of sixty-six inmates to be transferred from Sing Sing to Clinton, including leaders of the Mutual Welfare League, the conductor of the band Osborne had encouraged, and the head of his Education Committee. Clearly, Riley was trying to destroy the league and rid Sing Sing of men who respected and admired Osborne. Kirchwey again refused, and showed Riley's list to Governor Whitman.

The governor noticed that of the fourteen men Osborne had named as his defense witnesses, Riley had put eight of them on the transfer list. Riley's lame excuse, that Sing Sing was overcrowded, was exposed when it was shown that he was planning to transfer a score of Clinton inmates to Sing Sing. The governor dismissed Riley a few days later, with the scornful approval of a *New York Call* editorialist, who wrote that "Whitman isn't a great Governor, not even a fairly decent Governor—he's just a temporizing, fence-fixing little politician—but he may be thanked for kicking Riley out."[33]

Osborne received enormous public support, notably at a mass meeting in Carnegie Hall on January 16, 1916, attended by about thirty-five hundred members of the public, some of them former felons. A month later, Harvard president Charles Eliot, Judge William Wadhams, and several other men of distinction championed Osborne and his reforms in the same hall, at a meeting organized by ex-convicts, who also spoke in Osborne's favor.

Osborne himself was present at that second meeting, together with Sing Sing's head guard, Frederick Dorner, who had resisted threats and bribes and remained loyal to his chief.

Meanwhile, Whitman waffled. Under the subtitle "Whitman Forced Osborne Out," the *New York Times* quoted the governor as saying that although he "had received hundreds of messages from all parts of the United States, asking him to intercede in favor of Osborne," and that he both believed Osborne was innocent of the immorality charge and admired "the work the reform Warden had undertaken," he had decided that Osborne "must get out, without consideration of the why or wherefore of his return to Wardenship."[34]

Osborne felt betrayed by Whitman. He was also convinced that the governor could have prevented the case from going to trial. He suspected that the governor's motives in not doing so were Whitman's political ambitions.

So he took his fight to the public, speaking to enthusiastic standing-room-only audiences at colleges, churches, and public halls. Even the press, which had at first ridiculed his attempted reforms, now gave him a fair, and sometimes fervent, hearing. His policy of opening up the prison to reporters

Fig. 17. Death row. (Courtesy Guy Cheli)

was paying off: many respected him, after seeing for themselves how he had improved prison conditions. In fact, there was more press coverage on penal reform during Osborne's two years at Sing Sing than at any previous time in the country's history.

A supporter, Francis Hackett, believed that Osborne should be judged by results, writing in the *New Republic* for January 16, 1916: "In the hideous, obsolete, disgraceful environment of Sing Sing, handicapped within by physical conditions, handicapped without by multiple bitter enmities, Mr. Osborne has worked so effectively inside one year as to put a new heart into 1,600 condemned men. Knowing some of these men to be dangerous, some of them to be inimical to his experiment, Mr. Osborne has dared to regard his community as human. . . . He has trusted himself enough to give them the freedom by which fallen beings can learn to walk. Such limited leeway is easily misunderstood. It is easily garbled in reporting or describing. But go to Sing Sing, if you can, and see the convicts. See the system as it is working and ask yourself if the goal is receding, or nearing. It is the goal for which few prison officials have ever wisely striven, in the interminable and blundering history of prisons—the goal of equipment for society. In spite of the tuberculosis, the rheumatism, the filth, the vermin, the foul air, the infection which we still force on these men, are they closer to coming back with a fair mind? If they are, it is because of one man's unusual public spirit, imagination and grit."[35]

Osborne was charged with perjury, immorality, and neglect of duty, when his trial began before Justice Arthur Tompkins of the New York State Supreme Court on March 13, 1916. Assistant District Attorney William Joseph Fallon, of the resonant voice and perfect diction, later famous as "The Great Mouthpiece," led the prosecution, which he later admitted would more appropriately have been called a persecution.

The defense won the first round by establishing that Dr. Diedling had no authority to take Osborne's testimony on oath, and that Diedling's stenographer had either garbled or mistyped Osborne's words. So the judge threw the perjury charge out of court. That left the charges of immorality and neglect of duty. Osborne's attorney, George Gordon Battle, effectively discredited prosecution witnesses as either unreliable or disreputable convicts who had been offered sentence reductions for their testimony.

Five judges of the Appellate Division of the State Supreme Court unanimously agreed, and dismissed the charge of immorality. Having virtually lost its case, the prosecution dropped the final charge, neglect of duty.

Meanwhile, while Osborne had been fighting to save his job and restore his reputation, his friend Dean Kirchwey—filling in for him at Sing Sing—

had supervised the execution of two murderers, Roy Champlain and Giovanni Supe.

After their electrocution, the enterprising and ambitious Dr. Amos Squire, the prison's former consultant, now its head physician, began to perform an autopsy on one of the corpses, assisted by four trusties—low-risk prisoners given certain privileges. As he worked, Squire used a saw to cut through the man's skull in order to remove his carbonized brain. He was specially sensitive to the awful penetrating sound of the saw on bone, knowing that it spooked those in the nearby death cells, awaiting their turn to endure the same fate.

This was on Squire's mind when, above the noise of his saw, he heard wood being smashed, splintered, and pounded, followed by piercing screams. Because it sounded as if a guard was being murdered in the adjoining death house, Squire ordered the trusties to stay put, then rushed from the autopsy room into the prison yard to get help. The armed guards on the turrets of the outer walls had standing orders to shoot on sight anyone moving in the yard at night. So, as Dr. Squire raced through the still dark yard toward the office of head guard Frederick Dorner, he yelled frantically, "I'm Dr. Squire! I'm Dr. Squire!" praying that they'd take his word for it.

Relieved not to have been shot, he reached the head guard's office and gasped: "Quick. The condemned cells—something terrible!"[36] Dorner, with several other guards, soon reached the death house and found several condemned men smashing their stools and tables against their cell bars, while Oreste Shillitoni, aka Harry Shields, the most violent among them, was screaming hysterically and tearing his bedding to shreds. They trussed this twenty-four-year-old prisoner in a straitjacket, locked him in an adjoining padded cell, and quickly subdued the others.

Dr. Squire at first believed that Shillitoni had been driven mad by the recent executions and the sound of the autopsy saw opening a skull, especially as his appeal for clemency had just been denied.

Each day, after that, whenever the doctor visited Shillitoni—no longer in a straitjacket—he went berserk, tearing his hair and smashing his head against the cell bars while making ghastly, inhuman noises. As he kept it up throughout the night, preventing others in the death cells from sleeping, Squire had to give him a tranquilizing shot of hyocine. Still, the doctor often got late night calls to return to the prison to give him another injection.

Dr. Squire alone had the power of life and death over Oreste Shillitoni and all other condemned prisoners. If he determined that they were legally insane, they would be spared the chair.

Although he frequently wondered if the men he saw electrocuted were mentally unbalanced—and was, like Osborne, against the death penalty—he felt it was his duty to let the execution proceed. In his autobiography he claimed that "I never once saw a man go to his death who was definitely and legally insane, although I came very near to seeing that occur on one occasion."[37]

Warden Kirchwey was so impressed with Shillitoni's ravings, which included a threat to kill Dr. Squire, that he believed he was mad. Dr. Squire, at first, agreed, then changed his mind—after learning that a civilian worker at the prison had told Shillitoni that he couldn't be executed if declared insane, and that Dr. Squire made the vital decision.

However, the threat to kill Squire was no act: it was part of Shillitoni's escape plan for which he was well prepared. A woman visitor had smuggled in a gun and a box of cartridges.

Around midnight, he put his plan into action. Because his cell lacked a toilet, Daniel McCarthy, the only guard on duty, had no reason to be suspicious when Shillitoni asked for a slop can.

Being dressed only in his underclothes, the death-house inmate must have looked harmless. But he was holding a loaded revolver behind his back. As McCarthy unlocked and entered the cell to give him the slop can, Shillitoni shot him through the stomach—a fatal wound. Then he took McCarthy's keys and locked him in the cell.

Two guards, Ernest Bullard and George Nichols, taking a break in an adjacent room, heard the shot, and McCarthy's dying cries for help, and rushed to the rescue. As they did, Shillitoni shot Bullard in the arm and forced both men into a cell at gunpoint, took their keys, and locked the cell.

Some twenty other condemned cellmates, some due to be executed within a week, were too stunned to react, or perhaps hoped for a last-minute reprieve, because none of them asked Shillitoni to unlock their cells. Instead, he unlocked the door to a recreation court where he had exercised daily, up-ended a long bench to use as a ladder, and was soon in the prison yard. From there, under cover of the predawn darkness, he climbed a high fence at the west end of the prison and leaped into the Hudson River.

Although he had escaped in his underwear, a confederate had left clothing for him on the bank downriver and was waiting nearby to drive him away. But Shillitoni ended up at the wrong spot, and in the dark couldn't find the clothes left for him.

Meanwhile his escape had been reported and the shrieking prison siren so startled the confederate that he or she apparently drove off in a panic. Completely lost now, the escaped con headed for an illuminated building, which turned out to be Ossining General Hospital.

The only night nurse on duty had heard the prison siren and now, suddenly confronted by a gun-wielding man in soaking underwear, showed remarkable sangfroid. Speaking almost casually, she said: "Oh, you must have some dry clothes. Wait here, and I'll get them for you."

She went upstairs, returning, after a while, with just one laceless shoe and a shoelace. Shillitoni exploded: "What good is one shoe?" "That's all right, that's all right," she replied soothingly. "I'm going to find you another one somewhere—get into this one quickly while I'm hunting for another."[38] While he was preoccupied with lacing-up the shoe, she phoned the prison to say she would try to hold him until someone arrived. The nurse kept him there by pretending that, to avoid waking the sleeping patients, she had to sneak into the separate rooms cautiously, and could bring out only one piece of their clothing at a time. She successfully conned the conman, but it was touch and go. Shillitoni was almost completely dressed and about to leave when guards arrived and arrested him.

Dr. Squire had been at home when he heard the escape siren, followed by an urgent phone message to get to the prison fast. When he did, he was asked to take care of the wounded guards.

After attending to the guards' injuries, Squire went to see Shillitoni, who was back in his cell. He grinned at the doctor and said, "You are sure one lucky guy, Doc."[39] He explained that because the doctor had not declared him legally insane, he had planned to kill him the previous night, when he had expected the doctor to give him another tranquilizer. Fortunately, the doctor hadn't turned up the second time. Shillitoni also claimed that when he shot McCarthy, he was so desperate and agitated that he hardly knew what he was doing. Now he regretted it.

Guard Ernest Bullard's injuries were superficial, but a few days later Daniel McCarthy died in the prison hospital of peritonitis caused by the gunshot injury.

As the time neared for his execution, Shillitoni became more talkative, telling Dr. Squire about his life of crime during which he had killed four men. At thirteen he was found guilty of burglary and spent twenty-nine months in the House of Refuge. At seventeen, in 1909, he got a three-and-a-half-year sentence in Sing Sing for receiving stolen goods. On May 3, 1913, at twenty-one, while in New York City's Mulberry Street, he settled an angry argument about a revolver he'd borrowed from John Rizzo, by fatally shooting Rizzo with it. When two policemen, Charles Teare and William Heaney, tried to arrest him for the crime, he killed them, too. About a month later he turned himself in, was tried, and was sentenced to death.

The death house was crowded on June 30, 1916, with men eager to see Shillitoni take his last breath. Every Sing Sing guard had asked the warden for permission to witness the execution of the inmate who had killed one of their own. He surprised them all. The twenty-four-year-old "madman" went calmly to his death.

Three years later the law was changed. Instead of a prison physician deciding if a condemned prisoner was sane enough to be executed, the task was given to psychiatrists, then known as "alienists."

Three days after Shillitoni's electrocution, William Jennings Bryan, the former US secretary of state, appeared at Sing Sing to address the inmates. A band playing stirring patriotic music preceded him and Warden Kirchwey to the speaker's stand. Erected in the yard against the north wall of the mess hall, the stand was decorated with flags and buntings. Kirchwey introduced Bryan to over one thousand prisoners as a man who understood the American heart.

Calling his address "Plans and Specifications for Leading a Useful Life," which seemed to promise practical guidance, Bryan spoke of the relative importance of the physical, mental, and moral nature of man, and of the mysteries of life. "Life," he said, "was a mystery, love was a mystery, nature was a mystery. A child knew as much about natural phenomena as the most learned man"—which must have puzzled the scientifically minded in his audience.

"And patriotism is a mystery," he went on to say. Patriotism was a relevant topic, because World War I had been raging since 1914 and the United States would join the Allies against Germany less than a year after Bryan's speech, in which he also said, "I just left Peekskill. I saw there 1,200 men, all ready to do or die for their country. I saw groups of soldiers, like rivulets, all the way along the route as I came from Nebraska. I haven't any fear about patriotism in this country. If this country needed 1,000,000 men it would get them; 2,000,000 and they would be ready."[40]

The prisoners cheered heartily, but it wasn't clear if it was out of patriotism, or because they were unlikely to be sent to the fighting front, or just because Bryan had finished his long lecture.

Eleven days after Bryan's visit, the embattled Warden Osborne returned to Sing Sing in triumph. Forty-one ex-convicts, Mutual Welfare League graduates, caught the train to Ossining, along with their wives, sweethearts, and sisters, to welcome him back. Twenty-one of the men now worked in the Ford assembly plant thanks to Henry Ford. On a visit to the prison he had noted Osborne's ability to turn a scrap heap into a repair shop, and had kept his promise to employ every able member of the Mutual Welfare League on his release from prison.

They joined the crowd on the prison grounds which looked like a county fair, with flags and banners flying in the breeze, baseball teams starting a game, a parade beginning to form, and the prison's Aurora Band warming up. Prisoners stood on roof tops and looked through windows to get a good view. An account of the event on the front page of the *New York Times* was headed in part:

> Convicts' Carnival
> Welcome Osborne.
> Prisoners in Costume &
> Wild with Joy.

Eighteen hundred prisoners and about 300 sightseers cheered the Warden when he approached the north gate in an automobile shortly after 1 o'clock. Most of the people of Ossining had picked out spots on the hill back of the prison commanding a view of the ceremonies outside the prison, and they were the first to sight the Warden's car. Their shouts were soon overwhelmed by a great roar of approval from inside the prison. The north gate was opened. A band marched out playing "Tom Brown's Aurora Band." A big convict clad as "Uncle Sam" led the column of prisoners. After them came the pillars of civil government in the prison, the members of the Executive Board of the Mutual Welfare League, since it had been purged of influences hostile to the Warden, following the breaking of a chair over the head of the offending Judge. This section formed the most striking part of the parade. The Chief Justice and his yoke-fellows in equity were all dressed in black robes and wore the enormous fussy white wigs. . . . Some carried themselves with a deportment as stately as real judges. Frederick Dorner, the principal keeper . . . had shown himself so much in sympathy with the self-governing principles of the Mutual Welfare League that he was permitted to have the next station in the line. The Mutual Welfare League baseball team came next.

A long line of prisoners bore banners praising Osborne and Kirchwey. One read:

> With Tom and the Dean in the job,
> What care we for the political mob?

Then came a prisoner escorting a goat and carrying a banner reading, "Tom Brown's goat. Try to get it and see what happens." . . . The pre-Osborne period of prison methods was represented by a squad of convicts in the old-style, striped prison garments, doing the lockstep and supporting their roles by forcing a hangdog look, except when they stopped to cheer for Osborne.

Fig. 18. Warden Osborne celebrates his triumphant return to Sing Sing in 1916. (Courtesy Ossining Historical Society)

One delegation was made up of Charley (*sic*) Chaplins. Floats represented the difference between the old prison ways and the new followed. . . . After the procession . . . the 1,600 prisoners and a large number of visitors took their places around a platform.[41]

After speeches of welcome, Sing Sing conferred the honorary degree of Doctor of Humanity on Osborne and Kirchwey.

His voice trembling with emotion, Osborne told reporters that, as the reinstated warden, he intended to start a psychopathic clinic in the prison where trained psychiatrists would try to separate the feeble-minded, the degenerates, and the mentally defective from normal prisoners, and to send them away for treatment.

Osborne had already appointed the internationally renowned Dr. Bernard Glueck, director of the Government Hospital for the Insane in Washington, to head the project. The first clinic of its kind in the United States, it was to be endowed by the Rockefeller Foundation.

Back in control of Sing Sing, Osborne faced a summer of escapes and escape attempts. J. Kercher was recaptured on August 5, 1916, after being on the lam for three months. On August 17 F. Grabowski escaped and E. Totterman followed five days later. Curiously, one inmate, hearing that his father was dying, asked to be locked up because he was afraid that he'd be tempted to escape. Another was reluctant to leave his cell for an hour's recreation because he was scared of being attacked by Black Hand gang members. Nevertheless, Osborne still allowed trusted prisoners to play baseball and to picnic outside the prison grounds.

Two more prisoners, E. Kelly and T. Winters, escaped in early October. That same month Osborne oversaw the execution of another man he believed was innocent—Thomas O'Neil aka Thomas Bambrick. At the time, Osborne said, "It is almost as certain that Bambrick is innocent as that the sun will rise tomorrow." Evidence later came to light that convinced him and the chaplain that another man had committed the crime. Osborne even knew his identity. Apparently so did Bambrick, but he had refused to "squeal."[42]

Days after Bambrick's execution, Osborne sent shock waves through the prison and various offices in Albany and Manhattan. Just three months after his celebrated reinstatement and return to Sing Sing, he resigned.

He blamed Governor Whitman for breaking every promise to him, for trying to discredit his reforms, for demanding less press coverage on Sing Sing, and stipulating that no inmate with a long sentence should be allowed outside the prison walls.

Whitman, a Brooklyn Sunday School teacher, whose string of convictions as a district attorney had helped him to win the New York governorship, was apparently badly served by his assistants, whose conflicting reports about Sing Sing confused him. Whitman was also a Republican with presidential aspirations. Some considered Osborne, a Democrat with a growing reputation, to be a threat to the governor's ambitions, which might explain why Whitman betrayed him—if he did, because others believed that Whitman was maladroit, rather than malicious.

An Osborne biographer, Frank Tannenbaum, suggests that "Had the Governor dismissed Riley [superintendent of prisons] when the nature of the attack became apparent, and had he appointed a commission to investigate Sing Sing as he had promised, the horrible scandal would have been averted."[43]

Osborne himself expressed his views in a blistering open letter to Whitman on October 25, 1916: "Thanks to you, sir, the name I inherited from my honored father, and from my mother, who was your mother's friend, has been linked in people's thoughts with the vilest of crimes: I have had to fight for what is worth far more than life itself, against a powerful and remorseless political organization; I have been indicted and placed on trial with the shadow of state prison sentence falling upon the court room. Yet for all this and more, I not only bear you no resentment—I am deeply grateful. You have been the means of bringing to me some of the wonderful experiences the world can give; renewal of old friendships, and troops of new friends; appreciation of my work far beyond its deserts; increased opportunity and power to be of service to my fellowmen. I would not alter the past two years, if it were possible to do so. But I do desire to influence the future . . . to the end that no man so weak as yourself—so shifty, so selfish, so false, so cruel, may be trusted with further power. The next public servant who stands in your way may not be as fortunate as I have been."[44]

On August 1, 1916, Osborne having left Sing Sing, the secretary of the navy commissioned him as a naval-lieutenant and put him in charge of the naval prison at Portsmouth. His instructions were to make it more like a school than a prison. When he arrived, 190 marines were guarding 180 prisoners. Osborne dismissed the marine guards and organized a prisoner's group to replace them. When he left two years later, he had been in charge of six thousand prisoners and had successfully carried out his mission.

His Sing Sing successor, Lewis E. Lawes, greatly admired Osborne and kept many of his reforms. But he also came to realize that Osborne's mistake had been to give the inmates too much power. As Lawes saw it, prisoners are "people who have quarreled with the law. That regardless of motivating forces or underlying causes, prisons are communities of nonconformists. . . . The defect of Mr. Osborne's administration was in the overlapping of prisoner self-government with the warden's responsibilities as an administrator. His intense desire to raise the prisoner to a normal plane, led him to surrender his prerogatives. He became an advisor instead of a leader and ruler. The swing of the pendulum from severity to liberality was too wide. It resulted in chaos. Mr. Osborne was not given the opportunity to correct this fault."[45]

The next four years proved a difficult time for the governor to appoint a suitable warden, especially after Osborne's ordeal. Several suitable candidates had doubtless left the country for less contentious work, fighting in the trenches of World War I. In fact, 1916 though 1920 gave real meaning to the inmates' joke: that the quickest way to get out of Sing Sing was to go in as warden.

Calvin Derrick took over on October 16, 1916, and lasted less than three months. William H. Moyer followed and was warden for under four months, and then Edward V. Brophy became top dog. After three years he was replaced by acting warden Daniel J. Grant—but for only eight months. Then, on January 1, 1920, Lewis E. Lawes was persuaded to take the job—becoming Sing Sing's best and longest-lasting warden of all time.

When Osborne died of a heart attack in 1926, two hundred convicts walked passed his coffin, some in tears. Although he had been warden of Sing Sing for less than two years, his influence endures to this day.

CHAPTER SEVEN

WARDEN LAWES AND THE ROSE MAN OF SING SING

1920–1929

During Warden Lewis Lawes's twenty-one-year regime (1920–1941), word spread that Sing Sing was a breeze compared with other New York State prisons. Convicted felons pleaded with judges to be sent up the river rather than to Auburn, Elmira, Attica, or the dreaded Clinton Prison at Dannemora, located in the wild and desolate country known as "Siberia."

Lawes believed that merit should play the same part in prison as it did in the outside commercial world, and he was always willing to take a chance on convicts who were prepared to work and to obey the rules. Even the most hard-boiled prisoner, in his experience, given a job with responsibility, rarely disappointed him.

The son of an Englishman and an Irishwoman, Lawes (a great name for a warden!) began his career as a guard in the fearful Clinton Prison in New York. Governor Al Smith made him Sing Sing warden in 1920, and soon after he returned to Clinton on what amounted to a rescue operation. Its warden had just died, and during his visit Lawes spoke with twenty-four men in solitary confinement for breaches of discipline or escape attempts. Most said that they regretted their crimes, and promised to obey prison regulations if they could get out of solitary and back to work. He offered to release them from solitary if they promised to work in the shops of other prisons, including Sing Sing, and to behave decently in return for the privileges granted other inmates. Not surprisingly, they all said yes. The man temporarily in charge at Clinton, doubtless glad to be rid of troublemakers, agreed with Lawes's pro-

113

Fig. 19. Hundreds of inmates attend a football game at Sing Sing. (Courtesy Ossining Historical Society)

posal. The men were freed from solitary and transferred to Sing Sing and other prisons. It was a daring experiment, which worked at Sing Sing.

This was just the first of many innovative, even audacious actions that Lawes took to control and care for two thousand-plus often bloody-minded individuals. He was, for example, the first man to have his wife and three young daughters live with him on the prison grounds, and to let them befriend the prisoners. Some, including murderers, became members of his household staff.

During his career Lawes had been in charge of a six hundred-acre Orange County prison farm—without walls—for delinquent boys, where he had allowed 150 of them to take part in a film about the Mexican-American War, as extras armed with guns and blank cartridges.

Lawes was helped enormously at Sing Sing by his exceptionally coura-geous, humane, and loving wife, Kathryn. Despite warnings from her friends and relatives not to go near the prison, she joined him, and brought their two young daughters with her. A third was born in the prison. At the first basket-ball game in the prison gym, she and her girls sat in the stands among the inmates. When she learned that a murderer in the death house was blind, she taught him to read Braille. Later she learned sign language to teach a deaf-mute to communicate. The prisoners adored her. Many called her a saint.

Fig. 20. Warden Lewis Lawes, and his head guard,
James Connaughton. (New York State Archives)

In the beginning, after an exhausting and discouraging start, Lawes
needed all the help he could get. Almost as soon as he took over, a flu epidemic hit the prison and filled the hospital to overflowing, which forced him
to spend his first month more as a doctor than a lawman. Soon after, he
uncovered a plot to torch the prison.

Because Lawes feared a riot, the American Legion Post in nearby
Ossining was put on alert, in case extra help was needed. But it didn't
happen.

Days later, when two convicts overpowered their guards, got hold of
guns, and escaped in a stolen car, Lawes left the prison to lead a posse that
captured the men, found hiding in a New Hampshire forest. He had hardly
locked them back in their cells when he was off again to the Rockefeller
estate at Pocantico Hills, where he helped bring back another escaped con.

While commending Lawes for his enterprising and successful leader-
ship, the press mocked the state troopers who, according to some, had
declined to join the hunt for escaped prisoners because it was raining.

During his first year, Lawes supervised death-house alterations to
accommodate women, as well as men, awaiting electrocution. According to
the *New York Times,* one woman already there, Mrs. Hattie Dixon, was

costing New York State $700 a month (a small fortune in those days) while she waited her turn to be put to death. Lawes also made the prison more escape-proof. And he refused an artist's macabre request to visit Sing Sing to make a painting of the electric chair.

In March 1920, a group of Elks entertained the inmates. And in April, Lawes lost his personal waiter, murderer William Perry, whose sentence was commuted. Perry celebrated by hosting a dinner for his prison pals.

The following month, inmates entertained fellow prisoners in a vaudeville show, and controversial ex-warden Thomas Mott Osborne returned to address them. His high-minded, socially conscious attitude was hardly shared by the prison's pudgy executioner, John P. Hulbert. He complained that so far in 1920, having electrocuted sixteen individuals at $150 per killing, he already had a record high income, and would now have to pay income tax for the first time in his career.

In July, fifty bigamists were shown a movie, *Why Change Your Wife?* but there is no account of its making any of them single-minded. And a prisoner escaped.

Later in the year, an inmate eligible for parole refused to leave the prison, regarding the place as his home; some prisoners submitted their poems for publication; and Lawes identified a drug smuggler as a convict's relative, and put an end to that source.

Lawes had been puzzled to see the occasional drunk staggering around the prison yard. An investigation revealed that the men had been drinking alcohol-laced hair tonic from the prison barber shop—and, from then on, the product was banned.

In a risky experiment, Lawes took away the guards' weapons to encourage pride and confidence in their job. It proved effective. No guard was attacked, not even when supervising the most dangerous inmates in the yard.

Among the prisoners were two men Lawes sometimes pointed out to visitors as prisoners who had taught him never to judge by appearances.

One, Dr. Henry C. Meyer, a mild-mannered former doctor with an almost visible aura of sanctity, was still idolized by many ex-patients as a mixture of Jesus Christ and Dr. Schweitzer. Curious to know what had sent this paragon to Sing Sing, Lawes checked the records, and discovered, yes, he had been extremely considerate to some patients, even treating a few for free. But he had also murdered others, after insuring their lives and making himself the beneficiary. His weapon of choice was a poison that caused them to die slowly and in intense agony.

Lawes had characterized the other man as Sing Sing's most softhearted inmate. With the warden's okay, he had adopted a small stray dog and fussed over it like an anxious, loving parent, often going hungry to feed it. Checking this "softy's" record, Lawes discovered that as an armed robber he had butchered his victims under the most revolting circumstances.

Before the executions of notorious prisoners, Lawes was bombarded with crank mail and phone calls from ghouls eager to watch, from volunteers wanting to pull the switch, from others anxious to stop the killings, or from would-be suicides offering to change places with the death-cell inmate.

Though news reporters were invariably invited to executions, in the early years especially, women were excluded. But when Nellie Bly persisted in her request to witness an execution, Lawes gave in. The *New York World*'s Bly had become internationally famous many years earlier for her much-ballyhooed seventy-three-day race around the world by sea and land, when she beat Jules Verne's fictional hero by a week. Her editor, Arthur Brisbane, had dared her to attend the execution. As she was a respected veteran reporter, maybe Lawes thought she could take it. He sent her an official invitation to watch murderer George Hamby put to death. Hamby had killed bank teller DeWitt Peel in a holdup at the Brooklyn Savings Bank. The warden himself supervised the arrangements for the execution but, being opposed to the death penalty, was not among the spectators. Yet, although he never witnessed the victim's last moments, as he stood only a few feet from the electric chair, he could not escape the stench of burning flesh or the ineffective rattle of an overhead vent meant to dissipate the fumes. At the last moment he turned his head away or closed his eyes and so could honestly say that he had never seen an execution.

Bly, in her ringside seat, wished she could have said the same. She had been corresponding with Hamby who kept a sense of humor to the end: ordering a last meal of lobster salad, he quipped that at least he wouldn't have to worry about indigestion.

The experience was so traumatic that, according to her editor, Bly turned green and declined to attend the official autopsy. Another account has her collapsing and guards having to carry her out. In any event, she recovered before her deadline in time to write of the horror of the occasion. (Other women reporters who covered Sing Sing were Ada Patterson, Grace Phelps, Julia McCarthy, Isabelle Keating, and Dorothy Kilgallen.)

In October 1920, Governor Al Smith arrived to lay the cornerstone for a new prison to be located on a hill overlooking the old one. The old prison covered fourteen and a half acres, encircled by a wall. The two combined prisons took up forty-seven and a half acres. During the ceremony, Lawes pointed to

Fig. 21. Reporter Nellie Bly witnessed an execution—to her regret. (Library of Congress)

the prisoners in the courtyard below, near the river front and the old prison, and said: "It may surprise some of you people here today to see those men down there playing ball and having a good time in the sunshine. But it doesn't surprise me. That is the kind of treatment they deserve and are going to get as long as they merit it."

Lawes explained his modus operandi as follows: "It became quickly apparent to me that under conditions as they were, the prison warden, to be effective, would have to constitute himself not as an instrument of punishment but as a firm, frank friend in need. He would have to stretch humanitarianism to the limits of the law, with a stiff punch always in reserve. My job is to hold men, and, as far as possible, to win them over to sane, social thinking. And I judge the effectiveness of that job not so much by obedience to rules, for rules can be enforced, but by the humor of the general prison population."[1]

With that in mind, Lawes made himself available to any inmate with a pressing problem, on call twenty-four hours a day, seven days a week. (He slept naked, but kept his clothes at the foot of his bed ready for emergency calls.) He also allowed prisoners a measure of self-government, as Osborne had done, and let them decide how to spend their leisure hours. Lawes even let them leave Sing Sing to attend a funeral, or to visit a dying relative, making them honor-bound to return. Remarkably, they rarely tried to escape. He often lent money to discharged prisoners which was usually returned, some coming to the prison gate with the money years later. This explains why he dedicated one of his books "To those tens of thousands of my former wards who have justified my faith in human nature."

And what a mixed bunch they were! Among the 36,750 inmates in his charge during his twenty-one years as warden would be a sky-writing pilot, a prison warden, a radio announcer, a judge, lawyers, newsmen, a preacher, policemen, bankers, a bartender, a boxer, a masseur, the head of the Wall Street Stock Exchange, doctors, dentists, ministers, Communist spies, a pretzel peddler—the guilty and the innocent. Almost without exception

Fig. 22. As Warden Lawes allowed pets, this prisoner shares his cell with his pet bird. (Courtesy University of South Carolina Newsfilm Archive)

Lawes admired and trusted them, without excusing their crimes, and made this surprising statement: "If I should ever need a man upon whose courage I would rely in the face of the gravest danger, I know of hundreds of men, prisoners and ex-prisoner, upon whom I would stake my life."[2]

Lawes believed that "if you treat a man like a dog you will make a dog of him," and consequently he treated them like friends. And he shared the opinion of a Sing Sing chaplain that, though some inmates were monsters, others were "living the lives of saints."[3] He found that some murderers who used guns were tenderhearted, some thieves to be honest, and a few bold robbers to be timid men when not on the job.

Lawes himself was certainly bold: he eventually employed a prisoner as his cook, was shaved by a prisoner who had cut a man's throat, and allowed a kidnapper to drive the Lawes's youngest daughter, Joan Marie, known as Cherie, outside the prison in her pony cart. (Born in the prison in 1921, Cherie had a black male prisoner as her nurse.) Still, Lawes admitted that he wasn't a flawless judge of character, citing the two monsters mentioned earlier, whom he had once characterized as the kindest men in Sing Sing.

He was hardly as admiring of humanity at large, disturbed to find a list of seven hundred applicants for the job of executioner, some even willing to pull the switch for free.

When Lawes disarmed the guards, even took away their clubs, and emulated Osborne in walking unarmed among the prisoners, willing to listen to their requests or complaints, the atmosphere of threat and confrontation largely disappeared. Lawes's attitude even mellowed thirty-one-year-old Carl Panzram who claimed to have murdered twenty-one people and to have committed sodomy on more than a thousand. He boasted of having no conscience, believing in neither God nor the Devil, and of hating the entire human race, himself included. Panzram blamed his sadistic cruelty on his treatment at age twelve in a reform school, where he claimed to have been whipped, raped, hosed with water, frozen, and isolated. He worked in the coal pit during his brief stay at Sing Sing, before his bloodthirsty record caught up with him, including his recent murder of two boys. Then he was transferred to the Clinton Prison at Dannemora, the dreaded "Siberia" twenty miles south of the Canadian border, where Sing Sing banished its drug addicts, most dangerous criminals, and those who had tried to escape.

A man who went mad in Sing Sing's death house was escorted to Dannemora's Hospital for the Criminally Insane, where he spent the rest of his life. Had he been crazy enough to recover his sanity, the inmate would then have been shipped back south for execution.

One of the most unexpected comments from a man about to go to the chair was made by Walter Jankowski, who had killed a guard in an escape attempt. Now in great pain from incurable tuberculosis, he broke away from guards escorting him to the execution chamber, kissed the chair, and cried out, "I was never so happy to see anything!"

A condemned man named Ronny, who had murdered a bartender, hated the thought of his five-year-old son going through life "as a little bastard" and he got Lawes's permission to marry the boy's mother twelve hours before the execution, with guards as witnesses. His last words to the warden were: "At least I can go knowing I tried to do one decent thing in my life. Too bad I didn't try to do more."[4]

In his book *Meet the Murderer!* Lawes tells how a twenty-three-year-old man who had killed a young woman for rejecting him had asked for a stiff drink of whiskey before his execution. He deeply regretted his act and still loved the girl he had killed. Lawes had grown to like the unnamed man and, as he wrote, "For the first time in my life the sight of a man going to his death gave me nausea. He was young, virile, brave. It seemed a sacrilege that so very soon this clear-eyed young man would become a corpse." As he left his cell for the chair, Lawes handed him a small bottle of whiskey. He glanced at the warden, smiled, and handed it back. "'You need this more than I, Warden,' he said. 'Please drink it.' I did, and he went to his death—smiling." The young man's mother had phoned Lawes before the execution saying that she couldn't bear to come, but asked him to do what she would like to do: "'When my boy is dead please put a white rose in his hand.' Of course, it was done."[5]

One doctor inmate, Julius Hammer, a skilled and caring practitioner, had been sentenced to prison for up to fifteen years for killing a woman during an abortion, which she had assured him that she desperately needed for her physical and mental health. The *New York Times* covered his arrival at Sing Sing, noting that he "was fitted out in a suit of convict gray and assigned to the idle company, until he can be sent to the yard company to heave coal and do other rough work temporarily. More suitable employment will be found for him later."[6] The paper pointed out that this was strong refutation of the charge that there is one law for the rich and another for the poor. (Lawes, of course, knew that there was.)

Lawes considered the abortionist as "more than a radical. He was an intellectual communist who adored Lenin and sought every provocation to talk about him. . . . He never criticized America, nor the capitalist system. 'It's an experiment, Warden,' he would say. 'A lesson in self-control. Can the proletariat measure up to it? Time will tell. It may be wrong but it's worth the try.' He would argue (as elected secretary of the Mutual Welfare League) for the lowliest of his fellow prisoners. Never missed a trick. But he would never present a request that was objectionable. He argued it out with the dissatisfied prisoner before he came to me. The respect which he commanded among the prisoners helped to weed out petty and unreasonable demands and complaints."[7] Although he was later pardoned, his twenty-one-year-old son, Armand Hammer, shattered by what he considered his father's grossly unfair punishment for a tragic accident, rarely spoke of it, and grew up to be a famous multimillionaire business tycoon with friends in high places, especially the Soviet Union.

It was hard to find anyone sorry for sixty-two-year-old Charles Chapin, editor of Joseph Pulitzer's *New York Evening World*, when he landed in Sing Sing. A cold, cantankerous autocrat, he boasted of having fired 108 men in his time. When his paper's investigation helped to arrest a murder suspect, he gleefully cried out that he had started a man on his way to the electric chair. Chapin risked the chair himself for what he called a mercy killing. After shooting his wife in the head, he left a Do Not Disturb sign on their hotel-room door, walked out into the street, and surrendered to police. He had big money problems, he explained, and meant to kill her and then himself as a way out, but after shooting her, he lost his nerve. He escaped the chair but got a life sentence.

Soon after Chapin's arrival at Sing Sing, Warden Lawes received this letter expressing the general distaste for the wife killer: "I knew Mr. Chapin long and from a certain angle intimately in the years he was at the *World*. That is, I knew intimately the anguished stories of the hundreds and thousands [hyperbole obviously] of the writers whose lives he made a living hell. I used to think him a sort of devil sitting on enthroned power in the *World* office and making Park Row gutters glow red with the blood of ambitious young men. If you enjoy him, I hope you keep him long and carefully."

Lawes realized that "the devil" had undergone a personality change as he lay in the prison hospital ward, frail, feeble, deeply depressed, and not expected to live. Lawes found a cure by encouraging him to edit the prison paper, the *Bulletin*, which restored his health and spirit and in which Chapin eventually published his life story. Lawes also gave him a free run of the prison and okayed his changing the paper's title to the *Sing Sing Bulletin*. Chapin eagerly wrote most of the paper himself under various pseudonyms, until the authorities at Albany threatened to censor the paper, saying he was writing too much about himself, which was true, when Chapin chucked it.[8]

The great illusionist Harry Houdini occasionally entertained the inmates, once giving a three-hour performance of magic tricks and half an hour of his movies, showing how he could escape from anything. He often told interviewers that if he had been born to different parents he might have been a dangerous criminal. One Christmas night's entertainment consisted of him escaping from a hangman's noose, and answering questions supposed to come from the spirit world. As Houdini's wife, Beatrice, recalled, that night the convicts also "nailed him in a packing-case they had prepared, and in twelve minutes he stood outside, and the case was still soundly nailed together. Then, to their awe and delight, he produced personal spirit messages from notorious departed inmates of Sing Sing and from Ben Franklin, and performed diverse 'spirit' manifestations."[9]

Houdini had known Chapin before his imprisonment and, after the show, chatted with him for half an hour. They hit it off, and the warmhearted Houdini asked Chapin to put him on his visitors' list, promising to come see him whenever he was in the area.

Lawes's second year, 1921, presented him with a crop of new problems: A convict named J. Cohen, due to be released, kept Lawes puzzled for some time, while he sorted out if he was the right man to set free—because four other convicts had the same name. Death-house chef Blanche quit, complaining that condemned inmates were too picky about their food. Two convicts escaped, one under guard on a visit to New York City to see his dying

Fig. 23. Sing Sing's visitors included escape artist Harry Houdini. (Library of Congress)

son. Lawes reprimanded a convict for paying another to clean his cell, and had to remove another inmate, who went mad, to a padded cell.

But it wasn't all grim news from Sing Sing. New York's popular mayor, Fiorello La Guardia, famous for reading the comics over the radio, paid a visit. So did the great Italian tenor Benjamin Gigli from New York's Metropolitan Opera. Accompanied by Enrico Rosati, he went up the river to perform before a packed and eager house in Sing Sing's prison chapel. There, he sang nine songs from *Tosca*, *Pagliacci*, and *Marta* to a wildly cheering audience of a thousand inmates. He promised to return. Before leaving, he toured the prison and glanced at the electric chair.

More visitors began traveling to Sing Sing to teach, preach, entertain, or to satisfy their curiosity. The movie actor–director Charlie Chaplin first went to the prison with a writer friend, Frank Harris, to meet Jim Larkin, a radical Irish rebel and labor leader now working in the shoe shop. "A handsome man, about six feet four, with piercing blue eyes and a gentle smile, Larkin was a brilliant orator who had been sentenced by a prejudiced judge and jury on false charges of attempting to overthrow the government," Chaplin wrote in his autobiography. "So Frank claimed, and this was proved later, when Governor Al Smith quashed the sentence, though Larkin had already served years of it. Prisons have a strange atmosphere, as if the human spirit was suspended. At Sing Sing the old cell blocks were grimly medieval. . . . What fiendish brain could conceive of building such horrors!" After Chaplin had stepped into an empty cell, he "was appalled by the horror of claustrophobia. 'My God!' I said, quickly stepping out. 'It's inhuman!' . . . The warden, a kindly man, explained that Sing Sing was overcrowded and needed appropriations to build more cells. 'But we are the last to be considered in that respect; no politician is too concerned about prison conditions.'"[10]

When Lawes later showed the pair the death house, Chaplin found it even more sinister than the scaffold. And he was horrified when the prison doctor, Amos Squire, told him that if the electric chair hadn't quite killed the prisoner, then he was surgically decapitated.

Among other visitors was a Protestant minister, Dr. A. N. Peterson, apparently intent on quick conversions: he got a big laugh from the inmates when he stated the shaky proposition that very few Protestants went to the chair.

Wife-killer Chapin had been in the prison three years when, in the fall of 1923, he went to the warden's office and offered to take care of the prison lawns. Lawes said it was okay by him, but he had no idea what he was in for. Next day Chapin asked for a lawn mower, a sickle, a hose, and a pair of slippers. Lawes went along with that, too, especially as the tall, kindly, Catholic chaplain, Father William J. Cashin, offered to foot the bill. Despite the sterile soil, the former editor made a good job of it.

The following year, Chapin stopped Lawes in the yard near a desolate wasteland of stone, sand, and piles of old bricks. On one side of it was a cellblock, and on the other two sides, dilapidated buildings. "I have an idea, Warden," Chapin said. "I'd like to build a small garden, a flower garden. How about it?" Impressed by how Chapin had cared for the lawns, Lawes said, "Tell you what, Charlie. Let's have a real garden, trees and flowers. The boys will get a thrill out of it." Chapin's eyes lit up. "That's fine, Warden," he replied. "I'll make roses grow in that desert. Wait and see."[11]

And that, as Lawes recalled, was how Charles Chapin became the famous Rose Man of Sing Sing.

In fact, Chapin knew next to nothing about gardening, having spent most of his working life in newsrooms, his home life in Manhattan's luxurious

Figs. 24, 25. The desolate prison yard, above, before Charles Chapin got to it. Below, some of the flower gardens Chapin created, which earned him the name "the Rose Man of Sing Sing." (Courtesy James McGrath Morris, *The Rose Man of Sing Sing*)

Plaza Hotel, and his leisure hours yachting and at the races. But he knew how to get information from the experts. He was a newsman, after all. A gardening friend sent him instructions and eight volumes of the work of Luther Burbank, the Californian gardening aficionado. That winter, after devouring the books, Chapin got thirty volunteers to help him clean up the future garden site, driving them hard to remove massive piles of wood, stones, and bricks in time to have the earth ready for spring planting.

Watching the progress with growing interest, the warden rewarded Chapin with a pair of overalls and a farmer's hat, and gave him permission to order a wagon-load of loam and squares of grass. One volunteer, a young Italian inmate who loved flowers, worked beside Chapin every day from five in the morning until dinner time.

With the little cash he had available, Chapin ordered a few geraniums and gladioli from F. R. Pierson in nearby Tarrytown. When a friend told Pierson of Chapin's plans, he came to see the prison-garden-in-the-making for himself, gave some advice, and, when he got back, sent a gift of a truck-load of plants.

Philanthropist Adolph Lewisohn had also shown an interest in the garden, and Chapin wrote to him: "I hope to have some very beautiful flowers next Spring if only I can procure what I need in the way of bulbs, shrubs and plants. Seeds I am able to buy out of our slender funds. Do you know I actually get a heartache every time I look through the catalogue and read of the many fine plants in the greenhouses and nurseries that I covet?" He also mentioned the gift of plants from Pierson, adding, "Encouraging isn't it? It's the greatest happiness I have found in the three and a half years I have been in prison. I am up at five every morning and am at it almost constantly until it grows too dark to see."[12]

Lewisohn got the hint and sent Chapin a load of plants. When news of the prospective garden spread throughout the country, more people sent him seeds, plants, rosebushes, a dozen varieties of cannas, and peonies. Chapin was overwhelmed and thrilled, directing his volunteers to make room for the gifts in over an acre of land that awaited them. He filled one long border near the cell block with peonies and other flowers. He planted seeds in places where prisoners could rest during recreation periods, and watch them grow. He filled the center of one plot with thousands of rosebushes, and, in the center of a ten-foot-square lawn, he built a cement water fountain.

On another plot near the Hudson River, Chapin created a lawn and flowerbeds of snapdragons, phlox, and asters. When the asters first appeared, his young Italian helper said they reminded him of his own baby. What used

Fig. 26. Chapin probably reading a seed catalog on the porch of Warden Lawes's home. Lawes treated the wife-killer as a friend, allowing him to wear his own clothes and to sleep in an unlocked cell. (Courtesy James McGrath Morris, *The Rose Man of Sing Sing*)

to be a garbage dump in time became ablaze with tulips. And Chapin arranged it so that the last things prisoners would see, as they walked toward the death house bound for their execution, would be a strip of grass and a colorful border of flowers.

Chapin had been a tyrannical editor, to say the least. He was almost as tough on his garden volunteers, complaining in a note to Lawes: "Most of the [men] disappear if I am not around an hour before the whistle blows. I expect them to work from 8 AM until 11:30, and from 1 PM until 3:30, except in stormy weather, and they should be given to understand that shirking will not be tolerated."[13]

One morning, later in the year, Chapin walked into the warden's office with a bunch of roses. "First choice, Warden," he said, handing them over. "A Thanksgiving offering to you for your cooperation."[14]

That afternoon the two men inspected the gardens, now a riot of color, as well as greenhouses that Chapin had built near the river front. One greenhouse was the former prison morgue. Potted flowers were on the slab where autopsies had taken place, and in the sink, where the doctor had washed his instruments, sheaves of cut flowers lay in cool running water. Nearby, canaries chirped in their cages.

Every day Chapin brought flowers for the warden's office, home, and the prison hospital. On the days he didn't appear, Lawes knew that it was because Chapin was confined to his cell, or a hospital bed, with heart trouble.

In time, Lawes gave Chapin the use of his own carpeted, curtained, and book-lined office with its three windows overlooking the Hudson River. In this unbarred office in an alcove, sunlit by day, electrically lit at night, he worked for as long as he liked. He often stayed from seven in the morning until ten at night, and even had his meals there, served by his own private inmate-cook. As James McGrath Morris, author of *The Rose Man of Sing Sing*, described it, "There was probably no inmate in the world . . . with a more luxuriant workplace . . . many an afternoon [Chapin] could be found reading magazines in a wicker rocker on the warden's porch overlooking the river with the warden's daughter playing at his feet."[15]

At night while other inmates were locked in their cells, Chapin's own inmate-cook served him supper in his unlocked office, then, after closing the greenhouse, he was free to write or read letters, roam the prison yard, and inspect his flower garden by moonlight, before returning to sleep in his unlocked cell.

The cold winter of 1925 did not deter Chapin from working in the gardens and Lawes was concerned for his precarious health. So, at midnight on

Christmas Eve, carrying a flashlight and dressed as Santa Claus, the warden woke the sleeping Chapin and handed him a gift-wrapped windbreaker.

Almost as extraordinary as his exceptional privileges was Chapin's changed personality from almost diabolical to benign—though he was still a hard taskmaster. "Do you think that growing flowers did it?" he once asked Constance Nelson, the young editorial worker at a Cleveland bank to whom he had become romantically attached through correspondence.

Newspapers and magazines featured glowing accounts of the Rose Man of Sing Sing and his fabulous gardens. Visitors flocked to see the thousands of flowers, the trees, a birdhouse that took three years of hard work to build, and a fountain, and were astonished by the transformation. Such life, color, and fragrance in a prison setting seemed almost miraculous—like another wonder of the world.

The *New York Times* applauded Chapin for adorning "the gruesome place with flowers, trees and shrubs, and the yard which five years ago was desolate and littered with stones and rubbish is now a thing of beauty. The rose garden is an inspiration to dark and troubled souls."[16]

Of course, not all the inmates appreciated it. Joseph Valachi, the first man to break the Cosa Nostra oath of silence by revealing the secrets of organized crime, was briefly incarcerated in Sing Sing as a young man on October 26, 1923. What concerned him was how to keep warm and dry. What delighted him was not the sight or scent of flowers, but to be released from his cold, damp cell, and then to see, in comfortable surroundings, a special prison showing of a Broadway musical, *The Plantation Review*. He enjoyed it so much that he could hardly believe he was still in Sing Sing. He had mixed feelings about a later imprisonment there. Despite this, Valachi rated Sing Sing the place to go if you had to be incarcerated.

He was back again in April 1925 for a three-year term, when he was almost fatally stabbed in the back, the wound requiring thirty-eight stitches. But he came out smiling because, while in prison, he had learned to read and write. "Before I went back to Sing Sing, I could hardly make out the street signs," he said. "But the real education I got was being worldly-wise. . . . It's just all the things you learn about human nature in another world, and believe me, Sing Sing was another world."[17]

A big treat for Valachi and other inmates happened in 1925 when the New York Yankees played the New York Giants on the prison's baseball field, and they saw Babe Ruth hit a home run 629 feet over the field wall.

There had been almost as big a crowd rooting for the Roman Catholic chaplain Father William Cashin when he left Sing Sing the previous year.

The inmates had persuaded Lawes to let "Spare Ribs" Cohen, a jewel thief, travel to Manhattan unescorted to buy a farewell gift on behalf of the Welfare League. He came back with a gold crucifix, inscribed "To the Bishop of Sing Sing, From the Saints of Sing Sing," to replace the one so worn down with the kisses of the condemned that the Christ was hardly recognizable. The chapel was packed with prisoners and the altar bedecked with Chapin's roses. Outside the band blared Irish favorites. In his farewell mass and service, conducted with the help of an altar boy lifer and an organist who had murdered his sweetheart, Father Cashin apologized: "I had hoped to make my work here among you my life's work. I am sorry to leave you all. Give to my successor the same loyalty you have given me. There is more loyalty, sympathy, and understanding inside these walls than in any other place of equal area in the world. Bring out the good in you. It is there and I have worked here long enough [twelve years] to see what others cannot. Be square with yourselves and you'll be square with God."[18]

Father Cashin was succeeded by the Reverend John P. McCaffrey, a six-footer with wavy brown hair and a youthful manner. It was soon his task to escort two men, John Rys, nineteen, and John Emieleta, twenty-three, to their executions. Rys had been singing in a saloon when he met Emieleta. The ex-con persuaded Rys to accompany him to collect a debt from a Chinese laundryman. During a confrontation, Emieleta shot and killed the laundryman. As author Ralph Blumenthal reveals,

> Emieleta had vouched for Rys's innocence, but now both were slated to die. Rys, with fifteen cents to his name, had not had a visitor in his seven months on death row.
>
> Lawes found Rys pathetic and vented his outrage to a reporter: "Johnny is being crushed by the realization that the world has no heart and will not lift a finger to help him because he is poor. I have been ordered to kill in the chair this child of poverty and misfortune. If he were rich and could have engaged first-class counsel he might have escaped this, somehow. He might have been acquitted and served no time at all or, to satisfy the State, he might have been guided to plead guilty to the second-degree charge. He might now be working in the prison shops under a lighter sentence. But because he was penniless, he was railroaded to fatten a District Attorney's list of convictions. His poverty is the only reason for his plight. Did you ever see a rich man go the whole route through to the death house? I don't know of any. Have you ever seen the sons of the rich in Condemned Row, no matter what they do? I don't know any."
>
> But by then Rys was dead.[19]

Two years later, Sing Sing's chief physician, Amos Squire, resigned. He never explained how he resolved the moral dilemma of taking the Hippocratic oath to never knowingly harm anyone, and being part of a death-dealing team. Like others involved, he expressed opposition to the death penalty but persisted in taking part in its execution.

Here's his view of it: "Standing by the electric chair at Sing Sing, I have given the signal that sent killing current through the bodies of one hundred and thirty eight men. The prongs of a stethoscope in my ears, I have listened intently for the last heartbeat of each of those men, and many times I have been so overwrought I was alarmed by the thought that what I heard was my own pulse rather than that of the dying man. I felt that all of my other duties were constructive. But the horror of that one duty of participating in executions grew on me until it was more than I could endure. In looking back on it, I am amazed that I stood it for as long as I did." For eleven years. He added: "Even though I had the respect and cooperation of the prison population in general, there were times when I knew the inmates had a deep, inexpressible feeling of revulsion toward me—owing to the fact that I was about to take part, or had just taken part, in an electrocution. Never with words, or overt act, would they reproach me, but they did it with their eyes—which was worse—and by an unaccustomed silence. It was as if they were accusing me of having betrayed them, after leading them to believe I was their friend."[20]

Squire did save the life of one prisoner, writing to the governor that the man was in his view insane and had to be permanently restrained in a straitjacket. The doctor wrote to the governor to that effect but got no reply, so he went to Albany to appeal in person for the man's life. But the governor was out of town. Eventually Squire reached him by phone and the governor gave the condemned man a two-week reprieve. Experts then examined him, agreed he was insane, and sent him to a mental asylum.

After that emotional ordeal Squire wrote that he went to bed for a month: "During that time I lost thirty pounds. (Then) I went to the Adirondacks to recover my strength. But a change had come over me. I was oppressed by a feeling of anxiety and menace. I did not realize the trend of my subconscious thoughts, until duty took me to the death chamber again and I stood on the edge of the rubber mat, within reach of the chair. On that occasion, just after I had given the signal for the current to be turned on—while the man in the chair was straining against the straps as the load of 2,000 volts shot through his body—I felt for the first time a wild desire to extend my hand and touch him. Afterwards I subjected myself to severe self-analysis. I decided that the wild and irrational desire was merely a vagrant impulse, and that it would not

Fig. 27. Tea tycoon Thomas Lipton on his annual visit to Sing Sing. The warden's daughter, Cherie, is sitting in his lap. Warden Lawes stands directly behind Lipton. (Courtesy Guy Cheli)

occur again. But I was wrong. At each subsequent execution the impulse became stronger. It finally got so compelling, that I was forced to grip my fingernails into my palms in order to control it. Each time I had to stand farther and farther away from the chair. But even then, I would feel a sudden urge to rush forward and take hold of the man in the chair, while the current was on."[21]

Squire probably saved himself from suicide by quitting.

When Dr. Charles Sweet took over from Squire he did not have to struggle with the same moral dilemma because, from then on, the warden and not the doctor signaled the start of an execution. However, Sweet did watch the executions.

One innocent inmate, Edward Larkman, just missed being executed on the night of January 13, 1927. A family man and a petty thief, Larkman had been arrested for the robbery and murder of a paymaster in Buffalo, New York. The only witness to the crime was a woman who glimpsed the murderer for about five seconds, and recalled that he wore dark glasses. Larkman had been taken to police headquarters and made to stand alone in a bright light, wearing dark glasses. He's the one, said the witness.

Despite Larkman's vigorous denials the witness reidentified him under oath at his trial, and he was sentenced to be electrocuted at Sing Sing. His death sentence was affirmed by New York's highest court, though two dissenting judges believed that Larkman's identity as the killer had not been established beyond a reasonable doubt.

Shortly before Larkman was due to die, Warden Lawes told him that, based on the doubts of the dissenting judges, Governor Al Smith had reduced his sentence to life. Larkman then left the death house and joined the prison's general population, where he languished for two more years until a Buffalo gangster, Anthony Klakiewicz, admitted that, with the help of four gang members, he had committed the murder for which an innocent man was paying the price. Larkman was then freed.

The chair that had been ready for Larkman early in January 1926 did not stay empty for long.

The old death house, a small stone building attached to the main prison, was constructed so that condemned prisoners could see the little green door that led to the electric chair. Those awaiting imminent execution who had been moved to cells closer to the chair could see the man or woman walking to their electrocution and hear the hum of the deadly motor and the gruesome noise of the drills and saw used in the autopsy. The noise drove some insane.

Three desperate escape attempts to avoid execution had been successful, but only for a time. One man who killed a guard to escape was recaptured and executed, two others were found drowned in the Hudson River.

A new death house, known as the slaughterhouse, and finished in 1922, had cost almost $300,000, and was a prison within a prison with its own kitchen, hospital, exercise yards (with concrete on which to walk or play handball, and a view of the sky), visiting room, and a morgue. It was out of sight and sound of the autopsy room. One wing had twelve cells for men, and a separate wing had six cells for women. The women's section also contained a pre-execution cell, to which the condemned were removed on the morning of the day of their execution. On the second floor there were six isolation cells for the mentally disturbed, one of them padded for violent inmates.

In his *Miracle at Sing Sing: How One Man Transformed the Lives of America's Most Dangerous Prisoners*, Ralph Blumenthal explains that each cell "had a toilet and sink, but with the plumbing and faucets out of reach to thwart mischief. Drinking water came at the push of a button. Prisoners used their hands to slurp it up—there were no cups to be fashioned into weapons. The light bulbs were set high in the ceiling, unreachable to prisoners looking for a way to slash their wrists. The keyholes were protected so prisoners could not stuff them with paper, delaying guards while they attempted sui-

Fig. 28. Lawes (at left) and his head guard, John J. Sheehy, at the prison gates. (Courtesy Ossining Historical Society)

cide. And every ten feet along the corridors were alarm buttons for the guards to summon urgent help."[22]

Violent deaths not only occurred inside the slaughterhouse but outside as well, within sight of the prison. This happened on July 4, 1927, soon after about a thousand inmates had been released from their cells to exercise in the prison yard. It was a stormy day and hundreds of them were drawn to the high, iron-barred fence, fronting the Hudson River, to watch three young men fighting for their lives as they tried to keep afloat in a canoe five hundred feet offshore. There was a great shout from the onlookers as they watched the canoe capsize and hurl its occupants into the raging current. Several convicts yelled to the guard on the wall pleading to be allowed to rescue the young men struggling in the water. It was so rough that it was unlikely that even a professional lifesaver could rescue them. The guards, obeying orders, refused to open the gate and all three drowned. As Lawes explained later, the guards weren't to know if it was a "staged" attempt to bring about an escape.

News of the drowning reached the press, and there were critical letters from the public and suggestions that the inmates who had offered to risk their lives to rescue others should be pardoned. Lawes agreed with the guards, but he does not say in his book *Invisible Stripes* how he would have reacted if the water had been less rough, making it possible for inmates to have rescued the drowning men.

Three years later, in August 1930, a similar event occurred. Some two thousand inmates were in the exercise yard when two men and two women in a rowboat on the Hudson River yelled for help as their boat began to sink. Once again, inmates pleaded to be allowed to help them. This time a sergeant guard chose four short-term prisoners, and opened the gate for them to go to the rescue. While two of the inmates plunged into the river and swam toward the sinking boat, the other two had found firemen's grappling hooks and waited on the dock. The swimmers, slowly pushing the boat and its occupants toward the dock, eventually reached it, and the men with grappling hooks pulled the quartet to safety. The rescued boaters, writes Ralph Blumenthal, "were the chief of police of the New York Central Railroad lines, his brother-in-law, and their wives. Some of the prisoners were disgusted. (Others said that a railroad cop wasn't a real cop and it was okay to rescue him and his relatives.) Lawes hailed his four Sing Sing heroes, one a career larcenist with eleven arrests, in prison since 1910 serving two five-to-ten-year terms for forgery. Another was serving time for robbery and assault. The third was in for robbery and carrying a pistol; the fourth for grand larceny. It proved again what he had always said. There was good in every man."[23]

Actor Jimmy Cagney would surely have agreed. Strangely, Sing Sing had been a place for Cagney, the future movie star, to have fun when he was growing up. He and his pals were on a baseball team, the Nut Club, that often played against the Mutual Welfare League team on the prison grounds. When they first arrived, they were advised not to talk to the convicts, but soon after Cagney walked onto the field an inmate greeted him with: "Hello, Red." When Cagney pretended not to hear, the man said, "What's the matter, you getting stuck up?" It was a kid who had sat next to him in school.

As Cagney recalled in his autobiography, he broke another rule by shaking hands with "Bootah," as Peter Heslin was known. Heslin was in for five to ten for assault, having wounded a cop during a stickup, and his friend, Russell, a good-looking youngster standing a few feet away, was in for the same rap. Cagney knew him from school, too. When the innings began, to Cagney's amazement, the first to step up to the plate was another neighborhood youngster, "Dirty Neck" Jack Lafferty, a friend of his dad's. Seeing him there, Cagney remembered how Lafferty, a bar brawler, used to swear that one day he'd kill somebody. And it happened when a man named Bull Mahoney tried to stop Lafferty from stealing his car. Lafferty got the car by fatally shooting

Fig. 29. An aerial view of Sing Sing, also known as Hell on the Hudson, taken from the south. (New York State Archives)

its owner, but he also got twenty years to life in Sing Sing. That is, until Cagney's father—an alcoholic bartender and gambler—stepped in and, using his Tammany Hall contacts, got Lafferty's term reduced to fourteen years.[24]

"Later in the game," Cagney wrote, "I went down to coach first base, and a man there said, 'Hey, Red! You go down to the East Side House any more?' Another old chum, and before the game was over, I had met two more. . . . That is proof, if proof be wanted, that our neighborhood produced something more than ex-vaudevillians."[25]

Some time later, a cop with a sick wife, on his way home to take care of their four kids, came upon Cagney's friend Heslin, recently released from Sing Sing, pulling a stickup on East 102nd Street. Heslin turned his gun on the cop and killed him.

There were three reasons Cagney never forgot Heslin or July 21, 1927. On that night, heavyweight boxing champ Jack Dempsey fought James Sharkey, Cagney himself was acting in a Broadway play, and his friend, "Bootah"—Peter Heslin, "a quiet, reasonable, decent human being," was how Cagney thought of him, went to the electric chair.[26]

Few thought of Ruth Snyder and her lover, Judd Gray, as quiet, reasonable, decent human beings, especially news reporters at their trial. Snyder, a Long Island housewife, and her married lover, Judd Gray, a corset salesman, were facing the chair for killing her husband, Albert Snyder, a workaholic art editor for *Motor Boating* magazine. After several failed attempts, they had finally battered him to death.

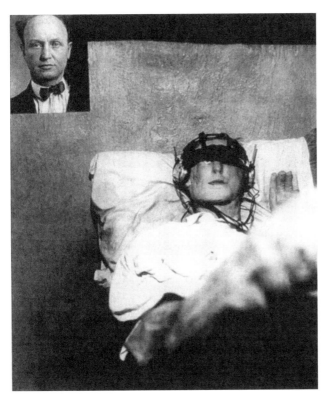

Fig. 30. An ingenious but failed escape attempt by inmate George Petersen (inset), who left this life-like dummy with sleeping mask and earphones in his bed. Afterward, inmates had to stand at their cell doors for the 6 PM head count. (Courtesy Michael DeVall)

Writer Damon Runyon saw Ruth Snyder as "a chilly-looking blond with frosty eyes and one of those marble, you-bet-you-will chins. She is not bad-looking. I have seen much worse." He saw Judd Gray as "an inert, care-drunk fellow that you couldn't miss among any hundred men as a dead set-up for a blond, or the shell game, or maybe a gold brick."[27]

Covering the trial, Runyon wrote:

She has a good figure, slim and trim, with narrow shoulders. She is of medium height, and I thought she carried her clothes off rather smartly. . . . Her parents are Norwegian and Swedish. . . . An assistant attorney asked her, "Mrs. Snyder, why did you kill your husband?"

"Don't put it that way," she said. "It sounds so cruel."

"Well, why did you kill him?" persisted the curious Peter M. Daly.

"To get rid of him," she answered simply, according to Daly's testimony.

Gray, a spindly fellow in physical build, entered the courtroom with quick, jerky steps. . . . You couldn't find a meeker, milder-looking fellow in seven states, this man who is charged with one of the most horrible crimes in history. Right back to old Father Adam, the original and perhaps the loudest "squawker" among mankind against women, went Henry Judd Gray in telling how and why he lent his hand to the butchery of Albert Snyder.

"She-she-she-she-she-she," the burden of the bloody song of the little corset salesman as read out in the packed courtroom in Long Island City yesterday. "She played me pretty hard. . . . She said, 'You're going to do it, aren't you?' . . . 'She kissed me.' . . . 'She did this. She did that.' Always she-she-she-she," ran the confession of Henry Judd.

True, she herself squawked on Henry Judd, at about the same time Henry Judd was squawking on her; but it's a woman's inalienable right to squawk.

Their sympathy is for Henry Judd Gray! There is no sympathy for Mrs. Snyder among the women and very little among the men. They all say something drastic ought to be done to her.[28]

The trial ended their passion and their prospects. Gray, the man Snyder had once called "lover boy" and "you darned lovable cuss," was now "that Judas who spells his name with two d's." During their eight-month wait on death row, literally feet apart, they neither spoke nor wrote to each other. However, they both had huge amounts of mail from strangers, especially Snyder. Many letters to her were from sadists relishing her predicament, from moralists saying she'd got her just deserts, or from the religious begging her to repent. Hundreds were from apparently intelligent and educated men proposing marriage should she beat the electric chair.

Warden Lawes gave her only those letters he thought wouldn't upset her, which did not include the ones from the lunatic fringe, including one threatening that "When Ruth Snyder is executed, the Heavens will heave forth in storm and I shall blast the wicked from the earth," and another that "The executioner will never reach the prison alive. Will bomb him before he gets there." Another message came from "The Lord God Almighty," written in a shaky hand and simply forbidding the execution.

Gray had fewer marriage proposals but more business propositions. One man wanted to buy the Bible Gray was reportedly constantly reading, offering half the profit from its sale to charity. The warden said no, and eventually sent it to Gray's family. Another, eager to buy the beds and chairs the couple used in their cells, was told they were state property and not for sale. A barber offered to buy Snyder's hair, willing to pay $100 to a prisoners' welfare fund and $100 to Snyder's relatives. When Lawes refused the offer, the barber phoned the prison and asked for the address of Snyder's mother. "Don't you think it would be indecent to disturb the grief-stricken old woman with such a request?" the warden asked him. The barber thought it over briefly and then said, "I guess I'll forget about it."

Callous money grubbers were outmatched by Snyder herself. A convicted husband-killer, she was in lively correspondence with an insurance company, insisting that when she was reprieved, as she anticipated, they must cough up the victim's $96,000 to her as his widow.

A fantastic rumor reached the warden that, even without a reprieve, Snyder would live to claim the cash. He was told of an extraordinary plan to restore her to life after the prison doctor had declared her dead. Rescuers, according to the rumor, intended to claim her corpse and resurrect it with adrenalin injections. Even if possible, the warden knew that they would have revived a zombie, because the massive electric shocks would have destroyed her brain cells. He quoted expert opinion that she would be shocked unconscious in less than 240th of a second, much faster than her nervous system could register pain. Of course, none of the real experts with firsthand knowledge were around to dispute him.

The resurrection rumor heated up when the warden received a lawyer's letter forbidding an autopsy on Ruth Snyder. She, however, scoffed at the plan to revive her, and converted to Catholicism. Some regarded this as a blatant ploy to sway Al Smith, the state's Catholic governor.

Robert Elliott, the man hired to make sure she died and stayed dead, was a kind, soft-spoken son of an Irish immigrant father. He took over from John Hulbert, who had electrocuted 120 people before having a nervous breakdown in 1925 which was signaled by his yelling at the guards and throwing his equipment around during an execution. He had suddenly quit on January 16, 1926, without warning Lawes. (Hulbert committed suicide three years later, with a gunshot to the head.) When the need for a new executioner was announced, Lawes got the usual flood of offers from what he called "morbid fellows." He chose Elliott, who had been executioner Davis's assistant. Davis had pulled the switch on the very first disastrous electrocution—of Kemmler—long before Hulbert's time. Elliott jumped at the job offer, saying it was the call of destiny, although he opposed capital punishment!

As official executioner for six Eastern states, Elliott, the gray-haired and skinny electrician, would eventually execute some three hundred and eighty-two men and five women. A devout Methodist, he began his killing career in Sing Sing by electrocuting two men. The first was an immense Scandinavian who glared at Elliott as if he hoped looks could make them change places. The other had hysterics and was strapped to a plank and carried to the chair screaming hideously. He was sick all over Elliott, who said that as the man was a killer it didn't bother him too much.

Because Ruth Snyder was the first woman he would execute, he was nervous about it, but not nearly as much as she was. As the time drew near she had frequent fainting fits from which she recovered, screaming in terror. Lawes had decided to execute Gray first, thinking he was the weaker of the two and might give the most trouble. Now he changed his mind, and guards moved Snyder to the holding cell only twenty paces from the electric chair. She recovered sufficiently to eat a last meal of soup, roast chicken with celery, mashed potatoes, and coffee. Gray had the same, and asked a guard to make sure the coffee was really good. After dinner Snyder fell into a coma, but a few hours later she was playing cards with female guards, after which she read the Bible.

Late on the night of January 12, 1928, she dressed in a brown smock, cotton stockings, a black cotton skirt, and brown felt slippers. When the barber arrived and began to clip off a patch of her dark blond hair, to leave part of her skull bare for a better electrode contact, she asked if he'd make what was left of her hair look attractive, because she wanted to die looking her best. Before she left the cell, her right stocking was rolled down for a second electrode to be attached to the bare skin.

She was given neither opiates nor sedatives to ease her last moments.

At 11:01 PM, twenty-four invited witnesses, mostly reporters, had their first glimpse of the woman they had come to watch be put to death. She had become slim in the death house and looked, as she had hoped, as if she'd just left a beauty parlor—except that her eyes were red-rimmed from weeping, and, at thirty-three, she looked middle-aged. Six relentless overhead lights revealed her terror and bleached her already white face. She shuffled rather than walked and groped for assistance from the matrons walking on either side of her.

"Jesus have mercy!" she responded to the Catholic chaplain's litany, her voice subdued but high-pitched like a scared child's.

"When her eyes fell on the death instrument, she all but collapsed," Lawes recalled. "Her knees buckled. Two guards reached out to steady her, then she walked the rest of the short distance mechanically, woodenly, as if in a trance."

Out of sight in an alcove, executioner Elliott watched anxiously as guards urgently strapped Ruth Snyder into the high-backed wooden chair and covered her hair with a football helmet containing the upper electrode while she continued to respond to the priest's litany in a weak, quavering voice.

The matron who had agreed to act as a shield began to sob, and hurried out—leaving Snyder exposed to the witnesses. It was just what Thomas Howard had hoped for. He had been hired by the *New York Daily News* to try to evade the no-photographs rule and to snap Snyder's dying moment.

Warden Lawes had put all those present on their honor to obey the rule, not realizing that photographers have a higher allegiance to posterity.

Soon after Ruth Snyder responded "Father, forgive them," executioner Elliott moved a short copper lever and made contact. There was a buzzing drone and his victim shot forward against the straps. At that moment, newsman Howard hitched up a leg of his pants and squeezed the rubber bulb concealed in his jacket, which triggered the shutter of a camera strapped to his ankle. It recorded the image of the dying woman twelve feet from him—and the blurred, slightly out-of-focus photograph gives it an added touch of horror. Aware of public appetite, the *New York Daily News* filled next day's front page with it, increased the press run by 120,000, and sold out. The photo has since been reproduced in countless books and articles and on TV screens.

Her flesh had turned brick-red, then, slowly, as the seconds ticked away, her exposed arms, right leg, and the lower part of her face became deadly white again. Spirals of pale, wispy smoke rose from her head. Some witnesses retched, others turned their heads away or closed their eyes.

Three times Elliott increased the current, held it steady, and then finally shut it off.

The prison's Dr. Sweet put a stethoscope to her chest. As he listened for a heartbeat, an attendant vainly tried to screen her leg with a towel. Water dripped down her leg from the moist electrode and the burn had left a greenish-purple blister on her calf. The doctor's curt nod indicated that she was dead. Two white-clad attendants unstrapped the body and carried it, mouth agape and arms swinging limply, to a stretcher on wheels. The priest left, head bowed.

Ruth Snyder's mother and brother were part of the crowd of a thousand gathered outside the prison. They had been among those who had hoped for a resurrection miracle. The attorney's letter forbidding an autopsy was their last desperate attempt to save her. But the attorney general had advised Lawes to ignore the letter, and a routine autopsy took place.

In his holding cell, Judd Gray had just opened a letter from his wife, who had visited him surreptitiously during his trial. She forgave him in this farewell letter. So did his mother-in-law. After reading it, he looked up and said, "I am ready to go now. I have nothing to fear."

Three minutes after the cadaver of his mistress left the death chamber, Judd Gray entered as if sleepwalking. He wore a white shirt and, like Ruth Snyder, brown slippers. He walked stiffly, yet somehow retained an air of dignity, with the Protestant chaplain at his side.

"Blessed are the pure in heart," said the chaplain. Gray's response was incoherent.

The guards soon strapped him in the chair. With his eyes masked and electrodes attached, he couldn't see but could still hear the chaplain say, "For God so loved the world . . ." as executioner Elliott made electrical contact.

A blue spark flashed in the leg electrode and Gray's body shot forward. Smoke rose from both electrodes.

". . . that he gave his only begotten son."

Gray's throat was suddenly swollen and what could be seen of his face flushed crimson. After two surges, Elliott shut off the current and Gray's color faded. Dr. Sweet listened for a heartbeat, found none, and said that Judd Gray was dead. The men in white wheeled him away for an autopsy.

Thirty minutes after the double execution, eyewitness reporter Gene Fowler sat at his desk typing: "They led Ruth Brown Snyder from her steel cage tonight. Then the powerful guards thrust her irrevocably into the obscene, sprawling oaken arms of the ugly electric chair. The memory of the crazed woman in her last agony as she struggled against the unholy embrace of the chair is yet too harrowing to permit of calm portrayal of the law's ghastly ritual. The formal destruction of the killers of poor, stolid, unemotional Albert Snyder in his rumpled sleep was hardly less revolting than the crime itself. Both victims of the chair met their deaths trembling but bravely. . . . Their bodies, shrouded in white sheets, are in the prison morgue, a small room not fifty feet from the chair. This then was the end of the road, the close of their two years of stolen love."[29]

World-famous and revered author Thomas Hardy also died on the day of the Snyder-Gray executions. One paper covered his obituary in two inches. The pair of killers got 289 inches.

After the executions of Snyder and Gray, Lawes and his wife, Kathryn, went to relax in Palm Beach, Florida, staying at the Alba Hotel with their personal physician.

While they were away, Kirchwey, a former Sing Sing warden (for seven months in 1916) and former dean of the School of Law at Columbia, told a meeting of the Society for Ethical Culture in New York City that there had not been the slightest improvement in Sing Sing since it was built a hundred years ago: "Discipline is the same. There are still the same dark cells—dungeons freely used for the most trifling violations, such as the rule forbidding communication between prisoners. The prisoner quickly takes on the color of his surroundings and becomes in fact the crook and bandit that we have by that process forced him to become." His statements were published the next day in the January 17 *New York Times*.

In the fall of 1928, Charles Chapin was visited by Bess Houdini, the widow of the great magician who had died two years previously. She and "Rose man" Chapin "became friends, particularly after she came to Sing Sing to make arrangements for the transfer of the criminology collection that Houdini had willed to Lawes. The two took a sincere liking for each other and Bess came to believe that Charlie's crime was a 'mercy killing.' Every few months, Bess came to visit by taxi from her home in Inwood, New York. In turn, Charles regularly sent her flowers from his garden and even arranged for some of his inmate-gardeners to do some landscaping at her cottage in Rye, twenty miles away."[30]

In those days, Sing Sing inmates probably invoked the name of Leibowitz as often as that of God or the Devil. Attorney Leibowitz, after all, was a miracle worker. As defense attorney in seventy-five murder trials not one of his clients had gone to the chair. The secret of his astonishing success was not only his ability to make juries laugh and cry, but the fact that he represented only those he was convinced were innocent.

Sing Sing inmate Harry Hoffman learned of Leibowitz's infallibility after serving five years of his twenty-to-life sentence for what reporters called the fiendish murder of a housewife. In January 1929 Hoffman wrote to the attorney, saying that he was innocent, desperate, and broke. Leibowitz must have believed him because he accepted the case. Four months later, Hoffman was free. Leibowitz had done it again.

In the summer of 1930, the prison needed a new drainage system and, to make way for it, a large steam shovel demolished most of Chapin's gardens as he looked on helplessly. Gone were thousands of roses and other flowers, the blue spruce trees, and the pool with pink and white waterlilies. Lawes believed that the loss of his beloved gardens led to Chapin's death a few months later.

The famous Rose Man of Sing Sing, who wrote his autobiography in prison and carried on two romances, mostly by mail, died of bronchial pneumonia at age seventy-two, at a quarter to midnight on December 13, 1930. He got his last wish, to be buried with the wife he had murdered and always claimed to have loved.

At least two newsmen did not recall their old boss as the Prince of Darkness. One wrote to Warden Lawes, "As an old *Evening World* man who owes whatever success he has attained to the fact that he received his early training under the greatest newspaper general in the world, I send you this word in memory of Charles Chapin." The other wrote: "I cannot pass this opportunity to send this message of sympathy in the passing of Boss Chapin, in remembrance of many kindnesses shown to me when I was a young reporter on his staff."[31]

Fig. 31. Lawes's daughter Cherie sings "Keep Your Sunny Side Up" to an audience of happy prisoners celebrating the imminent release of one of them. She was born in Sing Sing in 1921; her nurse was a black inmate. (Courtesy University of South Carolina Newsfilm Archive)

Lawes mourned his death, having regarded and treated Chapin as a valued friend, as he did many of the twenty-five hundred prisoners and staff in his charge. Living within the prison with his wife and three daughters, he claimed, with justification to have "the most cosmopolitan retinue in any home in the world. The dominant races of mankind are represented in my white butler (previously Japanese), my Mongolian chef, my black-skinned porter. Catholic, Protestant, Jew, Buddhist are among the great religions. Murder, manslaughter, kidnapping, robbery, burglary, pick-pocketing, arson, forgery, larceny, are among the crimes for which the men assigned to the warden's home are doing time."[32]

CHAPTER EIGHT

MURDER INCORPORATED AND THE MOVIES

1930–1949

Life imitated the theater of the absurd in the 1930s—the era of Prohibition—when there appeared to be more corruption outside than inside the prison. While Sing Sing began to enjoy its golden years, New York City was strangled by organized crime and its enablers, crooked politicians. The near-miraculous changes in Sing Sing were brought about by Warden Lawes, an unpredictable mix of tough and tender, who continued to perpetuate much of Osborne's work and, like Osborne, came to regard many prisoners as friends.

Instead of punishment, which he said never reforms, Lawes stressed rehabilitation and even allowed prisoners to have pets. Some convicts showed extraordinary tenderness in caring for rats, mice, sparrows, and every stray cat or dog they found wandering on the prison grounds. Lawes also encouraged inmates to attend Sunday evening lectures by leading artists, athletes, and clerics. He let them have radios in their cells, play baseball and basketball, and enthusiastically supported what became a first-rate football team, the Black Sheep, its mascot a pony painted to look like a zebra.

Catering to public curiosity, Lawes welcomed cameramen from Pathé News and Fox Movietone News. They filmed prisoners from the moment they awoke at 6:30 AM and carefully made their beds, throughout their workday, and while walking in their hundreds, ten or so abreast, back to their cells in the fading evening light. One scene showed prisoners in white shirts and slacks marching to and from meals to the stirring tempo of the prison band.

Hollywood quickly got into the act, and Lawes let several companies use

Sing Sing for location shots for feature films, and allowed the actors cast as inmates or guards to visit the prison to steep themselves in the atmosphere.

Warner Brothers led the pack, almost cornering the market in prison movies. One of its stars, Jimmy Cagney, often cast as a hoodlum, had no need to travel to Sing Sing to make his performance more authentic. As a young street fighter growing up in Manhattan, he, as noted in the previous chapter, had often visited the prison to play baseball against a team of inmates, several of whom were his boyhood pals. Warner Bros.'s *The Big House* appeared in 1930, and *Angels with Dirty Faces* in 1938. Cagney's studio repaid Lawes for his cooperation with a gift of a gymnasium built in the prison with concrete stands and a parquet floor.

Lawes's book, *Twenty Thousand Years in Sing Sing*, became a film of the same name in 1932, with Spencer Tracy playing the lead as an inmate and Arthur Byron as the warden. In it Tracy, serving a five-to-thirty-year sentence for assaults with a deadly weapon, is let out to visit his girlfriend, Bette Davis, critically injured in a car crash. He later takes the rap for a murder she had committed and goes to the chair. The warden in the film comes across as a combination of Osborne and Lawes, a man who trusted the inmates and whose job was jeopardized by political enemies. A remake in 1940, retitled *Castle on the Hudson*, was directed by Anton Litvak, with John Garfield as an inmate who challenges the reforms of the warden, played by Pat O'Brien.

One whitewashed, but according to Lawes, essentially fair view of a day in the lives of Sing Sing inmates, as shown on newsreel screens, starts with a bell waking cell-bound prisoners at 6:30 AM.

They have half an hour to wash, dress, and make their beds.

At 7 AM a second bell alerts guards to open the cell doors on each gallery. Prisoners then leave their cells and walk up a 137-foot-high hill, sometimes in pairs, sometimes ten abreast, to the mess hall.

Dressed in regulation gray pants and open-neck white or gray cotton shirts, they could pass for members of the Elks or the Round Table on a summer outing. In fact, Warden Lawes would characterize most as decent individuals, the products of unfortunate circumstances and environments. He once estimated that only 15 percent of them were dangerous criminals. Of course, this meant that among some two thousand inmates, three hundred were violent antisocial types—the daredevils, the brawlers, the embittered, and the would-be big shots—at their most dangerous and vicious when trying to impress or intimidate others.

At breakfast, regardless of their crimes and sentences, other than those in the death house or in solitary, all inmates get the same treatment and the same food: cereal, fresh milk, bread, and coffee. They are not punished, as in the not-so-distant past, for talking or laughing while they eat. As they leave, they drop their eating utensils in baskets at the door of the mess hall, and walk downhill for a half hour of throwing a baseball or strolling around the yard.

At 8 AM a steam whistle sends them to their various jobs in the hospital, cookhouse, laundry, and library, to join the cleanup crew—or to the workshops where they produce some seventy articles which are sold to public institutions. One group of inmates is photographed climbing a rock pile, and a convict is shown leaving his cell, which he shares with birds in two cages. Trusted prisoners get to work outside the prison grounds.

The exceptions are inmates attending the prison school, with its eighteen inmate teachers supervised by two civilian instructors. School takes precedence over all work assignments.

They have a choice of a surprisingly large number of courses up to a fifth-grade grammar-school level, in Everyday Arithmetic, Elementary and Intermediate Arithmetic, Business Arithmetic, Applied Mathematics, Slide Rule, Algebra, Accounting, Bookkeeping, Economics, Plain English, Punctuation and Paragraphing, English for New Americans, Elementary English and Rhetoric, English Composition, Short Story Writing, Penmanship, Newspaper Writing, Commercial Correspondence, Elementary Spanish, Elementary French, Business English, Business Geography, Industrial Organization, Blue Print and Plan Reading, Salesmanship, and Gasoline Motors.

On this day of filming, 470 inmates are taking one or more of these courses. Those educated beyond the fifth grade are allowed to take advanced correspondence courses, and can study in the fifteen-thousand-book library on the top floor of the old hospital building.

At 10:50 AM the steam whistle calls the men to lunch and they again walk to the mess hall, making their ways—depending on where they've been working or studying, sometimes skirting the death house—through the entrance to the church building, along various corridors, to the mess hall.

The lunch menu is roast veal with mashed potatoes, turnips and gravy, bread, cornstarch pudding, and cocoa.

Lunch is followed by half an hour of activity on the prison recreation ground. Lawes is amused to see some inmates take off their shirts to sun themselves during this break. These men, knowing that they are about to be freed, are trying to convert their prison pallor into a healthy tan to make it appear, when they get out, that they're just back from an extended vacation.

The whistle calls them back to work or to study at 12:30, when guards count them to make sure that none has escaped.

Dinner is a repeat of lunch with a different menu, after which—if there is no entertainment that evening—the inmates return to their cells and are locked in for the night.

Just because they're prisoners does not deprive them of all their rights. They are legally entitled to attend the religious service of their choice and to get a specific food allowance. Everything else is a privilege, which Warden Lawes has the almost godlike power to give or take away.

As for the 208 guards, if caught sleeping, instead of being fired they are given the option of resigning. A guard or any of the ninety-five civilian employees caught bringing alcohol or drugs into Sing Sing is instantly dismissed.

Not shown in any of the documentary films are the punishments meted out to those caught flouting the rules, such as being absent from school without a reasonable excuse, leaving beds unmade, and singing in a loud or off-key voice to annoy their neighbors. For his first offense, the culprit gets a warning and suspended sentence. For a second or repeat offense, he has years added to his sentence. For the worst offenses, like brutally attacking or sexually molesting a fellow inmate, it's the isolation cell.

But, if the filmed documentaries tended to picture Sing Sing as the Waldorf-Astoria with a river view, some inmates saw it as a grim, even gruesome place, crawling with insects and rodents, although the new cells up the hill were relatively brighter and had their own toilets, compared with the damp dungeons of the old cellblock. Anonymous ex-cons told newspaper reporters of the overcrowding, the booze, and the gambling, especially among the old-time inmates doing big time, and of the frequent stabbings. Inmates accused the guards of knowing what was going on and of demanding a share of the gamblers' winnings.

The only time inmates felt comparatively safe was when locked in their cells. One con was given a knife by a prison acquaintance and advised to keep it permanently strapped to his arm and use it the first time anyone made sexual advances. Otherwise, he was warned, you will be branded a punk and molested the rest of your prison stay.

Teenager Frank Crowley was safe from such an attack, being housed in the death house, away from the general inmate population, and condemned to die for killing a policeman. A virtual army of over a hundred armed policemen and detectives with "shoot-to-kill" orders—after being tipped off by an ex-girlfriend—had flushed him out of his Upper West Side Manhattan hideaway after a barrage of some seven hundred bullets had convinced him that he was outgunned.

Locked in his Sing Sing cell, the skinny youngster cursed the guards and

Fig. 32. Teenage death-house inmate Frank Crowley. He made a model of a building with rooms, stairways, a working elevator, and a live beetle as the doorman. Before his execution in 1932, he set the beetle free. (New York State Archives)

refused to cooperate. But Lawes got through to Crowley by showing a genuine concern for him and an interest in his artistic talent. What impressed Lawes was the model of a building that Crowley had constructed in his cell, with rooms, stairways, and a working elevator. He had attached a beetle to the front door with a piece of thread and a wad of chewing gum, named the insect "the doorman," and for hours at a time watched it moving around, as if it were the doorman. Crowley told Lawes that he meant to kill the beetle, but then felt sorry for it and decided to give it a chance to live. Crowley wasn't as lucky.

For his last meal Lawes gave Crowley a quart of ice cream as a personal gift, which he shared with another inmate also awaiting execution. Then he made peace with the guards he had insulted by handing them cigars.

On January 21, 1932, twenty pounds heavier than when he arrived at Sing Sing, yet still hardly overweight, Crowley walked almost casually to the electric chair between Father McCaffrey and the chief guard, John Sheehy. Lawes wasn't there. He was too upset. It was the first execution he had missed in twelve years though he never actually saw any of them, being fervently opposed to the death penalty. Crowley asked the guard to tell Lawes to send his love to his mother, and to thank Mrs. Lawes for all she had done for him.

There were, of course, some inmates who could not be treated like human beings, such as "Mad Dog" Vincent Coll who was charged with killing a five-year-old boy and wounding three other children when he opened fire on rival gangsters on a crowded Harlem street. Lawes considered Coll and his cohort, Frank Giordano, so dangerous that he detailed four guards to accompany them in his private car to their "baby massacre" trial in Manhattan's General Sessions Court in December 1931. Despite his reputation, Coll was freed on bail, which, in fact, became a death sentence. As he was making a phone call in a drugstore, a man entered carrying a violin case from which he took a submachine gun and killed Coll with fifteen bullets. His killer was never caught. Five months later Dominic Odierno and Giordano, his partners in crime, were found guilty of another murder and went to the chair.

Willie Sutton, the notorious bank robber famous for his response to the question, "Why do you rob banks?"—"Because that's where the money is"—had been in his Sing Sing cell only four days when, on December 12, 1932, he smuggled in a hacksaw, sawed his way out, picked two doorlocks, and entered the prison's empty mess hall. There, Sutton picked the lock on a cellar door and found two ladders, which he lashed together to make a longer one. Then he headed for a shadowed wall where he placed the ladder. A confederate was waiting for him on the other side with an automobile. This was one of Sutton's many prison escapes.

Soon after, Edward Larkman also left the prison, but by the front gate. The problem of eyewitness identification had spurred Governor Al Smith to commute his death sentence to life imprisonment—just in time. Larkman's head had already been shaved for the electrodes. In 1929 another man confessed to the murder for which Larkman was still doing time. It wasn't until 1933 that the new governor, Herbert Lehman, unconditionally pardoned him and he was set free.

In the 1930s New York City had become a crook's paradise, with organized crime largely in control—and with the dreaded Murder Incorporated installed as its bloody Brooklyn branch.

Under the city's charming and corrupt mayor Jimmy Walker, who dismissed with winks and wisecracks press exposure of widespread graft and pervasive mob influence, it seemed that nothing could stop the mob's rule—until three men came to the rescue: Franklin D. Roosevelt, Fiorello La Guardia, and Thomas Dewey.

Governor, soon to be President, Franklin D. Roosevelt, risked the wrath of Tammany Hall Democrats by insisting that public officials must explain their sudden, suspicious affluence or expect a one-way ticket to Sing Sing. The announcement caused a flurry of early retirements, sudden departures for foreign climes, or claims to have been lucky gamblers. Among the first wave of crooked public officials to be sent up the river to Sing Sing was

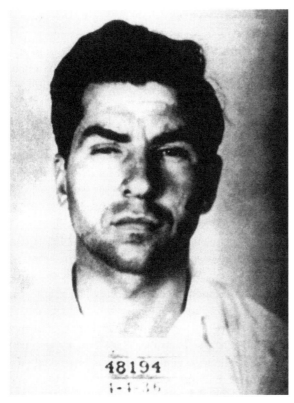

Fig. 33. Mafia chief Lucky Luciano. Although sentenced to from thirty to fifty years in prison, he got out long before that during World War II by helping the war effort. After the war, he retired to Italy. (New York State Archives)

Frank Warder, state superintendent of banking, who joined Bernard Marcus and Saul Singer of the Bank of the United States, already ensconced in Sing Sing cells. Mayor Walker might have joined them had he not found sanctuary in Europe, where he lived stylishly on his reputedly ill-gotten gains of over a million bucks.

A minute after new mayor Fiorello La Guardia was sworn in at midnight, on January 1, 1934, he immediately ordered the police to arrest the biggest crook in town, "Lucky" Luciano, a crime boss who had cornered the market in bootleg booze, illegal drugs, and prostitutes. Luciano boasted of having the cops and district attorney in his pocket and expected La Guardia to join them. He was bitterly disappointed. "I don't understand the guy," Luciano said, or words to that effect. "I offered to make La Guardia rich, and he wouldn't even listen to me." After seventy prostitutes had testified against "the whoremaster of Gotham," Luciano had to vacate his luxurious Waldorf-Astoria suite to take up residence in Sing Sing, facing a thirty-to-fifty-year sentence.

More high-ranking gangsters followed, thanks to Thomas Dewey, the new special prosecutor investigating organized crime, as eager as the feisty new mayor to clean up the city.

Hired killers, now Sing Sing inmates, found themselves among unlikely cellmates, such as Truman Capote's stepfather, in for fraud; and the once powerful politician Thomas Hines, in for conspiring to protect the notorious gangster Dutch Schultz.

But it was not a prison for men only. Eva Coo arrived at Sing Sing, dehumanized by headline writers as "Pig Woman," "Cave Woman," and "Tiger Woman"—sentenced to death for murdering a simpleton for money. The police kept their promise to her accomplice, Martha Clift: for helping to send Eva to the chair, Martha escaped the chair, getting twenty years to life.

Eva arrived in the death house as if returning to her brothel. She was cheerful, almost jaunty. Judging by appearances, the two matrons in charge of her were the condemned prisoners, and Eva was trying to keep their thoughts off their fates. Close your eyes and listen to Eva's cheerful chatter and you'd swear you were back in her Woodbine Inn and she was entertaining customers. The women guards soon cheered up; they had never had such fun with a prisoner or laughed so heartily.

Warden Lawes was astonished to find her radically different from the woman described in the press. In his benign eyes, the "Pig Woman" was neat and even attractive. In his presence she showed none of the tigerish qualities attributed to her. He saw her as a soft, ladylike, well-spoken woman who was never coarse or vulgar and who claimed that she was innocent—betrayed by so-called friends.

She simply sighed when her appeal was rejected, saying that she guessed that she wasn't in line for a break. But it devastated the two prison matrons in charge of her who had become Eva's affectionate friends. To them she was a warm, wisecracking woman who had refused a last meal because, she quipped, it would be bad for her figure.

Eva spent her last night in a holding cell, a large circular room where she could hear radio or phonograph music. Prisoners called it "the dance hall," "the walk to the chair," "the last mile," and the chair itself "the hot seat." They referred to electrocutions as "frying" or "burning," and whenever an inmate got a reprieve, they'd say, "The burner is out of a fee."

Eva Coo devoted her last few minutes to manicuring her nails and making up her face. When the prison barber began to shave her head to allow better contact for the electric current, she asked him to leave a little bit in front. She was pleased when a matron held up a mirror so that Eva could see the effect, saying that it looked real nice.

She was due to die at 11 PM on June 27, 1935. As the two matrons joined Eva to escort her on her last, short walk, one of them began to cry and Eva put her arm around the woman to console her.

When Eva sat in the electric chair, she saw that now both matrons were crying. She patted the head of one and thanked them both for being good to her. Then, her voice just above a whisper, she spoke her last words: "Thanks, darlings."[1]

Elliott the executioner checked the mask over her face and made sure that both head and leg electrodes were in place. He walked to the instrument panel behind the chair and threw the switch.

Eva jerked toward the witnesses as though in a violent car crash. But, instead of the noise of shattering glass and squealing tires, there was the familiar sputtering drone of the electricity and the smell of burning flesh. Her hands reddened, then drained of blood. Her neck veins seemed about to burst. After a minute Elliott reduced the current from 2,000 to 1,500 volts, and a wisp of gray smoke, fainter than from a cigarette, rose from the electrode on Eva's head. When Elliott switched off, Eva slumped back as if giving up a frantic effort to escape.

Once more he threw the switch. Now Eva's movements were an awful mockery of the laughing lady in her days at the Woodbine Inn, when her body had shaken, not in its death throes but in helpless merriment.

It took seven minutes to kill Eva Coo.

The woman who murdered for love of money died broke. She was buried in a pauper's grave.

Those going to die and those waiting their turn often played it cool. One man on his way to execution called out to a death-row neighbor, "See you tomorrow." Murderer Chuck Appel had an acute sense of timing and humor. He was about to be electrocuted for killing a New York policeman. Executioner Robert Elliott had already put the hood on Appel's head when the condemned man said, "Elliott, you are about to serve a baked Appel." But a woman, Irene Schroeder, was the coolest under pressure according to Elliott. She and her lover had killed a state policeman during an attempted robbery. The morning before she was to die—with her lover, Glenn Dague, following minutes later— her only concern was for him. And she asked a guard to make sure the cook fried Glenn's eggs on both sides, because that's how he liked them.

One expert more likely to know the murderer's mind than most was Frederick Wertham, a distinguished psychiatrist and author attached to Sing Sing who had studied and interviewed many murderers. One of his tasks was to determine if they were legally insane; if so, they would escape the chair.

He was not required to examine Irene Schroeder or her lover, Glenn Dague—murder for money was not considered a mental aberration. Nor did he speak with the killers of policemen. But he did check out Albert Fish, a mild-mannered little old man found guilty of killing and eating children.

Wertham's first impression of the sixty-two-year-old cannibal was of a meek, innocuous, gentle old man; the kind of person to whom you would entrust your own young children. Wertham made an in-depth study of Fish, tested him, and interviewed him and people who knew him.

At the trial, Wertham told the court that Fish suffered from religious insanity which manifested itself as visions of Christ and his angels and also of Hell. He said that Fish believed himself to be a very holy man who had to sacrifice and eat children to purge himself of his iniquities.

Four prosecution psychiatrists agreed with Wertham that Fish practiced many kinds of perversions, but disagreed that he was legally insane. After all, testified the chief psychiatrist for New York City, these same perversions were practiced by many people. Even the eating of excrement, he went on, was an appetite shared by some prominent citizens. Another psychiatrist for the prosecution estimated that a quarter of the people walking the New York City streets were psychopaths.

Fish, the sadomasochistic cannibal, sat impassively throughout the proceedings, smiling slightly, and absentmindedly stroking his mustache.

Fig. 34. A view of Sing Sing Prison from the east, the Hudson River beyond, and the Palisades on the western shore. (Courtesy Ossining Historical Society)

Crime reporters at the trial, who had seen their fair share of perverts and psychopaths, took a poll among themselves and decided that Dr. Wertham was right and that Albert Fish would be found innocent by reason of insanity.

They were wrong. The jury verdict was first-degree murder and the judge sentenced the lunatic to death. Smiling vaguely, Fish was taken to Sing Sing clutching a Bible, saying that he was looking forward to his execution with mounting excitement.

At his appeal hearing, the chief judge conceded that Fish was crazy, but not legally insane because he knew what he had done was wrong. Fish's attorney appealed to the governor for clemency, and suggested that Fish pay for his crime with life in prison.

Psychiatrist Wertham also appeared at the hearing where he said that Fish was incurable, unreformable, and unpunishable, and that in his distorted mind he was actually looking forward to the electric chair as his final experience of intense pain. He suggested that to execute a sick man was like burning a witch.

New York governor Herbert Lehman disagreed and decided that Fish should die.

Shortly before his execution, Fish had a lamb chop for lunch. He hid part of the bone and sharpened it on the cell's stone floor. With it he made two deep gashes in the shape of a cross in his stomach. He survived what was considered to be a last-minute suicide attempt.

Witnesses for his execution on January 16, 1936, saw a stooped, gray-haired man hobble to the electric chair. He looked twenty years older than his sixty-six years and was grinning as if about to take a thrilling Coney Island ride, behaving as if eagerly anticipating his last sadomasochistic thrill, and this time one that was perfectly legal.

A news reporter with literary leanings began his account of the execution: "Albert Fish, cannibal extraordinary, has gone the way of all flesh."[2]

Wertham was convinced that the state had electrocuted a madman "because the public was aroused over the murders, and the authorities needed to have him declared normal. I discussed the case with several members of the jury. What prompted their decision was their—not unjustified—fear that Fish might be released again to commit further crimes."[3]

Over the years, Wertham discussed Fish with other psychiatrists, as well as with attorneys and judges. Without exception, they agreed that Fish was legally insane. In executing him, Wertham thought that a great chance was lost in finding out how a man so severely mentally diseased, often in prison and twice in psychiatric hospitals, could persist undetected in his awful practices for decades. "What should have been done," he said, "was to use this case for an overhaul of the haphazard procedures which are still costing the lives of children."[4]

Another notorious killer, Frances Creighton, a 165-pound Long Island housewife who wrote poison-pen letters, and her neighbor Everett Applegate, were found guilty of the arsenic poisoning of his 286-pound wife, Ada. They were sentenced to die in Sing Sing during the week of March 9, 1936. Frances denied the charge but admitted that some twelve years previously she had fatally poisoned her nineteen-year-old brother, Raymond Avery, because, she said, he was tubercular and a pervert and better off dead. She also admitted she had been tried for the arsenic murder of her mother-in-law but had been found not guilty through lack of evidence.

Many believed that Appelgate was innocent, including Warden Lawes. Even the district attorney, Martin Littleton, had his doubts, but when New York State governor Herbert Lehman called Littleton the night of the double execution to say he might grant Appelgate clemency, the DA refused to go along with him. Both executions would proceed as planned.

But they didn't. Creighton was so terrified that when guards went to her cell to prepare her for death, they found her in a coma. They carried her, still unconscious, and gently placed her in the chair at 11:01 PM. She was dead three minutes later.

Appelgate entered the room at 10:09 PM, turned to the twenty-two witnesses and said: "Gentlemen, I want to say something. Before God I am absolutely innocent of the crime. I hope the good God will have mercy on the soul of Martin W. Littleton."

When executioner Elliott returned to Sing Sing a week after the electrocutions, he noticed that a death-chamber guard had a bandage on his arm. He explained that he had been badly burned when he lifted Frances Creighton's corpse from the chair, and his arm came into contact with her unusually hot flesh. The burn had been severe enough to have it treated in the prison hospital. Previously the heavy clothing that condemned prisoners usually wore had protected him, but Creighton's had been comparatively flimsy. Elliott wasn't surprised. He knew that the electric current made the electrodes so hot that one night it melted the copper in the leg electrode.

In 1937 Warden Lawes's wife, Kathryn, was killed in an auto accident. Many inmates were deeply upset by the news. They had thought of her as an angel of mercy who had written letters for the blind and illiterate, visited them in the prison hospital, and helped their families. When they heard that her funeral service would be in a church outside the prison, a committee of

Fig. 35. A formal photo of Sing Sing guards in the 1930s with the head guard, John J. Sheehy (far right). (Courtesy Ossining Historical Society)

prisoners insisted on the right to pay their last respects to someone they had loved. Lawes took an incredible risk in agreeing to it.

The night before the funeral, Sing Sing's front gate was opened and a procession of inmates—murderers, burglars, muggers, frauds, rapists, and petty thieves—left the prison grounds and walked to a house a quarter of a mile away. No guards trained their guns on the silent procession, and no guards accompanied them. Once inside the house, they silently passed the coffin, some uttering short prayers or crossing themselves—and every one of them returned to Sing Sing.

On January 5, 1939, another apparently innocent man, twenty-nine-year-old Charles Sberna, was executed. He and Salvatore Gati had been found guilty of murdering a policeman. At their trial Gati testified that Sberna was innocent of the crime, but no one who counted believed him. After Sberna's electrocution, the chaplain remarked: "This is the first time I've ever been positive that an innocent man was going to the chair, and there was nothing I could do about it. If only people would make sure they know what they are talking about before they swear away a man's life."[5]

That same year, DA Thomas Dewey rated Murder Incorporated's top gun, Louis Buchalter aka Louis Lepke, as probably the most dangerous criminal in the United States and offered $50,000 for him dead or alive. Known as the Czar of the Rackets, Buchalter headed the enforcement arm of the

National Crime Institute, better known as Murder Inc., which hired contract killers to eliminate business rivals and fellow mobsters. Murder Inc.'s motto was "We Only Kill Our Own," which was largely true. Buchalter was believed responsible for some seven hundred contract killings across the nation and to have personally committed at least two murders.

Hoping to escape the electric chair by cooperating, or to escape from contract killers targeting him, he turned himself in, but not to Dewey. He surrendered to gossip columnist Walter Winchell—acting on behalf of his pal FBI chief J. Edgar Hoover.

Buchalter's emissaries dumped a quarter of a million dollars onto attorney Sam Leibowitz's kitchen table as an inducement to defend their boss. But the famed attorney refused even to discuss the case. Having promised to take his wife, Belle, to a Cary Grant movie, he was afraid they'd be late if he stayed to talk. So the couple went to the movies, and Buchalter went to the chair, said to be the only organized-crime boss ever executed in Sing Sing, although Martin (Bugsy) Goldstein and Harry (Pittsburgh Phil) Strauss were surely in the running.

Goldstein and Strauss were a very active part of the Murder Inc. operation and reputedly had killed eighty-three people between 1931 and 1950. Some sources put their death toll at five hundred! To carry out their deadly orders as contract hit men, they used car bombs, shotguns, arson, and ice picks. They hanged one man with barbed wire. They were charged with only one crime, and they were both sent to the chair on June 12, 1941, for the murder of a Manhattan bookmaker on September 4, 1939 (the day after World War II broke out in Europe). They had tied him up, doused him with gasoline, and then set him alight.

It was to be expected that when some people read the newspaper accounts of such gruesome killings, they would volunteer to personally execute the perpetrators. Lawes was never without a thick folder of those willing and eager to replace Elliott and to pull the switch themselves. One applicant listed his victims as Germans during World War I, chicken and cattle on his farm, and a man he had killed in self-defense. All he needed, he told Lawes, was a crash course in electrocution and he promised that anyone he killed would stay killed. He hoped to hear from the warden by return mail. He did—no thanks.

On the other hand, the softhearted—some might say the softheaded—and the suicidal, offered themselves as substitute sacrificial lambs. One man was prepared to take anyone's place in the electric chair for free if the warden would pay his fare to the prison. A seventy-year-old ailing, would-be martyr

Fig. 36. Mass murderer Louis Buchalter aka Lepke, the dreaded head of Murder Incorporated, who was executed in Sing Sing in 1944. (New York Police Department)

was willing to replace a young man destined to die, saying that the youngster might prove worthy of a second chance.

A married man with six children volunteered to switch places with the next person in line for the chair, in return for lifetime support for the big family he'd leave behind. And a father made an emotional appeal to the warden to let him die in place of his son. He felt that having neglected his boy he was to blame for his awful looming fate.

The most plausible rationale from voyeurs eager to watch an execution came from a henpecked husband. He explained that his wife nagged him nonstop day and night, made jokes at his expense, and ridiculed him in front of others. He had been seriously tempted to kill her three times, he told the warden, and feared he might not be able to resist a fourth provocation. Watching an execution, he speculated, might deter him from becoming a murderer.

In all such cases, the warden politely declined the offer.

Lawes was thinking of retiring at the time Richard Whitney entered Sing Sing. A former head of the New York Stock Exchange, he had stolen a whopping $5,600,000 from his father-in-law, George Sheldon, treasurer of the Republican National Committee, and from his friends and family. He had needed the money to sustain his luxurious lifestyle and to pay for his country estate, a 495-acre farm in Far Hills, New Jersey; a townhouse; eight cars; forty-seven suits; thirty-two walking sticks; and five pink foxhunting coats; not to mention his flock of servants. The charge was reduced to stealing a mere $225,000 and for that he was sentenced to Sing Sing for from five to ten years.

He arrived handcuffed to a rapist. After he was free of the cuffs, fellow inmates nodded respectfully, moved aside to let him pass, called him "Mr. Whitney," and soon after, when he was behind bars, a guard called out, "All men who came in Saturday, Monday or Tuesday, and Mr. Whitney, please step out of the cell."[6]

Many who followed the case resented the fact that Whitney had been indicted for only two of his many larcenies and it spurred a St. Louis judge, who was about to sentence a young man for stealing $2 from a gas station, to remark: "Some people think there's one law for the rich and another for the poor. We'll correct that right now." Obviously a whiz at math, he quickly made a few calculations on a pad and announced: "Richard Whitney got five years for stealing $225,000 over five years. That would be $45,000 a year, $120 a day, $5 an hour. You stole $2. That would be 24 minutes. And that is your sentence."[7]

Lawes was obviously impressed by Whitney after knowing him for a few weeks. Without going into the question of his guilt or innocence, he saw Whitney as "an old gentleman, gray haired, soft eyed, with his benevolent smile and deliberate stride and neat appearance. You could hardly believe that he was, in his prime, the man who presided over the destinies of the greatest and most powerful aggregation of banks in the world. For years he sat with the mighty. . . . I marvel at the fact that he answers with an indulgent smile and ready ear when the lowest among his fellow prisoners greets him by his Christian name. Is this man doing penance? Is he paying his debt to society? . . . I remember the voice that was raised in loud protest that this sixty-year-old prisoner was assigned to a 'soft berth' in the prison library where he daily guides lesser intellects in their reading and study. I wonder if that vociferous critic would have assigned a thick-fingered and slow-thinking, untutored hod-carrier to the library and this cultured old gentleman to the rock pile."[8]

Whitney served three years and four months, eventually leaving his library tasks to take on a tougher assignment: scrubbing cell walls. He also did some clerical work and played first base on the Sing Sing ball team. When he was paroled in 1941, his brother, George, one of his victims, who had become president of JP Morgan, picked him up outside the prison gates. He didn't return to Wall Street but became manager of a dairy farm, then took a lowly job in an explosives plant, where he rose to be the vice president's executive assistant.

There were rumors that Whitney had promised fellow cons to find work for them when he and they got outside, and that ultimately he found employment for a hundred. This was not true, said Lawes. It was just for one man.

Shortly before Lawes retired, in the early hours of April 13, 1941, three prisoners in for armed robbery—Joseph Riordan, Charles McGale, and John Waters—tried to escape from the prison hospital. They were armed with revolvers that had been smuggled in to them, attached to the undercarriage of a truck that made deliveries to the prison. Seeing guard John Hartye ahead of them on his nightly rounds, they killed him with two shots in the back. Convict patient McGowan Miller was so stressed by witnessing the murder that he suffered a fatal heart attack.

The trio then forced another guard to lead them through a tunnel, where they handcuffed him, punched their way through a preloosened metal plate, used a rope to lower themselves thirty feet to the railroad track, and finally reached the street.

As they approached a getaway car parked near the prison, two Ossining policeman, James Fagan and William Nelson, stopped them and began questioning them. All three responded by firing their revolvers and the cops fired back. Waters died on the spot with two bullets in his head. Officer Fagan was fatally wounded with a bullet in his heart. Nelson drove him to a hospital where he was pronounced dead on arrival. Meanwhile, the getaway car had left without the two surviving fugitives, who hurried on foot to the Hudson River. There they forced an early-morning fisherman to row them to the western bank where they jumped out and headed for a wood.

The top half of the front page of next day's *New York Daily News* read: "3 DIE IN BREAK AT SING SING; GANG AT LARGE." Below it was a photo of the Easter Parade on Fifth Avenue.

Thousands of police, coastguards in a seaplane, two launches, a cutter, and bloodhounds joined the hunt for the killers. The bloodhounds found the men after a few hours

Author Ralph Blumenthal reports: "The fury of the police was unleashed on the shackled prisoners, who were beaten so brazenly that news photographers were able to show them being punched, knocked down, and yanked around by the hair. One photo showed a jackbooted officer astride the two men on the floor of the station house, a frightened-looking McGale clutching his crotch. Between interrogations by the prosecutor, Riordan and McGale, cuffed together, were brutalized by troopers and detectives for hours at a time. The assaults stopped briefly when someone called that the prosecutor was coming, and resumed after he left."[9]

At his trial in June 1941, Riordan testified that the police had beaten a confession out of him. McGale claimed that state troopers had joked that by the time they were finished, he would admit that he had killed Abraham Lincoln. The two men who had smuggled the guns into Sing Sing for the escape were also arrested.

Lawes, of course, as the man in charge was blamed for the escapes and the killings. Because the guns and handcuffs used in the escape had been smuggled on the undercarriage of a truck, to prevent any copycat escapes Lawes had installed an illuminated pit at the prison entrance, from which the undercarriages of all trucks entering and leaving Sing Sing would be inspected.

An investigation virtually exonerated Lawes, finding merely a few weaknesses in his administration.

Riordan and McGale were executed on Riordan's twenty-sixth birthday—June 11, 1942. Their two accomplices got life sentences.

By then the fifty-eight-year-old Lawes had been retired for several months. He had been Sing Sing's warden for a record twenty-one years. Hundreds if not thousands of prisoners and former prisoners considered him their friend. Two thousand four hundred inmates had packed the chapel to hear Lawes's farewell address—only those on death row and in disciplinary confinement were not admitted. There was so much cheering, applause, whistling, handshaking, and hugs that his "God bless you" was one of the few phrases that anyone could recall.

During those years as warden, Lawes had found time to edit a magazine, *Prison Life Stories*, as well as to write several books about prison life, all now out of print, including *Man's Judgment of Death* (1924), *Life and Death in Sing Sing* (1928), *Twenty Thousand Years in Sing Sing* (1932), *Strange Stories from Sing Sing* (1934), *Invisible Stripes* (1938), and *Meet the Murderer* (1940). In 1935 he traveled to England where Scotland Yard detectives welcomed him as a distinguished colleague. And as a leading advocate of the prison reform movement, he had frequently lectured throughout America as a passionate opponent of the death penalty.

According to admirer Henry Pringle, Lewis Lawes did more than any other prison administrator in US history to spread the gospel that vengeance is not a cure for crime, that rehabilitation is possible if convicts are treated like men instead of beasts.

Sing Sing's head physician, Dr. Sweet, was also on his way out. When he had taken over from Dr. Squire, he never had to struggle with the same moral dilemma that plagued his predecessor: it was now the warden's duty,

Fig. 37. B-Block at night in the 1940s ablaze with lights.
(Courtesy Ossining Historical Society)

Fig. 38. The prison band. On their release many of them became
professional musicians and some played with major recording stars.
(Courtesy Ossining Historical Society)

not the doctor's, to signal for an execution to take place. Sweet had merely to check that the inmate's heart was no longer beating and to perform the autopsy. But he had many more agreeable duties, having, during almost a quarter of a century at Sing Sing, operated on over five thousand inmates and saved the lives of hundreds.

One of his triumphs was to fashion a new nose for a convict who arrived at Sing Sing without one. Another was to cure an inmate's perpetual headache by removing a bullet from his brain.

Dr. Sweet made headlines for Sing Sing when a lifer, Louis Boy, volunteered to give his blood to an eight-year-old girl dying of cancer. Sweet conducted the medical experiment and, although the child died, Boy was rewarded for his part by being set free.

Whenever Sweet called for more blood, especially during World War II, he was never disappointed, although convict blood donors were warned that they would not be recompensed.

The youngest person ever executed at Sing Sing was eighteen-year-old Edward Haight, who went to the chair on July 8, 1943. He had abducted and murdered two girls aged seven and nine, killing one with a hunting knife and throwing her body off a bridge, and repeatedly running over the other girl with his car.[10]

That same year all prisoners in the damp, overcrowded, and unsanitary old cellblock were moved to the new building on the hill. The old cell bars were removed and donated as scrap metal for the war effort.

During the war, the US Navy feared that New York Harbor presented a likely target for enemy agents and thought that the underworld might be able to prevent an attack. Lucky Luciano, who had been moved from Sing Sing to Dannemora, was considered to have great influence on the waterfront. Early in 1942, Captain Roscoe McFall, the naval officer in charge of intelligence in the harbor, asked Governor Lehman to move Luciano back to Sing Sing. There, intelligence agents could be in frequent contact with him. Lehman agreed, and for the rest of the war Luciano remained in Sing Sing—helping to protect America.

Bertram Campbell was also a wartime Sing Sing inmate, serving a five-to-ten-year sentence for forging checks totaling seventy-five-hundred dollars. He repeatedly professed his innocence, but two witnesses had given sworn testimony that Campbell was the guilty party. He had been inside for three years, while his wife and three children survived on welfare, when drug addict Alexander Thiel, who slightly resembled Campbell, admitted that he was the forger. Thiel's confession turned out to be true. Thomas Dewey was

DA when Campbell had been prosecuted. Now, in July 1945, as he had become New York State's governor, Dewey freed Campbell and awarded him $115,000 for "shame, humiliation, loss of liberty," and loss of income.[11]

Nothing could restore Campbell's lost health and he died eighty-two days after getting the money. Fortunately, most Sing Sing inmates belonged there, among them pickpocket, Frank Germano, who appeared before Judge Samuel Leibowitz in 1947.

After the district attorney had reported Germano's long record as a pickpocket the judge said to the accused: "Your face looks familiar. It seems to me I've seen you in some crowd at Ebbets Field. Aren't you the fellow who knocked down Umpire Magerkurth?"

"Yes, Your Honor," replied Germano.

The judge recalled how, several years before, he was at Ebbets Field when the Brooklyn Dodgers were playing the Cincinnati Reds—and due to a decision by umpire George Magerkurth, the Dodgers lost. As the six-feet-three, 250-pound umpire was heading for the dressing room, Leibowitz saw Germano, a short but muscular man, leap on his back, knock him to the ground, and continue punching him, until others came to the umpire's rescue.

Now seeing him again, this time in court, Leibowitz declared, "You are a professional pickpocket. I'm firmly convinced that it wasn't the umpire's decision that prompted you to knock him down. You undoubtedly had in mind to have a crowd collect and then have your partner go through their pockets. I'm going to send you to Sing Sing for two and a half to five years. On Sundays you will attend ball games up there at the Big House. The umpires come from the outside, so don't you dare try to assault them. Stay in the stands and when you get out, if you get the urge to pick pockets, the best advice I can give you is never to leave your home unless you put on a pair of boxing gloves. Then you'll be absolutely safe from arrest. Do you promise that you will wear gloves summer and winter when you go out?'"

"Yes," said the prison-bound Germano.[12]

It's not surprising that there was often more laughter in Judge Leibowitz's courtroom than at Broadway comedies.

When Germano arrived at Sing Sing, Lawes was no longer in charge. And its chief doctor, Charles Sweet, was contemplating his own retirement. His work had taken its toll on him. At times he was awakened in the middle of the night to save the life of a man on death row who was either dangerously ill or who had attempted suicide, only to see him executed when he had recovered. He hated, he said, to see a healthy person die. That was his one major regret about the job.

Executioner Robert Elliott seemed to have had no regrets. Obviously many people envied him, because when he died in 1949, an avalanche of applications arrived on Warden William Snyder's desk, offering to replace Elliott. One in five of the letters came from women.

Two widows wanted the job. One said she had plenty of nerve, could repair her own radio, and felt sure she could soon learn the "little trick" of electrocution. But, if the warden turned her down, she asked him to find her a "nice honest husband," though not one from the prison population.

Her rival for the job, a former nurse, wanted to be an executioner because it was "odd and different." She claimed to be in perfect health, to have no bad habits, and, she concluded, "I am not hard-hearted, neither am I chicken hearted."[13]

A male applicant modestly requested one shot at an execution, needing the $150 fee to send his son to college, and another wanted the cash for a dowry to marry off his daughter.

The man the new warden, William E. Snyder, hired to be Sing Sing's last executioner was Dow B. Hover, a deputy sheriff from Germantown, New York. He was a married man with a son and a daughter. His identity was such a well-kept secret that it was only revealed in 2005.

When Warden Snyder oversaw the execution of Murder Inc.'s top gun, Louis "Lepke" Buchalter, and four of his mob, Hover pulled the switch.

Snyder held the job for almost seven years—until December 1950, when he was replaced by Wilfred L. Denno.

CHAPTER NINE

THE LONELY HEARTS KILLERS AND THE ROSENBERGS

1950–1982

On the theory that treating inmates humanely would improve their characters, Warden Wilfred Denno instituted new programs that kept Sing Sing inmates busy and trained them for honest work. They could learn to repair motorcycles, make ceramics, handle machinery, or become photographers or draftsmen. They had a choice of lectures on black history and Italian culture, Dale Carnegie courses for prospective business tycoons, and Gamblers Anonymous meetings for compulsive gamblers. Inmates were also allowed to have picnics.

The benign treatment had a remarkable effect on Edward Kelly, a divorced forty-two-year-old machinist, awaiting his turn to be electrocuted. He had admitted to having killed a woman, Elouise McHugh, after shooting her with a rifle on Main Street, Kingston, in broad daylight. When his sentence was overturned on appeal, he wrote to Warden Denno on June 12, 1951, as if he'd been staying at a pleasant holiday camp:

"Dear Sir, due to the fact that I'm leaving the 'Death House' I cannot say I have any regrets, nor will I recommend it to any one, but I can inform them that, if they are ever unfortunate enough to go to Sing Sing, they will be very well treated. I have no fault to find with anything or anybody during my stay, every reasonable request was granted. The entire staff of the prison are a credit to New York State. The Officers and Guards are as fine a group of men as you could find anywhere. 'Dick' and 'Freddie' go about their duties as if they had a part interest in the place, always helpful and ready with a word of

Fig. 39. Edward Kelly was executed in 1952 after telling the warden that he had enjoyed his time in the death house. (New York State Archives)

cheer if needed. I enjoyed 'Terry's' homelike meals. It would certainly be a pleasure to meet everybody, including yourself, under different circumstances. I extend my best wishes to all. But I hope I never come back."[1] Unfortunately for him, he did. He was retried and again found guilty of murder, for which he was electrocuted on October 30, 1952.

When Kelly's sister read a disturbing account of his last hours, she went to Warden Denno to complain. He investigated, and wrote to her on May 11, 1953, that the article "The Man Who Begged to Die," written by Russel Travers, in the July issue of *Vital Detective Cases* magazine, describing her brother's actions on the day of his execution was inaccurate "and it is apparent to me that the author of the article has a vivid imagination or was misinformed."[2]

Of course, not many had the same reaction to Sing Sing as Kelly. And, despite Warden Denno's concessions, there was no significant reduction in crime in prison. Gang rapes went unreported; bloody fights broke out over food being served too hot, too cold, too spicy, or too late; or because someone was bored. And there was a steady flow of former prisoners making the return trip up the river.

Nor was there any letup in the public's voracious appetite for murder trials, as demonstrated outside the Bronx Supreme Court when a crowd of mostly women pushed and screamed to get seats at the Fernandez-Beck murder trial. Only seventy out of several hundred got in.

The two on trial, Raymond Fernandez and Martha Beck, believed to have killed at least seventeen women and a two-year-old girl, tried to use the insanity ploy—but in vain.

Con man Fernandez had deserted his wife and children in Spain to make a killing in America, but found slim pickings. Needing a steady supply of suckers, he found a rich source in women, often widows, looking for soul mates at Lonely Hearts clubs. He first married them bigamously, then took all their cash before disappearing to hunt for his next conquest. If his victim proved to be a problem or tried to recover her money, he killed her.

He found more than his match in six-feet, 240-pound Martha Beck, the former head nurse of a home for handicapped children in Pensacola, Florida. She had also worked in a mortuary. After three failed marriages, she was declared an unfit mother and had her two children taken from her. Instead of his victim, she became the con man's willing partner in murdering women for their money.

The tabloid press dubbed them "The Lonely Hearts Killers."

Dr. Richard Hoffman, chief defense psychiatrist, believed Beck was a victim of physical and psychological abnormalities that made her Fernandez's slave. He testified that she was a pathological liar and the victim rather than the perpetrator of a compulsive and obsessive act.

Psychiatrist Frederic Wertham disagreed. After examining the guilty pair, he initially speculated that she might have fallen under Fernandez's hypnotic-like spell. But he changed his mind when he sat with Beck in the Women's Detention Center in Manhattan and asked about her drowning a little child in a bathtub. She surprised him by laughing. It wasn't a bathtub, she corrected him. It was a washtub in the basement.

Figs. 40, 41. Police photos of "The Lonely Hearts" killers, Raymond Fernandez and Martha Beck. Between them they were believed to have killed at least seventeen women and a two-year-old girl. They were executed in 1951. (New York State Archives)

During several conversations I had with Dr. Wertham in 1985, he said that he thought their motive for the cold-blooded killings was greed.

The insanity defense having failed, Fernandez put all the blame on Beck, saying that as a gentleman he wouldn't hurt anyone, but that Martha was evil and ought to die.

The jury found them both guilty and they were sentenced to Sing Sing's electric chair.

Camilo Weston Leyra had arrived in the death house not long after Fernandez was lodged there. Leyra's eighty-year-old mother, Catherine, and seventy-five-year-old father, Camilo, whom he regarded as loving, decent, useful, and harmless, had been savagely beaten to death in their Brooklyn apartment in daylight on January 10, 1950. The police immediately focused on their son, Leyra, and after grilling him for four days and four nights and having a doctor hired by the DA question him under hypnosis, said that they had his oral confession.

He was tried and sentenced to death.

Leyra had oddly mixed feelings as he rode in a brand-new chauffeur-driven car heading north along the road bordering the Hudson River en route to Sing Sing. True, a deputy sheriff sat handcuffed to him in the backseat while another sat in the front, holding the official papers, ordering his execution for the brutal slaying of his parents. But the sun was shining brightly, there were colorful flowers everywhere, and through gaps in the trees he occasionally glimpsed the sparkling blue river. Sometimes he felt numb, as if he weren't physically there. Other times he thought he was dreaming.

An appeal by his attorney, Frederick W. Scholmen, claiming that his client had been mentally coerced through hypnosis proved successful. The US Court of Appeals unanimously decided that he should have a new trial. At that trial the same judge who had first sentenced him to death did it again.

This time, Scholmen appealed the verdict before the US Supreme Court—and again won. And the judge who had twice sentenced Leyra to death dismissed the indictment. But, because the dogged district attorney had obtained a superceding indictment, Leyra underwent a third trial and for a third time was sentenced to death. Now the verdict seemed to stick, and Leyra found himself in a condemned cell in Sing Sing's death house in line for the electric chair.

Although his cell was windowless, a window in the wall outside his cell allowed him to see the exercise yard and beyond that the section of the death house that held the execution chamber known as the "Dance Hall."

It was a tradition for old-timers to size up a newcomer and decide if he was worth helping. For example, until his money was transferred to his commissary account, he could not buy toilet articles, candy, canned goods, or cigarettes from the commissary. In the meantime, if he created the right impression, the old-timers would help him out. Leyra passed the test. The day of his arrival guard John McGoey brought him a paper bag, saying that some of the boys had sent this down for him. In it were a toothbrush, toothpaste, soap, a washcloth, and cigarettes. He named Raymond Fernandez and two Swedes, Halberg and Jannsen, as the benefactors.

Although Leyra didn't know the Swedes, both convicted of killing a Chinese laundryman, he was astonished to hear the name Fernandez. He had pictured him from press reports as a monster involved with his partner, Martha Beck, in killing women and a child—the notorious "Lonely Hearts Killers." It seemed beyond belief that the man had a scrap of humanity in him, yet here he was acting like a friendly neighbor.

Leyra had little to do in his muddy, brown-walled, nine-by-twelve foot cell, No. 8, in the East Wing, but read and wait. Twice a day he exercised for half an hour at a time, while escorted by guards, but never in the company of another prisoner. To occupy his time, Leyra undertook an enormous task: reading the record of every murder trial in New York State and all the appeals before the US Supreme Court in the past forty years. As inmates were allowed to talk to one another, Leyra discussed the cases with Calman Cooper, who had studied the law for fifteen years while in prison and was something of an expert. Cooper was one of the three men facing the chair for the holdup murder of a *Reader's Digest* messenger carrying money.

As time passed, Leyra observed that every inmate in the death house eventually became mentally disturbed to some degree, if they weren't a bit off-kilter when they arrived: some developed persecution complexes, others heard voices or saw visions, and a few went stark raving mad.

Even though they faced the same terrible fate, there was not always harmony among death-row inmates. Stein, Cooper, and Wissner, the trio of killers who murdered a *Reader's Digest* money messenger, were the cause of some of the trouble because they often discussed their case in Yiddish. This infuriated wife-killer Lewis Wolfe, whose cell adjoined Stein's. A devout Jew, Wolfe yelled angrily that they were corrupting his beloved language.

Leyra was able to remain reasonably calm, sustained by the conviction—as he told the Catholic chaplain, Father Thomas J. Donovan, at their first meeting—that as he was innocent, the truth would eventually exonerate him.

The chaplain seemed surprised and asked why he was so confident. "Do you believe there's a Heaven?" Leyra asked him. "Of course," the chaplain replied. "So do I," Leyra said, "and I also believe that my parents are in Heaven. And if that's true, then nothing bad will happen to me, because my mother would never allow it."[3]

Leyra soon began to talk with inmate Raymond Fernandez every day and to hear intimate details of his life with Martha Beck.

Fernandez had switched from calling Beck a fat bitch with bad breath to declaring his undying love for her. He told Leyra that during his crooked career he had been corresponding with eight or nine women at the same time, and though determined never to be legally entangled with any woman, he eventually bigamously married at least fifty-five of his victims. He seemed proud of his ability to fleece so many women after meeting them through "Lonely Hearts" clubs.

He also admitted that Beck had originally been one of his victims, but she had fallen madly in love with him. Although he had skipped town, his usual modus operandi, she found him and persuaded him to hire her as his partner in the racket where she would pose as his sister. But she craved affection, was insanely jealous of his relations with other women, and had a violent temper, he said. And when he made her mad, she beat the hell out of him. She had even murdered one of his bigamous wives to prevent her and Fernandez from consummating their "marriage," and had drowned a little girl in a washtub out of spite, because she suspected that he liked the girl's mother.

When their last appeals failed, Fernandez admitted his guilt, said he had done terrible things, and was not afraid of the chair. But Beck broke down and sobbed that she was afraid to die.

Fernandez scoffed at reports that he had used magic to seduce hundreds of women, although he had boasted that by concentrating he could make a woman obey him, which he called "hypnosis at a distance." His vanity was sustained by women who wrote to him—and must have had a death wish—hoping he'd escape the chair and add them to his list of conquests.

Beck complained about newspaper headlines that characterized her as "The Obese Ogress" and "Overweight Juliet," as if she were being condemned not for murder but for being too fat. She, too, received stacks of marriage proposals in the mail.

The couple continued their love-hate affair in Sing Sing, waving and smiling at each other across the exercise yard. Some male prisoners, listening to Fernandez's lurid confessions, thought of Martha Beck as a frustrated beast. Once, after he had boasted of their steamy sex life, fellow cons spread a rumor that Beck was having sex with a prison guard in the women's wing of the prison. When Fernandez heard it, he went bananas.

They weren't the first to die in Sing Sing on the night of March 8, 1951. At 11 PM, twenty-two-year-old John Joseph King of Long Island City was executed for murdering an airline employee. Then Richard J. Powers, the same age, was executed for participating in the same crime.

Assuming Fernandez to be the weaker of the two, the warden had decided to execute him first. However, Fernandez promised Father Donovan that he would die like a man. He ate a last meal of onion omelet, followed by almond ice cream and coffee. Then he smoked a Cuban cigar.

Two hours before he was to die, Beck wrote a poem and sent it to him. He scribbled a reply: "I want to shout it out. I love Martha. What do the public know about love?"

After reading the note, Beck embraced the matron, saying, "Now I know that he loves me I'm ready to die."

When guards went to escort Fernandez to the chair, they found that he had collapsed, so they carried him into the execution chamber.

The first jolt of two thousand volts probably killed him, but the executioner followed the routine by sending three more blasts through his body. Each time, lights dimmed and flickered in the prison corridors.

Martha Beck waited in her holding cell, after a last meal of a double portion of southern-fried chicken and salad. A matron told her it was time to go. "Then what the hell are we waiting for?" she replied impatiently, but managed a smile. She had not lost her bouncy, almost jaunty walk.

Dressed in a blue-gray housedress, she sat on the edge of the electric chair twelve minutes after Fernandez's body had been wheeled out. The thirteenth woman to be executed by New York State endured a few embarrassing moments as she struggled to squeeze her large body into the chair.

Just before a guard put a mask over her face, either a nerve twitched in her cheek or she tried a farewell smile to the two matrons nearby.

Unlike Fernandez, it took four shocks before Beck showed no signs of life, and Dr. Howard Kipp, Sing Sing's chief surgeon, officially pronounced her dead.

Writer Truman Capote knew Martha Beck when they were children. They had run away from home together to stay overnight at a hotel run by her uncle in Evergreen, Alabama. "After that her family took her away," Capote told me in 1972. "I didn't even realize it was the same person until years later all my relatives in that town said, 'Oh, Martha Beck's the girl who was here that summer. She's the one you ran away with.'"

I told Capote that psychiatrist Frederic Wertham believed Martha Beck's motive for murder was greed. "Yes," said Capote. "Sexual greed on her part, and financial greed on the man's part."[4]

That night Camilo Weston Leyra watched four people—King, Powers, Fernandez, and Beck—walk to their deaths. He was anxiously waiting to hear the result of his latest appeal before the US Court of Appeals. He didn't have long to wait.

On April 12, 1951, as John Salu was about to be electrocuted for murdering a boy he had criminally assaulted, and Chaplain Donovan was preparing to give Salu the last rites, Leyra got a phone call from his attorney, Fred Scholmen. The court had reversed Leyra's conviction and ordered a new trial based on their unanimous decision that he had been mentally coerced in his oral confession. Legally, an oral confession in such circumstances is invalid.

The following week Leyra left Sing Sing for Brooklyn's Raymond Street jail, buoyed by his attorney's belief that he would soon be a free man. But his long ordeal was not over. Despite the law that an oral confession is not admissible, the trial judge let the district attorney read the entire document, including the oral confession, to the jurors. And they found Leyra guilty of the brutal murder of his parents.

On January 2, 1954, he was back in Sing Sing's death house, again in line for electrocution.

Several men he thought of as friends were still there: Calman Cooper, Harry Stein, and Nathan Wissner, the trio convicted of murdering a money messenger; and Ed Kelly, found guilty of killing his sweetheart in Kingston, New York.

Among the newcomers was Ethel Rosenberg, now in Martha Beck's death cell in the women's wing. Her husband, Julius, hadn't yet arrived.

The trial of the Rosenbergs has been called the most sensational spy trial in history. It began on March 6, 1951, and lasted just three weeks, during which Julius took the Fifth when asked about his beliefs, membership in the Communist Party, and his associates. According to J. Edgar Hoover biographer Curt Gentry, Ethel, who "as a loyal wife and mother, might have been expected to arouse a certain amount of sympathy, came across as cold and unfeeling, her contempt for the proceedings barely concealed. In less than a day of deliberating the jury found them both guilty on all counts."[5]

The judge called the crime—feeding atomic-bomb secrets to the Soviet Union during World War II—"worse than murder," adding, "By your betrayal you undoubtedly have altered the course of history to the disadvantage of your country." American troops were fighting in Korea when the Rosenbergs were arrested, and many feared that war with the Soviet Union was imminent. Some claimed that they enabled the Communists to have an

Fig. 42. A serious Julius Rosenberg and his smiling wife, Ethel, arrive at New York City's Federal Courthouse on March 21, 1951, for their trial under the 1917 Espionage Act. (AP Photo)

atomic bomb of their own by September 1949, years earlier than experts had predicted was likely.

After Ethel's arrival in her death-house cell, isolated from the men's section, she wrote to her attorney, Emanuel Bloch, that she was the sole women in the women's section of the death house and had the "distinction" of occupying the same cell as the late Martha Beck. She had recently read, she told him, that the only woman condemned to death by a federal court had been Mary Surratt, who was hanged for her part in assassinating President

Abraham Lincoln. Didn't he agree, she wryly concluded, that she was in good company?

She couldn't sleep much because of severe migraines. Before her arrest, she had received psychiatric treatment for emotional problems. In prison a psychiatrist visited her every other week. When asked if he had any opinion of her guilt or innocence, he said he was not an objective witness but had no reason to doubt her innocence.

Five weeks after Ethel entered the death house, Julius arrived there escorted by two heavyweight detectives. After his mustache was shaved off and he took a shower, he put on his ill-fitting gray prison uniform.

For over two years the couple awaited execution, while their lawyers launched twenty-three appeals before one hundred and twelve judges. Finally, the Solicitor General remarked that not only had all legal procedures been exhausted once, but many times.

Before the couple spoke together for an hour once a week, wire mesh screens were placed in front of the bars of Ethel's cell to prevent them from seeing each other. But, in the final months, they were allowed to speak twice a week. They also exchanged some four hundred letters—stamped as "okay" by the prison censor. The first, from Julius, addressing her as "darling," informed her that they were only thirty feet apart but their steel doors made it an infinity.

Prison chaplain Rabbi Irving Koslowe gave a sermon to his death-house congregation while they remained behind bars—except for Ethel. Being the only woman in the death house she was allowed to leave her cell and sit in the corridor with the rabbi. At the end of the service, when the participants sang, Ethel's lone feminine voice was clearly distinguishable. According to lawyer-writer Louis Nizer, "Julius was particularly thrilled with it and considered it not merely an ode to God, but a personal message, to which he responded by drowning out the spiritless voices of his fellow prisoners. Then they wrote to each other of the vocal contact they had achieved, he lavishing praise on her 'magnificent singing,' a tribute she could not return, but instead expressed her excitement at being 'touched by your voice.'"[6]

As if to sustain life in the midst of death, a fellow prisoner planted an orange pip in a crack in the cement of the exercise yard, and when Julius took his daily fifteen-minute breather, he and others helped to keep the orange pip alive by watering it. The pip eventually grew into an eight-inch orange tree with small oranges. He began to collect insects and soon had a dragonfly, locust, small brown butterfly, and a white moth. He also hunted cockroaches and played chess with a prisoner he couldn't see in an adjoining cell, holding the board between them.

Although the light in his cell was dim, Julius read some six newspapers a day, including the *National Guardian*, which proclaimed his innocence, and the *New York Post*, which didn't, as well as Thomas Wolfe's *You Can't Go Home Again,* and Forbes's *History of Technology and Invention*. He scrubbed and cleaned his cell, and made picture frames from cardboard to hold photos of his young sons.

On December 9, 1952, Julius wrote to his attorney, Emanuel Bloch, that like everyone else in the death house, each day he was allowed two fifteen-minute exercise periods when he occasionally played boccie-ball, but mostly he enjoyed the chance to walk around the yard of the death house, enthusiastically belting out his favorites songs, such as "Peat Bog Soldiers," "Joe Hill," and "Freiheit." Singing those songs brought back old memories, thoughts of other innocent inmates, he said, and gave him fresh courage.

Again, on December 27, 1952, he shared with his attorney little details of his life as a condemned prisoner: how gently the guard who escorted him outside his cell—and played handball with him—reminded him that his fifteen minutes in the fresh air was up, and how he reluctantly returned to his cell, with its steel door, padlock, and concrete shell.

Julius had become a chain-smoker, proud of his acquired skill of unfailingly flipping the butt into the toilet bowl from wherever he was in the cell. And he was delighted when he got a better mattress.

His teeth were in bad shape and, after the prison dentist had extracted them, Warden Denno got him a temporary plate. This may have been a simple act of kindness, but Denno was no Lewis Lawes. UPI reporter Jack V. Fox described him as "a medium-small, rather diffident man, more suited to a drugstore counter than keeper of the toughest criminals in New York."[7]

If anything, Denno was Lawes's opposite: he believed in the death penalty and was against the dormitory or cottage-type prisons. He said that it cost $2,000 a year to keep prisoners in Sing Sing and that the other types of prisons would cost twice as much and be harder to guard. He was especially exasperated by movie and television portrayals of prison life in which the warden was a pleasant, compassionate soul played by the likes of Spencer Tracy, who knew all the inmates by their first names. This was a pretty fair description of his famous predecessor. Despite his tough talk, Denno didn't treat the Rosenbergs harshly.

Two weeks before their date with death the director of the Federal Bureau of Prisons, James V. Bennett, called on the Rosenbergs, and afterward their lawyer issued this statement: "We were offered a deal by the Attorney General of the United States. We were told that if we cooperated with the

Government, our lives would be spared. By asking us to repudiate the truth of our innocence, the Government admits its own doubts concerning our guilt. We will not help to purify the foul record of fraudulent conviction and a barbaric sentence. We solemnly declare, now and forever more, that we will not be coerced, under pain of death, to bear false witness and to yield up to tyranny our rights as free Americans. Our respect for truth, conscience and human dignity is not for sale. Justice is not some bauble to be sold to the highest bidder. If we are executed it will be the murder of innocent people and the shame will be upon the Government of the United States. History will record, whether we live or not, that we were victims of the most monstrous frame-up in the history of our country."[8]

Judge Kaufman had scheduled their executions for May 1951, but their appeals took two years.

In early January 1953 Judge Kaufman granted them a stay of execution, awaiting President Dwight D. Eisenhower's decision on their petition for executive clemency. He turned it down in February.

On May 31, 1953, Julius wrote to Ethel that he wondered what he could write to his "beloved" when they both faced a grim reality: in eighteen days, on their fourteenth wedding anniversary, they were to be executed. He advised her that as that day grew near, they should both do their utmost to remain calm and avoid "hysterics" or "false heroics."[9]

Just before her execution, sons Michael, ten, and Robert, six, brought a bunch of marigolds and roses for their mother. But these were taken from them because flowers were forbidden in the death house.

After the boys' visit, Ethel wrote to her attorney that when the boys left and she was alone in her cell, she cried like a baby at the thought of what an ordeal it must be for her sons. With the little time left to her, she said that she intended to do as much work as possible to persuade others that theirs was a test case, and to warn of the danger of the United States becoming a fascist county. Her last words were a direct plea to Bloch that he not let her and Julius be murdered.

Meanwhile, in the White House, President Eisenhower awaited word from Hoover that the Rosenbergs had agreed to talk—he would then commute their sentences. To persuade them to talk, Rabbi Koslowe had been recruited. His task was to ask them separately if they would be willing to "confess" to save their lives. It had been agreed that if either showed a willingness to talk, even after they had been strapped in the electric chair, then the whole process would be halted. Two FBI agents would be waiting in the death house to get a signal of yes or no from the chief guard. A direct phone

Fig. 43. After visiting Julius and Ethel Rosenberg in Sing Sing on June 16, 1953, their defense attorney, Emanuel Bloch, talks to reporters as he leaves the prison with the Rosenbergs' sons, Michael, ten, and Robert, six. (AP Photo)

line kept the prison, FBI director Hoover, and the Justice Department in contact should either "confess."

It was a sweltering evening when everything was set for the double execution. Heavily armed guards and state troopers stood at wooden barricades that had been hastily erected across roads leading to the prison.

Five thousand protesters gathered in Manhattan's Union Square for a prayer meeting fifteen minutes before execution time. Police turned off a loudspeaker, fearing it would be used to spark a riot. There were demonstrations in England, France, and Italy in support of the Rosenbergs. Even FBI director Hoover had been against executing Ethel Rosenberg, warning the judge that the public would be revolted by the execution of a wife and mother. He also wrote to the Attorney General, pointing out that her execution would make orphans of her two young sons.

The Rosenbergs' attorney, Bloch, made a final appeal to Judge Kaufman to delay the execution as planned because it would take place on the Jewish Sabbath. Kaufman made a small concession changing the time to 8 PM (before sunset), but the executioner wasn't expected to arrive until 9 PM.

Then FBI chief Hoover had a change of heart, and was so intent on killing the couple on time that he ordered a helicopter to go and get the executioner. As it happened he arrived by car in good time, escorted by FBI agents and state troopers to speed his journey.

Being a federal, not a state, execution, there were only five witnesses: US Marshal William Carroll; his deputy, Thomas Farley; and after being searched for hidden cameras, three reporters: Bob Considine of the International News Service, Relmin Morin of the Associated Press, and Jack Woliston of the United Press.

Joseph Francel, an electrician in Cairo, New York, had been a part-time executioner at Sing Sing for fourteen years. Now he stood before a glass panel in an alcove of the death chamber. By eight that evening, thirty-five-year-old Julius Rosenberg, who had refused to "confess," had been strapped in the electric chair. Warden Denno nodded to Francel who pulled down a large switch in a firm, steady movement. Forty-five seconds later Julius was dead.

When Rabbi Koslowe went to Ethel's cell, she asked, "Did it happen?" "Yes, he is dead," he said. Then he asked her, for the sake of her children, to say something that still might save her.

"I have nothing to say," replied thirty-seven-year-old Ethel. "I am ready." She followed him, as he read Psalm thirty-one, which begins:

> For I have heard the slander of many;
> Fear was on every side:
> While they took counsel together against me,
> They devised to take away my life.

Before she sat in the electric chair, Ethel held out her hand to Matron Helen Evans, who had become her friend, and kissed her lightly on the cheek. The matron hurried away wiping her eyes. Ethel then shook hands with the other matron.

It took four minutes and thirty-six seconds to kill her. It was one day after her fourteenth wedding anniversary. She and Julius were the only husband and wife ever executed at Sing Sing. For the double killing the executioner was paid $300.

The *New York Times* also reported that "They went to their deaths with a composure that astonished the witnesses."

FBI agent Robert Lamphere said, "We didn't want them to die: we wanted them to talk."[10]

One well-placed witness to the last years of the Rosenbergs was their death-house neighbor Camilo Weston Leyra, three times convicted of the murder of his parents. He was in the cell next but one to Julius and often heard him talking about his two sons and his mother, who was looking after them. Leyra, with his Hollywood-inspired conception of a spy, could not imagine the mild-mannered Julius Rosenberg—a simple man with simple tastes whose idea of a good time seemed to be to take his family out to eat—as being the real McCoy. He certainly didn't fit the newspaper description of the paymaster of a Russian spy ring. In fact, Leyra was convinced that Ethel was the mastermind who led her husband into the spy business, a dyed-in-the-wool Communist and a frustrated woman who enjoyed beating people in political arguments.

He saw the couple at religious services when, said Leyra, "She seemed to go looking for arguments [and] sometimes led the rabbi in discussions intended solely to demonstrate her intellectual superiority."[11]

Leyra had read in the papers of Ethel's early ambition to be an opera singer and sometimes heard her singing lustily in her death-house cell. He once mentioned to three other inmates, Cooper, Wissner, and Stein, that she invariably sang in Yiddish. All three men understood Yiddish and Cooper confided to Leyra that Ethel's loud singing in Yiddish was a subterfuge: it allowed her to communicate with her husband, undetected, from her cell in the women's wing on the west side of the death house, some twenty feet away from his. "Don't say anything about it to the guards," Cooper warned. "It's the only way Ethel and Julius can talk to each other without the guards finding out."[12]

What she was saying remains a mystery. The night before their executions, FBI agents were present, hoping the Rosenbergs would confess. And that was the night, Leyra recalled, when Ethel sang for more than an hour, and again, according to him, she was trying to bolster Julius's courage and warn him not to talk about their crime. (Ironically, somebody "singing" is as everyone knows a euphemism or code word for squealing. But that was evidently not true in Ethel's case.)

If Leyra's account can be trusted, this is the only occasion when Ethel, confident that none of the listening lawmen would understand Yiddish, may have admitted their guilt. To the end, at least in English, both she and Julius insisted on their innocence. Leyra believed that Julius was about to crack as the time for his execution approached, and felt that if the authorities had offered to free Ethel to care for their young sons, Julius would have broken and talked.

Of all the thirty-eight people executed during Leyra's time in the death house, Ethel alone needed two more than the customary three shocks to kill her. A guard told Leyra that after the third time, when the doctor put his stethoscope to her breast, he heard her heart still beating. So the executioner gave her two more shocks. They stopped her heart.

The latest evidence is that Julius was a spy for the Soviet Union and had given them some not very valuable information about the atomic bomb. What is still in dispute is how much Ethel helped him. Many believe that the death penalty was excessive punishment for either of their crimes. Many others believe it was appropriate.

In a phone interview with the author on August 19, 2005, the Rosenberg's son, Robert Meeropol, said that he does not think Leyra is a reliable witness. He pointed out that he and his brother, Michael, are not looking for sympathy, but are interested in discovering the facts of the case. They both still believe that some of the government's evidence against their parents was fabricated and that their father never revealed any atomic secrets. Robert continued that the record indicates that the government imprisoned their mother, despite knowing that she was not a spy, and sentenced her to death in a vain attempt to pressure their father into confessing to something he did not do.

Leyra was still awaiting execution more than eighteen months after the deaths of the Rosenbergs. Then his never-say-die attorney got the US Supreme Court to hear the case and it reversed his conviction with a 5 to 3 vote. (Justice Robert Jackson didn't vote as he was in the hospital after a heart attack.) But the district attorney was persistent, too, and he moved for a reargument before the Court. They turned him down. Yet Leyra still wasn't set free.

Although the Brooklyn judge who had sentenced him to death now dismissed the indictment against him, he had not reckoned with the dogged DA. Some time before, this DA had asked a grand jury for a superseding indictment against Leyra and got it.

Samuel Leibowitz, having been the judge in Leyra's previous two trials, disqualified himself, and Judge Hyman Barshay took over. He ruled that the coerced so-called oral confession would not be allowed as evidence. But one of the jury asked for the transcript and the request was granted. It persuaded a third jury to sentence Leyra to death.

In July 1955 Leyra was back on death row—having already spent five years there—but now, at Harry Stein's request, in cell No. 1. Stein was in the next cell, No. 2.

Leyra still believed that his lawyer could get him out through the court of appeals. But it would be a long wait.

During his stay, he listened to a new inmate, John Francis Roche, admit to having killed at least three people, and express his fury against the world in general, and against one guard in particular. This guard had declined to tune into the radio program over the public address system that Roche wanted. In a voice that was apparently terrifying, Roche threatened to kill the guard. His threat was taken seriously and the guard was reassigned out of the death house. Still Roche continued to rage and attempt to intimidate others until it became time to kill him in January 1956.

It eventually became clear why Stein wanted Leyra to occupy the adjoining cell—to hear what amounted to Stein's death-bed confession. In July of 1956, at about nine on the night before Stein was to go to the chair, he told Leyra that he had something important to tell him that would solve an enduring mystery—the disappearance of a New York State Supreme Court judge named Crater, with which, he claimed, he was personally involved.

Twenty-six years previously, Judge Joseph Force Crater, a popular, handsome judge, and something of a ladykiller, after drawing a total of $5,150 from two banks, had left a Manhattan restaurant on Forty-fifth Street, entered a taxi waiting at the curb, and vanished. His wife believed that he might have fallen overboard unobserved and drowned while on a boat trip. Some believed he had left with his mistress to live in Nova Scotia, but that theory proved a dud when the mistress was seen around town. Others suggested that the powerful Democrat had been kidnapped and killed by political enemies, but there was no persuasive evidence that he had any.

The conventional wisdom of the time held that he was being blackmailed because of his liaison with Vivian Gordon, a former showgirl who had become the madam of a high-class brothel. When Crater handed over money to the blackmailers, they demanded more. In a struggle that followed, he was accidentally killed, carried to the Hudson River, and sunk there in a barrel of concrete.

The true story according to Stein was as follows: Judge Crater had taken a $5,000 bribe to keep a crook out of prison, but failed to do so yet still held onto the cash. Stein and two Philadelphia hoods were hired to get the money back but came up with a more rewarding scheme: to kidnap the judge for a $25,000 ransom. Informed by Vivian Gordon that Judge Crater would be dining at Billy Haas's restaurant on the evening of August 6, Stein borrowed a taxi from a friend, had one of the team drive it and the other sit in the back. They parked outside the restaurant with Stein watching nearby from the sidewalk. When Crater emerged from the restaurant, he was forced into the cab at gunpoint and Stein saw him being driven off to Eleventh Avenue as planned, where they left the cab and took off with their captive in a panel truck. They drove to Philadelphia where they kept him prisoner in a flat. Far from being afraid, the well-connected judge laughed at their phoned attempts to raise $25,000, warning them that every cop in the country would be looking for him.

When the Philadelphia police got a tip that he was in the area, they put the heat on local mobsters and rounded up many of them. Stein's confederates began to panic and Stein, still in Manhattan, told them to tie up Judge Crater and take him in the panel truck to Clifton, New Jersey. From there they phoned Stein that Crater was getting too hot to handle. Stein was reluctant to set him free, suspecting that the judge had spotted him while he watched the kidnapping from the Manhattan sidewalk. Instead, Stein ordered the men to whack him.

The judge laughed in disbelief when they untied him and gave him the chance to get down on his knees and pray if he wanted to. At about 3 PM on August 13, 1930, when he declined to kneel or pray, one of the gang put two bullets in the back of his head, killing him instantly. They dumped his corpse in a rusty bathtub bought from a garbage dump, poured hydrochloric acid bought at a local store over his body, waited until there was little left of him, and dropped the remains in the Passaic River.

Having got the secret of Judge Crater's disappearance off his chest, Stein apparently went to his own death peacefully.

Another death-house inmate, Romulo Rosario, was sentenced to die for murdering Michael Gonzales in Manhattan in 1953. He hoped to escape the fate of his cellmates by handing over a letter to a detective that outlined a plot to free the prisoners by friends outside, who meant to kidnap Warden Denno and his wife and take them hostage. Rosario, whose crooked career included drug pusher and police informer, expected clemency as a reward for exposing the plot. Investigation by the authorities concluded that he had concocted the whole thing to escape the chair. He didn't. He was electrocuted on February 17, 1955.

In the late 1950s Sing Sing held some eighteen hundred prisoners, all over twenty-one years old, slightly less than half of them Caucasian, serving time for felony murder, aggravated assault, rape, robbery, burglary, and other major crimes. The most dangerous prisoners were in the maximum-security block, where the eight hundred cells all faced outward so none could see each other. Warden Denno strongly supported this arrangement, especially one cell to each man, which, Denno maintained, discouraged homosexual assaults, though it was still a big problem. As was the crime of sexual assault outside prison.

Sexual assaults on women landed many men in Sing Sing. It landed Edward Eckwerth on death row.

The terrified screams of his woman victim on crutches didn't bother him when he tore the handbag from her shoulder and left her lying on the sidewalk crying in fear and pain. She remembered him vividly: a slight, nice-looking, brown-eyed guy. With his long crime record, he was a natural for a lineup, and she had no trouble picking him out.

A judge gave him five to eight years in prison, but then a clergyman stood up in the courtroom to tell of Eckwerth's miserable childhood in which he was brutalized and half-starved by an alcoholic mother. He had known almost nothing but pain. The judge was moved to pity, canceled the prison sentence, and set him free on probation.

Eckwerth resumed his old job as a coffee salesman to, among others, Rosemary Spezzo. She was a frail, twenty-four-year-old diabetic parochial schoolteacher, a customer on his route, with whom he enjoyed a friendly acquaintance. One evening she accepted his offer for a ride in his car. It ended near a wood in Yonkers, where they had sex. Whether it was consensual seemed unlikely because he used a flashlight and a rock to batter her to death. At least this witness would never identify him. After taking her money, Eckwerth went home to his wife and child. And the very next day he headed, alone, for California, his trip financed by the dead woman's money.

En route, he picked up a young woman hitchhiker. She, too, was a schoolteacher and she, too, was charmed by Eckwerth's friendly manner.

Detectives investigating the death of his first victim discovered that Eckwerth had delivered coffee to her shortly before her murder. They tracked him down and arrested him before he could harm the woman hitchhiker.

At this trial there was no clergyman to plead for compassion, so Eckwerth did it for himself: speaking in a calm, soft voice he recounted his awful childhood. It didn't work a second time.

His next stop was Sing Sing, where he was on death row for twenty-seven months. During that time, his only visitors were his attorneys who delayed his execution six times. Neither his wife, child, relatives, nor friends came to see him.

Two days before he was due to die, his attorney asked Gov. Nelson Rockefeller to commute the sentence to life in prison, saying that "No public benefit would be served by putting the man to death."[13] The district attorney told the governor that there was nothing in Eckwerth's long criminal record, considering the chances he had been given, to justify clemency. Rockefeller agreed. All the argument had gained Eckwerth was an extra six weeks of life on death row.

An hour before midnight on May 23, 1958, a guard opened the oak door leading to the room with the electric chair. A Catholic priest walked ahead of Eckwerth, who wore a white shirt and neatly pressed, well-fitting gray denims. His footsteps muffled by felt-soled slippers, he took short steps, as if playing for time. To a *New York Times* reporter, Eckwerth looked like a young boy following his priest to the altar.

He sat quickly in the electric chair, took a deep breath, and closed his eyes, crossed his heart, and murmured incoherently. Then he opened his eyes and looked at the twelve witnesses in their churchlike wooden pews.

When the two thousand volts hit him, Eckwerth strained forward with clenched fists as if making a superhuman effort to escape. After a while, the priest anointed his body and left. There were no mourners.

In sharp contrast with the unrepentant murderer Eckwerth was Pietro Matera, who had been in Sing Sing for thirty years. He must have been grateful to Gov. Franklin Roosevelt for commuting his death sentence to life in 1932. But, in fact, he shouldn't have spent a day in prison. On her death bed in 1960, the wife of the real culprit confessed that she had "fingered Matera to save her husband."[14] Soon after, Matera was set free.

Frederick Charles Wood was the next-to-last man to be electrocuted in Sing Sing. He received a long prison sentence for his first murder committed when he was fifteen. He was paroled in 1931, and killed again two years later. After a long stay in prison he was paroled in 1960, despite public protests. Just weeks after his release, he killed two men, one with a knife, and the other by smashing him over the head with a shovel. The parole board was condemned by the press for allowing Wood to kill repeatedly. After his final arrest he admitted to both murders.

When asked for his last words, the fifty-one-year-old Wood said with a smile, "Gentlemen, observe closely as you witness the effect of electricity on wood."[15]

Eddie Lee Mays, an African American, was the last Sing Sing convict Warden Denno watched die, before the death penalty was generally outlawed in New York State late in 1963. Mays, a violent career criminal who had killed a woman during a robbery in an East Harlem bar, said that he would rather fry than go to prison. And he got his wish, together with the requested two packs of cigarettes instead of the traditional last meal. It took three minutes of electricity to kill him on August 15, 1963.

It had seemed a sure bet that George Whitmore Jr. would go to the chair for the 1963 murders in Manhattan of two young women, Janie Wylie and Emily Hoffert. He was saved and freed when another man was charged with the murders. It was the fact that an innocent man came so close to execution that persuaded Governor Rockefeller to abolish the death penalty in New York State, except for anyone killing an onduty policeman or committing a murder in prison while serving a life sentence.

Between 1891 and 1963, 606 men and 8 women had been electrocuted in Sing Sing prison.

In *Condemned: Inside the Sing Sing Death House*, Scott Christianson wrote that about one-third of those condemned to death had cheated the chair for some reason or other and in later years the percentage of prisoners winning their appeals became so high that the legal machinery jammed and put the executioner out of work—at least for a time.

Samuel Williams was one of those who cheated the chair. He had been sentenced to death—although the jury had recommended a life sentence—for killing a teenage girl. Gov. Thomas Dewey saved him by commuting his sentence to life, and, in 1963, a federal court reversed his conviction as the only evidence against him had been his coerced confession. After a year on death row, and almost sixteen years in Sing Sing, Williams was free to go. New York City awarded him $40,000 in compensatory damages for "malicious prosecution."[16]

Warden Denno retired in 1967, at sixty-two, after sixteen years in Sing Sing, to settle with his wife in Florida. He had witnessed sixty-two executions, and told UPI reporter Jack Fox that the hardest inmates to rehabilitate were

> the ones who are in here for only a couple of years. They don't want to learn. We try to tell them. "Let time serve you, don't serve time." But most of them don't even understand.
>
> We have schools that bestow a high-school diploma, psychologists, sociologists, workshops where a trade can be learned, but it is up to the man to rehabilitate himself. It's not something you can force on him.[17]

John T. Deegan took over from Denno.

Three years later, in 1970, Sing Sing's death house was closed to make way for a proposed expressway that never was built. The electric chair was moved upstate to Greenhaven Correctional Facility, a maximum security prison some twenty miles southeast of Poughkeepsie in Dutchess County. The Sing Sing death house became a visiting center.

In 1970 euphemisms were being adopted for many jobs in an attempt to increase prestige without increased compensation. Housewives had become domestic engineers, for example. Prisons now became correctional facilities (also to emphasize rehabilitation rather than punishment), wardens became superintendents, and guards, correction officers. And, to separate Sing Sing from its unsavory past, it was renamed Ossining. But neither the press nor public bought the changes.

Whatever it was called, "Crazy" Joe Gallo treated the place as an equal-opportunity employment agency and private club. One of Sing Sing's most colorful inmates, Gallo was in for seven to fourteen years for attempted extortion and conspiracy. It ought to have been for life without benefit of parole, according to Albert Seedman. As New York City's chief of detectives, Seedman was an expert on killers, having questioned hundreds of murder suspects and visited almost two thousand homicide scenes. To Seedman, Gallo was Brooklyn's most ferocious gangster who got away with murder.

Gallo had no rival as Sing Sing's resident intellectual, reading Flaubert, Balzac, and Kafka; eagerly absorbing the contents of two newspapers a day; and painting the occasional picture. His friendly conversations with African American prisoners were not to break the color bar, but to make sure they had jobs when they hit the streets—as recruits for his dope-pushing enterprise.

Freed in 1971, Gallo traded his gun for a typewriter or tape recorder to give his version of life in Sing Sing. Another gangster gave him permanent writer's block, however, after following him to Umberto's Clam House in Little Italy. This hit man shot him there, while Gallo was celebrating his forty-third birthday. His bodyguards returned the gunfire while Gallo was dying outside on the sidewalk, a few steps from police headquarters. Police there reported that he "bought it" at 5:20 AM on Friday, April 7, 1972.

Novelist John Cheever just missed seeing Gallo in Sing Sing because he arrived at the prison in the late spring of 1971, just after the gangster left the place. Cheever, who lived near the prison, entered it not as a prisoner, but as a somewhat nervous volunteer to teach inmates creative writing. He had been encouraged to do so after someone at a party told him that the prison had only six teachers for some two thousand inmates.

Cheever wrote to his son, Ben, on May 9, 1971: "Dear Ben, Tomorrow I go to Sing-Sing to talk with the warden about giving a course in the short story to convicted drug-pushers, etc. If you don't hear from me you'll know what happened. Clang."

According to his fictionalized recollections in *Falconer*, his brilliant novel about Sing Sing, the guards did nothing to reassure him, with a grim warning that the inmates "Rape, they stuff babies into furnaces and they'd strangle their mothers for a stick of chewing gum." This was no exaggeration, two Sing Sing insiders told me, one of whom added: "And you can't believe a word they say."

On his first day, Cheever was taken inside the prison walls by bus. Guards escorted him through five gates that clanged shut and were locked behind him to a classroom with a worn American flag, where twenty inmates awaited his arrival.

Cheever was relieved to find that sociopaths and sadists were banned from his class, and that the rapists and murderers had chosen to stay away.

At the end of May, he wrote enthusiastically to his son, "The class was great on Thursday. The high point came when a Puerto Rican drug pusher (aged 24) got up and exclaimed, 'Oh what a cool mother-fucker was Machiavelli.' It isn't always that good. Yesterday Fred and I took three boxes of books over for the prison library. As soon as we got the books (the Harvard Classics) in the (stifling hot) processing room they locked us up. We would have to wait until the proper authority had examined the books. I wasn't as bad as I might have been. I mean, I didn't go around saying, 'Will you *kindly* give me your name etc.' When I asked if I could go to the car and get a cigaret [*sic*] the guard made a face at me and I damned near hit him, which would have made everything dandy. We were in for about half an hour (while guards went through the books searching for forbidden material, and pulled out two Christmas cards) but the warden called this morning to apologize."[18]

He told his novelist daughter, Susan, who interviewed him later for *Newsweek:* "First I went there as a do-gooder, but then the horror of prison—an imponderable . . . the blasphemy of men building stone by stone, hells for other men—got to me. After that I went there very unwillingly. It seemed to me to be participating in an obscenity."[19]

Cheever was still teaching in Sing Sing when the bloody Attica riots broke out in upstate New York. Half of its twenty-two hundred inmates revolted, seized forty guards and a few others, and took control of four of the five cellblocks. After four days Governor Rockefeller ordered state troopers to attack. They killed twenty-seven inmates and injured some two hundred. Eleven of the hostages were killed. As most Attica convicts were black and so were Sing Sing's inmates, Cheever feared that they might riot in sympathy. And more than one convict told him that he'd make a great hostage. But he didn't lose his nerve, and continued his weekly visits, prompting one of his class, Donald Lang, to say to him: "I wondered where a little shit like you gets the balls to come here." Cheever replied that he didn't expect anyone to hurt him. And they didn't. Nor did anyone start a riot at Sing Sing while he was there.

Cheever emerged after just over a year of teaching, pregnant with an idea for a novel about the prison. He decided not to return after suffering a heart attack in 1973. But when he recovered he tried to capture in his writing what seemed to him a prison's mysterious atmosphere and the unnatural, inhuman situation of one group of people imprisoning another.

Still, Cheever's personal experience of prison life was limited. During his weekly visits he had walked through the five gates that were locked behind him, to go straight to and from the classroom. He had never witnessed what went on in the cellblocks, mess hall, or even the workshops.

Fortunately, he had a great source of information in thirty-one-year-old Donald Lang, who had spent most of his life behind bars. When he was paroled from Sing Sing, Lang frequently called on Cheever at the writer's Ossining home to give him a sardonic and pungent old lag's account of the prison terrain and the inside dope on what went on there, from which the writer took off and turned low life into literature.

Lang told him about the stray cats, a sadistic "asshole" of a guard named Tiny, the brutal fights, and the homosexuality. And how a goon squad of guards eliminated troublemakers by beating them to death and having the death certificate certify natural causes—a charge hard to prove or disprove.

Readers were stunned by the rare reflection of life in Sing Sing, in turn, moving, harrowing, raw, funny, sad, sickening, ennobling, corrosive, and nightmarish.

I asked Cheever's widow, Mary, if he had written anything factual in his Sing Sing novel.

She laughed and said, "He only wrote one way."

"With a fictional twist?"

"Yes."

"Did he go to Sing Sing with some trepidation?"

"At first. But he really enjoyed it and he loved what those guys wrote."

"They were entertaining him as much as he was entertaining them?"

"Much more. And he made friends of one who was on parole and he had him over night after night to talk about prison when he was writing *Falconer*. He had been in for something like armed robbery when he was a kid."

"Were you worried about having an ex-con in the house?"

"No, that was the least of my worries."

Cheever had been a bisexual alcoholic.

There was no one in the Sing Sing death cells during Cheever's time there, and in 1972 the US Supreme Court ruled (*Furman v Georgia*, 408 U.S. 238) by a 5–4 decision that in the cases before the Court, the death penalty was cruel and unusual punishment and therefore unconstitutional. The decision invalidated the death penalty throughout the United States and spared the lives of almost six hundred condemned prisoners. Justices William J. Brennan and Thurgood Marshall argued that executions are per se cruel and unusual punishment in violation of the Eighth Amendment prohibition. Justice William O. Douglas stated that the discretionary application of punishment affected the "poor and despised" unequally and therefore violated equal protection of the laws. Justices Potter Stewart and Byron White found the system then operating "so wantonly and freakishly imposed" as to be unconstitutional under the Eighth and Fourteenth Amendments.

In his dissent Chief Justice Warren E. Burger emphasized that capital punishment laws, which did not mete out death in a random and unpredictable manner, might ultimately be constitutional.

During the 1970s, after Sing Sing's ancient, decaying A and B blocks were judged to be unfit for human habitation, they were renovated at great cost.

In the same period, according to Susan Sheehan in her book *A Prison and a Prisoner*, most inmates in New York State prisons (which included Sing Sing) were poorly educated, unskilled drug users. Eighty percent had committed major crimes other than drug-related law violations. Over 78 percent had not graduated from high school, fewer than 7 percent were college educated, and most listed their occupation as unskilled laborer.

She discovered that 68 percent were from New York City, 82 percent were black or Hispanic, just under 16 percent were white, 62 percent had never married, and 22 percent needed to have their teeth extracted. The average inmate was aged thirty-two, capable of seventh-grade reading and sixth-grade math, and spoke English fluently.

Sheehan noted that "a significant number of men had missing teeth—visual evidence of the fact that it is the poor rather than the rich who are usually convicted and sentenced to state prison. Another is the small number of Jews. Still another is the number of men who have relatives in prison, and the large number of men who are tattooed."[20]

Prisoners and guards estimated the number of practicing homosexuals at 20 percent.

Sheehan continued: "Each new arrival is asked whether he has any enemies in the prison population. If he does, he is transferred elsewhere."[21]

A former New York policeman, Patrolman William Phillips, joined Sing Sing inmates serving life sentences in 1972. He had been a star witness during the Knapp Commission hearings on police corruption—which exposed a lot of it. The commission report described Phillips's fourteen-year police career as one of "virtually unrelieved corruption."[22] He was convicted at a second trial—the first had a hung jury—for the double murder of a pimp and a prostitute.

In 1977 New York State's court of appeals struck down the death penalty for the murder of a policeman or of a prison guard, with the exception of a murder committed in prison by a prisoner serving a life sentence. He could be executed, which must have been some comfort for Sing Sing's guards.

Even so, conditions in Sing Sing did not encourage wardens to stay long.

The quip that the quickest way to get out of the prison was to go in as warden remained true. No one ever approached Lewis Lawes's twenty-one-year record again. John T. Deegan put in three years before he was replaced by James L. Casscles in 1969 who lasted for two. Then Theodore Schubin became warden. After three years he handed over the reins in July 1975 to Joseph Higgins who was interim warden for three months, after which the new man in charge was Harold Butler. He, too, was an interim warden, and after one month William Gard was officially warden of Sing Sing—for two years, when another interim warden, Walter Fogg, took the job. Three months later, in October 1977, Sing Sing had a new warden, Stephen Dalsheim. But he held on only until 1980.

During his brief regime an inmate committed suicide in his cell by hanging himself and it was six hours before anyone noticed. Prison inspectors had reported an alarming increase in the availability of drugs (resulting in one or two overdose deaths), liquor, hypodermic needles, and homemade weapons; and extremely unsupervised movements of inmates especially in the tunnels leading to and from Tappan (the medium-security section of the prison), the bathhouse, B-Block recreation area, and the commissary, "resulting in a history of unusual incidents in those areas," including a deadly escape attempt.

A major complaint was that guards ignored such incidents to avoid confrontation with armed inmates. One of the inmates' many complaints was that female guards did not announce their presence on the block, and deliberately watched them when they were naked and taking showers, and while using the toilet.[23]

Wilson Walters, Dalsheim's replacement, had been warden for two years when in 1982 a Westchester County DA charged a correction lieutenant, four correction officers (guards), a cook, a commissary clerk, a former guard, an inmate, and a former inmate with bribery, receiving bribes, criminal possession of cocaine and marijuana, promotion of prison contraband, and other criminal offenses. All were found guilty except one defendant who died of natural causes during his trial. According to the charge, some guards had been given large amounts of money for drugs and other items. That same summer three-foot-high marijuana plants were found growing in the prison yard.[24]

CHAPTER TEN

RIOTS AND REFORMS

1980s AND 1990s

No visitor expected Sing Sing to be a rose garden except, of course, during the halcyon days of Warden Lewis Lawes and the former-editor inmate, Charles Chapin. To writer Steve Lerner, touring the place where they warehoused the most dangerous felons in the early 1980s, it looked like a giant zoo, or aviary, with the cages stacked five stories high. But, unlike the Lawes-Chapin era, when there was an actual birdhouse on the grounds, there wasn't much to sing about.

In a futile attempt at privacy, some prisoners had fixed cardboard partitions or hung clothes on the steel bars—futile because, as Lerner noted, guards periodically patroled "the catwalks knocking down these forbidden, makeshift walls with their nightsticks."[1]

Sing Sing had protected inmates from each other with wire fencing on the catwalks in front of the upper-tier cells, anticipating the danger of those who didn't pay for drugs or settle their gambling debts on time being pushed to their deaths. This, of course, didn't preclude other forms of violent retribution. The day before Lerner's visit, one inmate had beaten another senseless with a blunt instrument in one of the many prison corridors.

Race riots had been known to occur over someone turning the TV to an English- or Spanish-speaking station.

"Melees have been sparked," Lerner was told, "by disputes over how long someone is speaking on the only public telephone. Bad food, cold food, or food that isn't served on time can cause a prison to erupt. The drug traffic, protection rackets, sex, and arguments over poker debts can also incite bloody violence. . . . Although most inmates are probably more afraid of one another than they are of the guards, some inmates fear guard brutality the most."[2]

Lerner was barred from the disciplinary cells, where prisoners were punished by being deprived of their radios and other comforts. Because the inmates rarely took such measures meekly, guards had covered cell bars in that section with plexiglass shields to prevent angry inmates from spattering them with excrement, spit, and urine.

Yet when trouble came, it was not from these hell-raisers, but from the six hundred transients in Cellblock B, awaiting shipment—sometimes for six months—to other state prisons. Among them were Haitians, Cubans, Black Muslims, and neo-Nazis. Some were mentally disturbed: psychotics, schizophrenics, or manic depressives. Many needed drugs to moderate their moods. Others were veterans of the bloody Attica Prison uprising in 1971 in which ten guards and twenty-nine prisoners were killed when heavily armed state police had stormed the prison.

A major grievance of the waiting transients was that they did not enjoy the privileges given to long-term Sing Sing inmates as a sop after the Attica riot. They couldn't, for instance, take part in the popular arts and crafts program, making dolls selling for up to $65, which allowed doll-making inmates to keep a big chunk of the profits. And their movie-going was restricted to twice a week, while other inmates went more often.

They were certainly not pacified by news on the evening of January 8, 1983, that the local town clerk of nearby Ossining had reversed a previous ruling and was now willing to issue marriage licenses to Sing Sing inmates. Few, if any, in Cellblock B were in a marrying mood. An apparently tipsy guard lit the fuse that had been sputtering for weeks by cutting their few privileges, such as refusing to let some transients take their customary showers after dinner, and depriving others of recreation time. Their angry protests grew into a chorus of insults as they began to jeer in unison, "Take that drunken sergeant out of here!" varying his title from sergeant, to screw, hack, cop, and several obscene alternatives.[3] The shouts swelled to a roar of rage.

Warned of impending trouble in B-Block, a senior prison official, Lt. Lowell D. Way, hurried to the spot. After sizing up the situation, he ordered the guard to leave the area. But he had walked into a trap: the inmates were not consoled by the guard's departure and grabbed Lieutenant Way as the first of their nineteen hostages. Among the hostages, one had been on the job less than a month, six had been guards for just two months, and more than half had less than a year's experience.

Leaders of the riot then demanded a face-to-face confrontation with New York's very new governor, Mario Cuomo.

It was only his second week on the job, and Cuomo was at dinner with his family in a Manhattan restaurant. Before the dessert arrived, his body-guard warned him that he had a riot on his hands.

Resisting the urge to speak with them, Cuomo followed the experts' advice to go home to Queens. But he returned soon after to take charge of a specially trained Crisis Intervention Team—an innovation being put to the test—on the fifty-seventh floor of the World Trade Center. Keeping in touch through an open phone line with prison commissioner Thomas A. Coughlin and Warden Wilson Walters, who were at the prison, Cuomo learned that some inmates were threatening to kill or mutilate their captives.

Herbert McLaughlin, director of correctional guidance, anxiously sorted through six hundred records to spot which inmates were mentally disturbed and taking mood-altering psychotropic drugs, and who among them "would be leaders and create problems for the others."[4]

Fifty-six percent of the inmates were black, 25 percent were Hispanic, and 19 percent were white. Among them were the following:

"Bulla," leader of a Hispanic gang. A twenty-two-year-old drug-using Puerto Rican with a sixth-grade education, who was in for five to fifteen years for burglary.

"Iron Mike," a drug-using twenty-five-year-old white Catholic with a high-school education, doing six to life for robbery. At six feet six, he needed a cane to walk, was captain of B-Block House gang, and had emceed the prison's Christmas show.

"Alabama," a twenty-five-year-old black Protestant drug user with a ninth-grade education, in for 12½ to 25 years for burglary. He had been involved in riots in Alabama prisons and had been sentenced to life in Alabama for rape.

The Imam (spiritual leader) of B-Block Sunni Muslims, a twenty-nine-year-old black in for four to fifteen years for manslaughter.

"Cuba," a twenty-seven-year-old black/Hispanic Catholic with a sixth-grade education, who couldn't speak English. Castro had deported him from Cuba to the United States in 1980. He was in for from twenty years to life for murder.

Mr. Umina, assistant commissioner for health services and director of the Crisis Intervention Unit, dealt with the death threats by trying to get the rioters to talk about other issues such as their moral responsibilities, despite Dr. Raymond Broadus's warning that it wouldn't work with the inmates in for murder.

Anxiously glued to TV sets to see if their shouted demands would be announced, the inmates saw instead, along with news reports of the ongoing riot, repeated highlights from the Attica bloodbath. According to one inmate viewer, it scared the living hell out of them.

Cuomo had radical views about prisons and the death penalty. As a lawyer during the early years of his career he had been a pro bono counsel to poor criminal defendants. Twice he had represented men condemned to Sing Sing's electric chair. In both cases he was successful, and the death sentences were commuted. His visits to death row, "the sight of the electric chair, the growing knowledge of the fragility of the law and vulnerability of the justice system" made an indelible impression on him.[5]

He considered it a ridiculous waste of money to jail nonviolent people who could be on work programs or supervised probation. He agreed that violent criminals must be imprisoned and knew that New York State was spending a fortune doing so. "But," he wrote in his diary, "when we still need space for violent criminals who are not yet behind bars, it is foolish to use our expensive cells for non-violent petty criminals who can be more appropriately—and more inexpensively—punished through alternative methods."[6]

In his campaign for New York State governor, first against Mayor Edward Koch in the Democratic primary, and then in the general election against Conservative Lewis Lehman, Cuomo, the son of Italian immigrants, felt that he was losing ground because of his opposition to capital punishment.

His mother, like many New York voters, believed in an eye for an eye, and, he put in his diary, "I won't even write down on this page what she suggests for sex criminals."[7] Nevertheless, she once suggested to him a winning tactic: "'You listen to me! You tell thema you changea your mind, you wanna the electric chair. Then, after you win . . .' And here she made an ancient Italian gesture, flicking the bottom of the chin, with two fingers, throwing out the whole hand, palm open, waving to a whole world, saying in effect 'After the election to h—— with them!' From anybody else I would call it cynical," Cuomo wrote, "from Momma, it's the way she's made it through 80 years of labor and pain." Sticking to his anti-death-penalty principles, Cuomo surprised himself by winning.

Now, as governor, he faced enraged demands from the kind of men that his mother would have gladly sent to the chair.

Inmates yelled their demands through bullhorns to newsmen gathered on rocks overlooking the prison grounds, while hostages added their pleas for help. Hostage Marcus Mendez, a guard, was brought to a window at knifepoint and shouted in an emotional voice, "Mr. Cuomo! I'm begging you to get me out. Help us. Everybody's Okay, nobody's hurt. Mr. Cuomo, you are my only hope." Followed by a prisoner also speaking through a bullhorn: "We're trying to resolve this peacefully. We want the officers' families to know there will be no harm to them, but we want to see Governor Cuomo with the media." He handed the bullhorn to hostage guard Barry Clark who called out: "Why do you keep playing with our lives? Don't you even have any sympathy? There are 16 bodies in here. You aren't even concerned about that. You want my job? You can have it. It's not worth much anyway if they take my life. They want the media in here. We want the Governor to come down here. I have respect for the inmates. They're keeping us warm. They're feeding us."[8]

The standoff and negotiations continued for fifty-three tense hours, during which Cuomo took brief naps on a conference table.

He finally let the rioters' shouted complaints and demands be shown on local TV news stations. And he accepted them as reasonable. That same night, all the hostages were released. None had been seriously injured, although some needed psychological counseling.

According to Dr. Roger Kalhoud, the prison's director of psychiatry, a significant number of "Latin Brothers" put their arms around captives, saying: "You want him, you have to cut me first." And probably saved their lives. "I also heard that some of the Black Muslims were very helpful," added Dr. Jacques Rambaud, director of emergency services at the prison hospital.[9]

A subsequent official 275-page report by Scott Christianson revealed: "Most of the inmates in B-Block that Saturday had been in prison before, for other crimes. Some had spent virtually their entire adult lives behind bars; others had never been in trouble with the law before being sent 'up the river' to old Sing Sing. To survive in prison, most inmates stuck together with others like themselves—Black Sunni Muslims with Black Sunni Muslims, homosexuals with other homosexuals, Hispanic street gang members with others from that background, whites with other whites, and so on. The most fundamental divisions were racial. Even within those groups, however, fierce differences and loyalties set some blacks apart from other blacks, some whites from other whites, and some Hispanics from other Hispanics."[10]

The warning signs of a potential riot had been blatantly obvious. Several gangs were trying to control the flow of drugs and various services in the prison. Sometimes they invaded another gang's turf or ratted on their rivals to the authorities. Reprisals were inevitable, from threats to beatings and stabbings. In the months before the riot, the violence had escalated and many scared prisoners had armed themselves with sharpened scraps of stolen metal which they hid in their cells.

As for the guards, according to a recent Commission of Corrections report, they lacked "training in interpersonal relationships with inmates. Some officers adopt a 'John Wayne' posture. This behavior perpetuates incidents. Also: Inmates are permitted to work in extremely sensitive areas of the facility. . . . This presence makes them privy to information which could compromise the security of the institution."

Although female guards were forbidden to strip-search the prisoners, they were allowed to pat-search them. They were also instructed not to gather around them when the inmates were taking showers. Apparently they had been flouting this second rule, although in emergencies, all the rules were dropped and guards, regardless of their sex, were allowed to perform any duties deemed necessary.

Fortunately, when the riot broke out, no females were on duty in B-Block, because inmates and male guards "alike strongly agreed that any women present in B-Block during the disturbance probably would have been raped and/or killed."

Christianson's official report of the riot and its probable causes stressed that the inmates had too much idle time, that violence was endemic in the prison, and that its warden lacked the capacity to take control. "The reality at [Sing Sing]," wrote Christianson,

> is that there is practically no educational program provided to anyone. At the time of the riot only 60 out of 1,500 prisoners attended school. (Though why more didn't attend, Christianson doesn't explain.)
>
> Employee hostages are the primary—sometimes the only—article of barter which inmates hold. Without hostages, they could not continue the siege, nor would they have any real chips in their negotiations. Many—perhaps most—of the inmates are also held against their will, and some of the inmates are much more likely to be beaten, tortured, raped, or murdered by other prisoners (New Mexico, 1980, is the most tragic example). Those inmates who are most likely to be victimized are usually individuals whom the convicts consider to be *undesirables*—child molesters, homosexuals, and other minorities.
>
> The inmate code specifies who is undesirable. It also demands revenge or punishment for informers and other enemies. Child molesters, for example, are generally detested by the inmates—in part, because such people run counter to inmate values such as toughness and physical courage. They are easily victimized, and not likely to receive support or protection from other prisoners. Nor is the State very likely to intercede. . . . During the Attica riot of 1971, an unpopular inmate was observed running around screaming that his throat was being slashed. Police did not intercede. However, when it was thought that the hostages were in danger of being cut, the State responded forcefully.

During the Sing Sing riot, most of the rioting inmates "were armed with kitchen knives, street knives, crudely-fashioned shivs, spears, and a wide assortment of other potentially lethal tools," with which they often attacked each other. Some assaults were between Hispanics and blacks "and the widespread fear was that some of them could have escalated into a full-fledged race riot, along the lines of the New Mexico State Penitentiary in 1980." Then, fueled by drugs and hate, inmates had overpowered the fifteen guards on duty and butchered thirty-three fellow inmates. All the guards taken hostage survived, though some were brutally beaten.

According to a report signed by Warden Walters, "Shortly after the takeover of B-Block by the inmates (one inmate claimed) that he was dragged in to a cell and forced to commit oral and anal sex acts. He was then told that if he did not do the same for the (six) other inmates waiting outside the cell that he would be killed during the riot."

Lieutenant B. A. Kessler wrote that he had received a sick call from an inmate who "began making frantic gestures cautioning me not to say anything that would expose the true nature of his request. He was standing three to four feet back from the cell bars, in turn shaking his head, pointing to his ear, and placing his forefinger in front of his mouth in a gesture of silence while holding a note with his right hand. It stated that he had been the victim of homosexual rape at least 25 times after the inmates had taken control of the block."

When Kessler escorted the inmate to the prison hospital, the man broke down and began to shake and cry. He was taken in protective custody to Westchester County Medical Center for examination and tests.

Another account of possible rapes concerned a known homosexual who claimed that he had been forced into the officers' coat closet at knifepoint and made to commit various sexual acts on two black inmates. Four more black inmates then took turns raping him. He said that he came out of the closet crying and saw some thirteen to fifteen guards being held hostage on the gallery. At least two hostages confirmed his account, saying that they had seen him crying.

John Burke, a prison official, "gave Governor Cuomo high grades for the way he handled the crisis" but called Warden Walters "an incompetent" and recommended his replacement with a more decisive warden. Burke also described some members of the media reporting the riot as "irresponsible . . . subversive . . . locusts . . . out to sensationalize."

The president of Sing Sing's union local representing the guards, Wilfred Flecha, said that the riot was "not against the officers; it was against the system. . . . I'd categorize our relationship with the inmates as friendly." And he echoed Burke's charge that Warden Walters was incapable of taking decisive action to remedy problems.

Both guards and inmates considered Walters as an extremely passive and ineffective warden. Inmates viewed him as a "very aloof, unapproachable, non-communicative" man who so rarely toured the prison he was practically invisible. To many, his deputy, John McGinnis, who had been at Sing Sing since 1963, rising through the ranks, was "the one guy who was trying to run the place."

Yet Wilson E. J. Walters III had an impressive record: Sing Sing's warden since July 24, 1980, he had previously been a parole officer, parole administrator, and deputy superintendent of programs at Attica for three months after the bloody 1971 riot there.

But the Sing Sing riot put an end to his career. Three months after the outbreak, in May 1983, he retired and James Sullivan, a former deputy warden at Clinton, took over.

What started Sing Sing's riot? Was it Guard Cunningham's drunken, arrogant behavior? Witness Guard Romeros said that he "detected liquor" on Cunningham's breath. Guard McNamara explained that, having a cold, he couldn't smell anything very well, but Cunningham's "irrational behavior" seemed to indicate that he had been drinking. A third witness, Guard Coffey, who also couldn't smell if Cunningham was drunk, because of a cold, had noticed his fellow guard's "glassy eyes and hyper-appearance." The inmates were emphatic that Cunningham had been drunk, after smelling liquor on his breath, seeing his bloodshot eyes, and noting his wobbly walk and erratic behavior. One inmate reported: "Cunningham told me he had just come from a party, had been drinking and hoped there would be no trouble that night."

Christianson concluded in his report that although Sing Sing's

> disturbance ended without a bloodbath [The guard who had spoken of 16 bodies proved to have been mistaken], the conclusion of the Department of the Corrections Inspector General that the uprising "ended without serious incident" is not warranted by the facts. The Inspector General's chronology of events under-represented the full extent of inmate injuries, and his post-disturbance reports were also insufficiently detailed and contained factual errors, omissions, and distortions about other aspects as well. Defensive and self-serving posturing by the Inspector-General is inappropriate for a unit which should seek to determine, not deny, Department accountability.
>
> The Government's unplanned, unreflective approach to criminal justice in general, and corrections in particular, cannot continue. If it does, more prison disturbances are inevitable.

Governor Cuomo agreed. Having conceded that the inmates' complaints about overcrowding, "idle time," and primitive conditions were justified, during the next four years he built more prison cells than any other governor in the state's history, increasing the inmate capacity by 27 percent. He also proposed building two more prisons with room for fourteen hundred inmates.

His critics insisted that more reforms were urgently needed to prevent future riots among the ever-swelling prison population. And reforms were quick in coming. The former "death house" was converted into a vocational program space to teach inmates several trades, and an assessment shop was built to handle incoming inmates. A new visitors' room was built—with floor-to-ceiling windows overlooking the Hudson River—as well as an outside pavilion for use in the summer and a welcoming room for child visitors.

By 1985 Sing Sing had initiated a Special Needs Unit, which included the first prison medical ward for inmates with the HIV-AIDS virus. Hearing of the program, Mother Teresa went to visit the patients there. On arrival, she found that a new six-story medical center with a hundred beds and state-of-

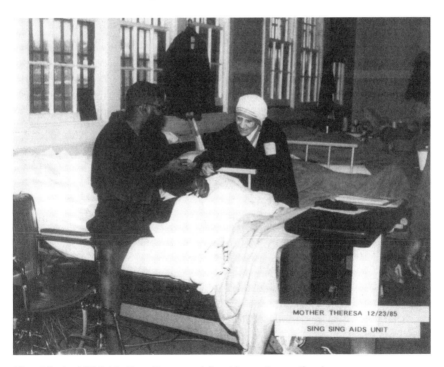

Fig. 44. In 1985 Mother Teresa visited inmate-patients in the AIDS ward of Sing Sing's hospital.
(Courtesy New York State Department of Correctional Services)

the-art equipment was in the works. At the time of her visit, the medical staff of thirty-five cared for sick prisoners in the main hospital with twenty-three beds and six isolation rooms. Psychiatrists treated convicts with severe mental problems in a psychiatric ward. There were also clinics for podiatry, ophthalmology, radiography, pharmaceuticals, and blood work.

Warden Sullivan who had welcomed Mother Teresa to Sing Sing, held the job for five years, after which, in December 1988, John P. Keane replaced him.

Inevitably, news of the various reforms brought complaints that life was too cushy for Sing Sing prisoners, that instead of being punished for their crimes they were the spoiled and pampered darlings of society, assured of free food, clothes, healthcare, accommodation, literature, and legal advice, counseling, sporting activities, and both live and canned entertainment. And each one was costing the state $25,000 a year.

The authorities agreed with the critics and, in 1991, Keane introduced a new get-tough policy. All inmates not hospitalized had to work to help pay for their keep and to attend educational and vocational classes to prepare them to survive without reverting to crime when they got out. They were paid sixty cents an hour, rising to sixty-five cents for a forty-hour workweek, repairing TV sets, making office furniture and cleaning supplies for state and local government agencies, and helping nonprofit groups outside the prison with painting and reconstruction.

But there was massive resistance. One thousand and seventy-one inmates refused to do work of any kind, and two hundred and sixty-seven refused to attend classes. The no-work inmates were locked in their cells for twenty-three hours a day, where they had all their meals, until they changed their minds. But they were allowed an hour a day to exercise. Those who still resisted were blackballed when they came up for parole. The no-classes group had various privileges revoked.

Justifying the new policy, Thomas Coughlin III, commissioner of the State Department of Correctional Services, said: "I've been troubled for years by the public perception that inmates sit around all day watching TV or pumping iron, while the average guy is trying to make ends meet. We fully intend to change the perception of inmates getting a free ride. We have a basic responsibility to teach inmates how to read and write."[11]

That summer a dozen black felons, some as young as fourteen, arrived at Sing Sing in a yellow school bus. Most were guilty of armed robbery. Judges had decided to give them a chance, however, and instead of locking them up had put them under strict supervision. It was hoped that the horrors of Sing Sing would shock them on to the straight and narrow.

But it didn't seem to be working. One fourteen-year-old boasted that his brother had been to prison, where "people get killed." And a fifteen-year-old added: "Prison's a badge of honor. You get respect." Vernon Manley, an assistant probation commissioner, countered, for the benefit of an accompanying reporter: "No returnee [to prison] is about to disclose the worst—that he was sexually assaulted, for example. They want to be seen as bad dudes."

Glen Williams, a substance-abuse counselor, pointed out the old death house to the group, then led them up flights of stairs to B-Block, where, on five levels, 643 inmates were housed in cages. As the group passed the cells to a cacophony of screams, yells, bells ringing, and the whistle of a distant train, the group was greeted with the customary showers of urine. Inmates yelled: "Educate the babies!" "Go to school, home boy!" "Punks!" and, "This is genocide!"[12]

For a taste of possible things to come, each youngster was locked in a maximum-security cell for five minute, then went to a room for verbal shock treatment—from the discomforting to the deadly. One old-timer told them that prison coffee was always cold and orange juice always warm, and that guards can strip-search you at any time. Another said that you can't kiss your kids goodnight and never know who your wife or girlfriend is sleeping with. A third told how the strong prey on the weak, fashion deadly weapons out of almost anything including tuna-fish cans, and kill on a whim—highlighting the fate of the murdered TV channel changer.

An old lag laughed at all the young criminals as they shook their heads after he'd asked them if they expected to end up in Sing Sing. "When I was your age," he said, "I didn't put in a reservation here and say I want Cell 6P 17." As they filed out of the room, a passing guard muttered, "They're all fleabags."[13]

A radically different group—in age, appearance, and motivation—arrived at Sing Sing in the spring of the following year led by eighty-year-old Rabbi Irving Koslowe. He had stood by the Rosenbergs during their electrocution in 1953, vainly pleading with Ethel to name names to save her life. Those were two of the seventeen executions he had witnessed in the death house.

His group were members of his five hundred-family-strong Mamoroneck congregation. He had been the Jewish chaplain at Sing Sing for forty-nine years and although this was his first year of retirement, he had continued to visit Jewish prisoners, bringing them Jewish newspapers, books, and food for the holidays. When he first arrived in 1954, there were some one hundred eighty Jewish inmates and eleven of the nineteen in the death house were Jews. Of the twenty-four hundred prisoners in 1992, some thirty-five were Jews but only about ten took part in the religious services.

"People ask me what I'm doing bringing matzo balls to a bunch of killers," he told a *New York Times* reporter. "But maybe we bring some good in their life. Some of the guards would say I'm crazy, but I do what I can. If I can have an inmate come into the chapel and put on a yarmulke and worship I think that shows there's a positive change in behavior, a real step forward."[14]

His attitude toward prisoners was: I didn't put you in here and I can't get you out, but while you're here I'll do what I can to help.

As he led his group from Westchester through the prison, the rabbi reassured the nervous by mentioning that he had never once been insulted or touched in anger by a prisoner—in almost fifty years. Still, he warned them to stay near the walls to avoid being jumped by inmates. After service in the synagogue, several Jewish inmates met the visitors around a buffet table and confided that through Rabbi Koslowe they had rediscovered their Judaism.

In 1993 the rabbi persuaded the state prison system to provide all Jewish prisoners with kosher meals.

Since 1994 relatives have been allowed to visit Sing Sing convicts for two days at a time, staying in inmate-built trailers on the prison grounds. The visiting room has floor-to-ceiling windows overlooking the Hudson River. The regular prison staff of almost a thousand—teachers, engineers, guidance counselors, clergymen—was augmented by up to a hundred volunteers.

Still, there were plenty of flaws in the system exposed in a damning official report which listed a shortage of nurses, an inadequately staffed and equipped psychiatric unit, poor security in the laboratory, and a large population of inmates with chronic kidney disease, severe heart problems, lung disease, and cancers not receiving the sophisticated medical care they needed.

The prison library was the bright spot. It was the first such library in the United States to have books other than Bibles, thanks to New York governor William Henry Seward who gave $300 to buy them in 1843. By the late 1990s, Sing Sing had a reference library of 3,274 volumes, according to its librarian Robert T. Richter, equal to that of a small-town library. It also had five thousand law books, three legal periodicals, together with inmate legal clerks available to help fellow inmates with their appeals and other litigation. There were fifteen thousand fiction and nonfiction books of general interest and fifty-seven periodicals to suit various tastes. Some sixteen hundred books were in Spanish, about one thousand focused on African American culture. Inmates could also borrow books from the Interlibrary loan system, including those in Chinese and Korean.

In 1995 New York State Theological Seminary sponsored a Masters in Theology curriculum from which thirty convicts graduated and obtained certificates in ministry, enabling them, when free, to begin noncriminal careers as assistant chaplains or counselors. Thirty more graduated in 1996, and another thirty in 1997. The program continues today.

When Rabbi Koslowe retired as Sing Sing's Jewish chaplain in 1999, the handmade farewell card he received showed a crayoned sketch of the synagogue with a bearded Jew waving good-bye at an unbarred window from which a bird was flying. One inmate had written, "Our moments shared were times of hope and joy."[15] Besides Jewish inmates, it was also signed by Muslims and a Chinese inmate of unknown religion.

Rabbi Koslowe died in New York's Mount Sinai Hospital City on December 6, 2000.

Along with the reforms of the 1990s came an attempt to prevent prison escapes. The original Sing Sing wall built of handmade bricks in 1877 was razed in 1994 to be replaced by a state-of-the-art cement wall. And a maximum-security perimeter fence was completed two years later, with nine towers, barbed wire, a tension line, and sensitive infrared sensors that might defeat even a modern-day Houdini.

On March 7, 1995, the families of police officers and others who were victims of capital crimes watched Governor George E. Pataki sign legislation reinstituting the death penalty in New York State. He then told them: "Under this legislation, those who murder a police officer, a probation, parole, court or corrections officer, a judge or witness or member of a witness's family can face the death penalty. Someone who murders while already serving life in prison or while escaping from prison, or who murders while committing other serious felonies can face the death penalty. Contract killers, serial murderers, those who torture their victims, or those who have murdered before can also be sentenced to death. And in determining whether the death penalty should be imposed on anyone convicted of first degree murder, the bill expressly authorized juries to hear and consider additional evidence whenever the murder was committed as part of an act of terrorism or by someone with two or more prior serious felony convictions. . . . For eighteen years, the Legislature overwhelmingly supported capital punishment. For eighteen years, the public will was thwarted by gubernatorial veto."[16]

In 1996 Alison S. Lebwohl interviewed Sing Sing guard David Luther, the thirty-three-year-old father of four daughters, about how it felt to work on "the toughest beat in the world," as he called it, where all he had to protect him were his radio, baton, wits, and fellow guards.

"Everyone around you is a criminal," he said. "A violent offender. Murder, rape, manslaughter, all the big ones. I'm outnumbered 75 to 1. We have assaults on staff, crimes committed behind the wall. Do men die in jail? All the time. And what about TB, AIDS, Hepatitis B and C? Those are the things you can't see. More than once I've had to throw my uniform away because there's been blood on it."[17]

Once an inmate threw cups of feces, urine, and caustic soap over him. Resisting the urge to beat out the inmate's brains, and temporarily blinded, Luther was hospitalized. There's no mention of the inmate's mental state, but Luther's was one of revulsion. Three showers didn't remove his feeling of being unclean or his fear of being infected with some deadly germ. A lunatic law allowed his attacker to keep his medical records a secret, so that prison doctors couldn't tell Luther to what dread disease he might have been exposed. However, Luther soon returned to duty, apparently still healthy.

A year later, in 1996, "throwing," as it was called, became a felony, although, strangely, inmates are still allowed to keep their medical records a secret. So, as a precaution, guards have their blood tested every six months.

What keeps Luther on the job, he said, apart from the need to support his family, is the fellowship among the guards: "No matter what your differences on the street, when you walk through that door [into Sing Sing], you would lay down your life for them." Yet he admitted, "I take a deep breath, then I put on my game face and walk in. At the end of the day, when I come out, I look at the Palisades and take another deep breath. It's good to be alive."

White-haired, soft-spoken Charles Greiner took over as warden on March 13, 1997. Following the tradition of most of his predecessors he stayed for three years, but his regime was well-documented. During that time, investigative reporter Ted Conover appeared on the scene, working undercover as a guard. In his subsequent book, *Newjack: Guarding Sing Sing*, he gave what is probably the first independent and in-depth account of life in a maximum-security prison.

CHAPTER ELEVEN

RECOVERING THE PRISON'S MISSING ARCHIVES

By the year 2000, New York State governor George Pataki had reinstated the death penalty and five men awaited execution. But there was no longer a death house in Sing Sing and its electric chair had been sent on loan to a museum in Virginia. Future executions in the state were to take place way north in the Clinton Correctional Facility near the Canadian border, and by lethal injections of potassium chloride. Although considered more humane than the electric chair, there were no survivors to attest to that.

In 2000, the year Brian Fischer took over from Warden Greiner, death-penalty opponent Scott Christianson published his book *Condemned: Inside the Sing Sing Death House*, using previously unavailable material about many of Sing Sing's executed prisoners. Three years previously, someone had unearthed the prison's official records which had been missing—stored away and forgotten for years. After several more years, some, but not all of this material became available to researchers at the New York State Archives in Albany. These records and photos, which Christianson published, give a vivid insider's view of life and death in Sing Sing.

They show that about one-third of the hundreds sentenced to die in the electric chair were, for various reasons, spared. And, over time, the flood of legal appeals for new trials or commutation of their sentences brought the system to a halt. The executioner was out of his 150 dollars a shot until things were cleared up. One of those saved, Isadore Zimmerman, had been accused of killing New York detective Michael Foley during a holdup at a Lower East

Side restaurant. He swore that he had not been at the crime scene, but a witness testified that he had provided the murder weapon. Despite Zimmerman's claim that he had been framed, he was found guilty. On death row in 1938, as his time approached, he watched with growing despair as other men walked past his cell to their deaths. The night before he expected to die, Zimmerman showed unexpected resilience, even using a touch of gallows humor. He had ordered a last meal of steak and blintzes, but the cook said that he didn't know how to make them. "Then," quipped Zimmerman, "I'll wait until you've learned."

Just two hours before his scheduled execution, the court of appeals ruled that the chief witness against him had lied and that the prosecutor knew it. Consequently Zimmerman's sentence and that of one of his codefendants were commuted to life. Three others involved in the killing were electrocuted that night. Long after, Zimmerman recalled his prison existence: "I saw thirteen men actually executed [unlikely that he actually witnessed their deaths], and out of the thirteen I believe four were totally innocent. Some couldn't take it, cried like babies. Others walked very calmly. I was terrified. When I first came there I couldn't eat and I couldn't sleep. Fear became the dominant emotion in my life. I was so frightened that I couldn't talk coherently to anybody, and I was ashamed of myself.

What bothered me was that I knew I had done nothing. I said: 'Why should I die for nothing at this age? Why me, why did they pick me out?' I used to feel so sorry for myself."[1]

"The years pass," he later wrote while still in prison, "and in the drab, gray world I inhabit, nothing changes but the dates on the calendar. I sit in my cell and try one night, after lights out to establish the chronology of all my wasted years: nine months in Sing Sing death house; eight in Auburn; three years in Attica; one year in Greenhaven; eleven years in Dannemora. Nothing changes; only the names."[2]

After twenty-four years in various prisons, new evidence proved definitively that the chief witness against Zimmerman had lied and the prosecutor had withheld that information. So, in 1962, the forty-five-year-old Zimmerman was exonerated and freed. Soon after, he married and took a job as doorman of a Manhattan apartment building.

Nineteen years later, in 1981, Governor Hugh Carey signed a bill which allowed Zimmerman to sue the state for damages. He asked for $10 million for twenty-four years of wrongful imprisonment, and on May 31, 1983, Judge Joseph Modungo awarded him $1 million. After paying his attorneys, he had $660,000 left. His god-awful luck seemed at last to have changed. The sixty-six-year-old Zimmerman bought a new car and took his wife for a brief vacation in the Catskills—and died a week later.

Salvatore Agron, aka "The Capeman," another death-row inmate who escaped execution after being reprieved by Gov. Nelson Rockefeller, became the subject of a Broadway show.

The recovered records show that until recent years the men guarding these inmates were invariably white men, mostly of Irish or German descent. Some had fathers and grandfathers who had been policemen or prison guards. For them, it was a proud family tradition. The male guards and death-row inmates generally regarded one another warily and sometimes resorted to violence. One fight erupted over a prisoner's complaint that he hadn't been given enough bread to feed birds in the yard. Some women guards, however, felt real affection for their female charges and cried at their executions.

The archives also cast more light on the Rosenbergs' time in the death house. They reveal that on December 5, 1952, Sing Sing's acting warden I. J. Kelly wrote to J. V. Bennett, director of the Bureau of Prisons:

> With relation to the pending execution of the Rosenbergs, procedure at this institution for State executions, is as follows: After the order from the Court of Appeals has been received fixing the week of execution for carrying into effect the original sentence of death, notices are sent as follows:
>
> 1. Condemned prisoner.
> 2. Governor.
> 3. Clerk of the Court of Appeals (Acknowledgement).
> 4. Commissioner of Correction.
> 5. Chairman of Governor's Commission, to examine into the mental condition of the condemned prisoner.
> 6. Various officials within the institution such as principal keeper, prison physician, Chaplain, steward.
>
> Meanwhile the Governor's Commission calls at the institution to examine the condemned prisoner. Invariably executions at Sing Sing occur on Thursdays at 11:00 P.M. Notifications for the scheduled execution go to the Governor, Commissioner of Correction, Chief Engineer at the institution, and the executioner. And invitations also go to the following approximately five days before the scheduled execution:
>
> 1. District Attorney of the County of Conviction.
> 2. Sheriff of the County of Conviction.
> 3. At least twelve reputable citizens of full age, selected by the Warden, and may include newspaper representatives.

Arrangements are also made for the Warden, two physicians, Chaplain, principal keeper, assistant principal keeper, Captain, two lieutenants and three sergeants to be present. All invited witnesses, including newspapermen who have been approved by the Warden, are assembled in the Warden's Office at 10:30 P.M., invitations are collected, and satisfactory proof of identity established. After this has been completed the Warden issues instructions to the invited witnesses to the effect that they have been invited . . . to attend the scheduled execution and that upon entering the death chamber they will refrain from talking, smoking, and making any unnecessary noises. Any person having in his possession any firearms is directed to leave them with the officer at the front door. They are also instructed . . . that upon their return from the death chamber to the Administration Building, they will be required to sign a certificate attesting to the fact that they served as an official witness at the said execution. A frisk of all witnesses is conducted in the Administration Building prior to their entering the bus to be escorted to the death house. The Warden's Certificate is prepared and signed by him immediately following the execution, showing the time and place of the execution, in conformity to the sentence of the court and the provisions of the Code.

Executioner Joseph P. Francel, hired to kill the Rosenbergs, wrote to Warden Denno from Cairo, New York, on June 14, 1953, "Your letter of June 12, 1953, informing me of the executions scheduled for Thursday, June 18, 1953 received, I will report in the usual manner on that day."[3]

Found among the recovered Sing Sing archives were letters from convicted atom-bomb spies Julius and Ethel Rosenberg to their attorney, Emanuel Bloch. One from Julius, dated June 18, 1953, who regarded Bloch as a beloved brother, said that he had made his will, about which Ethel completely agreed, to ensure that Bloch would be responsible for the future of the Rosenbergs' young sons. He continued: "Dear Manny, I have drawn up a last will and testament so that there can be no question about the fact that I want you to handle our affairs and be responsible for the children as in fact you have been doing. Ethel completely concurs in this request and is in her own hand attesting to it." And he asked Bloch to protect and love them with all his heart. He concluded: "Words fail me when I attempt to tell of the nobility and grandeur of my life's companion, my sweet and devoted wife. Ours is a great love and a wonderful relationship, it has made my life full and rich. . . . *Never let them change the truth of our innocence* . . . we face the executioner with courage, confidence—never losing faith."

The next day Ethel again wrote to her attorney: "The following letter is to be delivered to my children: 'Dearest Sweethearts, my most precious children, only this morning it looked like we might be together again after all. Now that this cannot be . . . Unfortunately, I may write only a few simple words, the rest of your own lives must teach you, even as mine taught me. At first you will grieve bitterly but you will not grieve alone. That is our consolation and it must eventually be yours. Eventually, too, you must come to believe that life is worth living. Be comforted that even now, with the end of ours slowly approaching, that we know this with a conviction that defeats the executioner! Your lives must teach you, too, that good cannot really flourish in the midst of evil; that freedom and all the things that go to make it a truly satisfying and worthwhile life, must sometimes be purchased very dearly . . . Your Daddy who is with me in these last momentous hours sends his heart and all the love that is in it for his dearest boys. Always remember that we were innocent and could not wrong our innocence. We press you close and kiss your with all our strength. Lovingly, Daddy and Mommy—Julie Ethel.

"'P.S. To Manny: The Ten Commandments, religious medal and chain—and my wedding ring—I wish you to present to our children as a token of our undying love. . . . All our love to all our dear ones. Love you so much, Ethel.'"

After the Rosenbergs' executions the executioner filled out his report card indicating that he had used 8 amps on Julius Rosenberg for 2¾ minutes and 6½ amps on Ethel for 4½ minutes. Their orphaned sons were brought up in a loving atmosphere by Abel and Anne Meeropol, whose name they adopted. As adults the sons wrote a book maintaining that their parents were innocent, but in 1997 former KGB agent Alexander Feklisov revealed that Julius had been a spy and had handed him dozens of military secrets. He told a reporter for Cox newspapers in Moscow that on Christmas Eve morning of 1944 in a Manhattan cafeteria, Julius Rosenberg had given him a radar-controlled proximity fuse, a "smart" weapon, which Soviet engineers replicated. And it was used to kill Americans. One, he said, was used to shoot down the U-2 plane piloted by Gary Powers in Soviet airspace in 1960. Feklisov also said that the atomic bomb information Rosenberg provided was insignificant. As for Ethel, he claimed that she was an innocent wife who never met a Soviet agent.[4]

The Rosenbergs' sons were naturally pleased that a KGB agent had exonerated their mother, although Soviet documents released in July 1995, known as the Venona documents, had fingered their father, Julius. The sons responded to that accusation with this statement:

> Nothing in the 49 VENONA documents released by the National Security Agency and the CIA on July 11 causes us to alter our positions.

1. Our parents, Ethel and Julius Rosenberg were not guilty as charged [With spying for the Soviet Union]. 2. their conviction was based upon perjured testimony and fabricated evidence; 3. that government agents and agencies orchestrated our parents' frame-up which resulted in their execution.[5]

Another revelation of the archival records shows that about one-third of Sing Sing's death-house prisoners who were reprieved or given executive clemency still spent much of the rest of their lives behind bars.

All death-house inmates, shortly before execution, were subjected to an examination by three doctors, known as the Governor's Lunacy Commission. They were charged with what seems like an impossible task: deciding if the condemned prisoner was sane at the time of the crime which may have occurred years before.

In one such case, Oliver Little, a one-eyed thirty-nine-year-old laborer, claimed that during an argument with Henry Beard he had stabbed him to death in self-defense. The examining psychiatrist, Carl Sugar, rated Little as mentally defective, borderline level, with an IQ of 64 on the Bellevue Intelligence Scale, and summed him up as a high-grade moron. Yet, Little was electrocuted.

Members of the Lunacy Commission were demonstrably men of few words and in their verdicts gave little to question or challenge them on, judging by this one-sentence report to Gov. Nelson A. Rockefeller on December 11, 1959: "As a result of their observation and final examination on this date, a consideration of the Record on Appeal, and a result of the testimony taken, it is the unanimous opinion of your Commission that the said prisoner is sane at the present time, and they have no reason to believe that he was not sane at the time of the commission of the crime for which he was convicted. John F. McNeil, M.D. Chairman; Leo F. O'Donnell, M.D., George F. Etling, M.D."

Other letters found in Sing Sing's archive include the following one from a compassionate fellow prisoner to eighteen-year-old Benitez DeJesus, a handyman who had stabbed Edwin Berkowitz to death during a robbery: "I heard that you have a new guard up there who is telling you that you have no chance—that you will certainly get the chair. I do not see how anybody can be that brutal. Even if he believed you would get the chair, he should not have told you, he should have used a little tact." DeJesus did get the chair, on July 8, 1943.

Another letter was to nineteen-year-old laborer Harley La Marr, a Native American from Buffalo, who shot Marion I. Frisbee with a rifle during an attempted rape and robbery. His motive? He said that he needed money: "A Friend" wrote to him: "Dear Harley, You probably have received many letters from Buffalo in the past two weeks. It is only natural that we should feel closer to a person of our own age. One thing that has bothered me since I saw you at the Erie County Court House. You put on a good act that convinced most people that you were tough and not afraid. But when I saw you I knew that you were afraid as any other person in your condition. I can honestly say that I believe the sentence was a mistake. It seems that every time I pick up a newspaper I see of a murder, but do they ever sentence these men and women to die? I haven't seen it happen yet. They wait till a boy of 19 makes a mistake till they decide that justice has to be done. This letter will be read before it

Fig. 45. Harley La Marr was executed in 1951. (New York State Archives)

gets to you. If it ever does and I hope that the one who reads it will have mercy on you. It was brought up at the trial that you have no friends. Maybe you had none then but I am sure that you have now. Not only girls but boys too. God Bless You." La Marr was executed on January 11, 1951.

Although Leonardo Salemi, a fifty-one-year-old plasterer, had a long criminal record, he denied that he was guilty of fatally shooting Walter Forlenza in a bar. Two days before his execution on February 19, 1957, he mailed this letter by Special Delivery to district attorney Vincent Dermody who had sent him to the death house. "I know this letter will come as a surprise to you, the last guy in the world you expect to hear from is me—Leonard Salemi. Anyway, since it appears that it's all over but the shouting I am sending you a little memento, which I highly prized and valued here! Something which I hope you will be big enough to accept in the good spirit and intent which they are meant. They are my now hand made, molded I should say—Rosary beads. They are made of 'Bread' Vince and no doubt the only ones of their kind in the world! Bread as you know is our secret commune with our beloved Lord Jesus Christ who died on the cross forgiving his executioners. They are as durable as any others and the pierced sacred heart and decades (divisions of the rosary) were colored in red by adding a small amount of cherry cool and concentrate into bread which worked into a doughy substance for molding purposes. There is also a small amount of sugar added to give the needed glucose which veritably turns the beads into stone-like substance when completely dried out. And please, Vince, even though I know you know better, don't let the press know about this letter, or especially about the beads. Goodbye, Vince—if it's not asking too much to offer up a prayer for me sometime. Except for that one bitterness and hate, I go in peace. I am, Sincerely and Respectfully Yours, Leonard Salemi."

Salemi also wrote to his "dearest friend. I know what you are feeling at this moment. I am sure it is the same kind of feeling that my own family feels right now! I've seen their faces Sal and felt their own pain with them. Long ago I foresaw their agony and unspoken suffering. And here is something else that may surprise you to hear, but as God is my judge, it is his own Gospel truth. As a boy, when my Dad was murdered cold bloodedly while coming home from work with my brother Joey one night I actually 'foresaw myself sitting in the electric chair.' I was only a lad of eleven years old then Sal— and of course took an oath to avenge his killing! Shortly after I had seen a picture of one of our local scandle [sic] sheets—I believe it was the N.Y. *Evening Graphic*, of a person sitting in the electric chair. Well, Sal, I remembered that picture 'and actually saw myself grown up and would for something that I had no part of. That's what really makes it hard. A guy don't give a damn when he goes out 'knowing he was guilty.'"

Unlike Salemi, Frank Newman, a fifty-year-old widower from Long Island with three children, admitted his crime. He had made himself a widower by fatally shooting his wife, Ethel, then blamed the killing on acute alcoholism and temporary insanity. The Lunacy Board didn't buy the "temporary insanity" plea and on August 22, 1956, the day before Newman's execution, he wrote to his soon-to-be-orphaned children: "It is so difficult for me to put in writing the sadness that is in my heart for you boys. I do want you to know that I have respect, love and affection for you. I could go on page after page but I do not believe I could describe how much I despise myself for this terrible thing. I loved Mother, I pray to God to forgive me and that my boys will try to soften the terrible hatred you have for me. . . . May God guide and watch over you always. Love, dad."

Relatives and friends who wished to visit Sing Sing's condemned inmates had to follow strict rules.

Close relatives (fathers, mothers, sisters, brothers, children) could visit twice a week except on Thursdays. The only exception was the Thursday before the inmate's execution. On that last Thursday afternoon and evening, only close relatives were allowed inside. If no relative applied to visit, friends were let into the death house for their last good-byes, but only those approved by the warden. Visitors were allowed two Sunday visits every month, less frequently if the building was crowded. Those intending to visit on Sundays and holidays had to hand their passes to the head guard on the Tuesday before their visit. Sunday visits were limited to three in the morning and three in the afternoon, each lasting no more than two hours. A married woman had to show her marriage certificate, or a copy, to confirm that she was a prisoner's wife. But she only got in after the document was examined under a detectoscope to determine that it wasn't a fake.

Of the more distant relatives and nonrelatives (aunts, uncles, cousins, in-laws, and friends), a prisoner was limited to five who had been been approved by the warden. Friends were restricted to one weekly visit. And *all* visitors to the death house were fingerprinted.

When it was time for Pablo Vargas to be executed for strangling Lillian Mojica, he stuck to his claim that he had been forced to confess. A thirty-four-year-old Puerto Rican–born cook-helper at Jewish Memorial Hospital and the married father of three, his case aroused public sympathy. Sergeant Byrne reported to Warden Denno that two pickets outside the prison were carrying signs of protest. One read "Though shalt not kill" on one side and on the other, "Clemency for Pablo Vargas. Vigil for His Life." The other sign read on one side, "The Death Penalty Is Legal Murder—Catholic Workers, 39 Spring, N.Y.C.," and on the other, "Clemency for Pablo Vargra [*sic*]. Join the Vigil for His Life at Sing Sing."

Vargas was not willing to cooperate in his own execution and put up a fight, the first time since 1891 that any of the more than six hundred condemned prisoners had resisted so strenuously.

The prison records reveal that Warden Denno gave his own version of what had happened to Corrections Commissioner Paul D. McGinnis, on May 17, 1960: "I wish to advise that it was anticipated that Vargas might pull some stunt due to the fact that his wife and other relatives were driven to the institution by a representative of a Spanish newspaper in New York City, and when the visit was completed the same newspaperman picked up the relatives in their car. It is also my understanding that one of the newspapers paid the expenses of attorney Nancy Carley to go to Washington to try to get a stay of execution. It would appear that apparently this inmate was reassured that he would get a stay of execution and when this did not come through he became very upset. As a matter of fact, he showed signs of getting jittery right after his wife, sister and half-brother left the institution. Therefore, I had some extra officers out of sight in the event that he did something unusual. He walked into the execution chamber in the usual manner, and when he got immediately opposite the chair he started kicking, but his arms had been held tight by the additional officers that I had. The whole incident was greatly exaggerated in the newspapers because, of course, it was something out of the ordinary. However, there was no prolonged struggle to get him into the chair, and I would say that the incident didn't last more than fifteen to twenty seconds before he was strapped in the usual manner."

The recovered records also show, what had not been published in the press, that there had been several attempts to escape from the brick-and-stone death house with steel-barred windows, which had been described as the most impregnable penal institution in the world. Gerhard Puff was one inmate who tried to escape. Aka Donald Jardine and Richard Rogers, Puff was a thirty-nine-year-old German-born truck driver whose wife was also in prison but not in Sing Sing. Puff had shot and killed an FBI agent, Joseph J. Brock, in a hotel while on the lam from a bank robbery. He claimed that he had fired in self-defense.

Head guard L. J. Kelley reported to Warden Denno on December 4, 1953, that diagrams of keys on a scrap of paper had been found in Puff's condemned cell, and that guards on all three shifts had all been warned that he might be planning an escape. Eight months later Warden Denno left no doubt that Puff had not escaped, writing to a US Marshal, in part to protect the identity and privacy of the man who had electrocuted Puff:

I am attaching herewith vouchers executed by Dow W. Hover, who officiated as legal executioner in the case of Gerhard A. Puff, #113970. One of these vouchers is in the amount of $150 which is the usual fee paid to the executioner. The other is in the amount of $12.80 which covers mileage of 160 miles at the rate of eight cents per mile. You will note that the voucher covering the mileage does not give the starting point of the return point from Ossining. This is done in order to protect the locality in which the executioner resides as we do not desire his name nor his place of residence to become public knowledge through the press.

However, you can use my letter as certification to the effect that the mileage claimed by the executioner is the mileage which the State of New York pays him and it is correct in all respects. Therefore, in order to protect the official residence of the executioner that is the reason why the starting point was not included in this bill.

Death-house inmate Romulo Rosario also had an escape plan. A married man of thirty-seven, with two children, he fatally shot Michael Gonzalez to death on the street, vainly claiming that it was in self-defense. Now, awaiting execution, he wrote to a prospective accomplice also in the death house: "It is impossible to get any guns in here and we have to have guns to get away. What we are planning to do is to have the warden's home taken over and him used as a tool to bring my boy in with him as a visiting cop. He will have all the stuff with him and we use the warden's family as hostages. It only takes 2 or 3 men outside and I have a boy out there who knows the whole plan with the times and all the details. Are you in? It's better than waiting around to just die like sheep. What can we lose? TEAR UP AND FLUSH IN TOILET!"

The letter was in Sing Sing's archive so, obviously, it hadn't been torn up or flushed down the toilet.

Rosario was executed on July 17, 1955.

The previously mentioned death-row inmate, fifty-one-year-old Frederick Charles Wood, was the next-to-last man to be electrocuted in Sing Sing. He had committed his first murder at fifteen and, after an extensive prison term, was paroled in 1931. Two years later, he committed his second murder. Again he was sent to prison and, in 1960, despite public protests across New York State, was paroled for a second time. Just weeks later, on July 30, Wood slashed one man to death and killed another with a shovel. After he was arrested and had confessed to both crimes, newspapers condemned the parole board for letting him free to kill repeatedly. When a Lunacy Commission member had asked him, "Is there any way we can help you?" he had replied, "Let me burn." Which they did, on March 11, 1963.[6]

The last and 614th person to be executed in Sing Sing's electric chair was Eddie Lee Mays, a thirty-four-year-old African American. He had killed thirty-one-year-old Maria Marini with a .38 caliber pistol during a nighttime stickup at the Friendly Bar and Grill in East Harlem, 1403 Fifth Avenue between 115th and 116th Streets. Mays had a long criminal history as a native of North Carolina, where he had served six years for killing a man, and was described in his prison record as aggressive and violent. After relocating to New York he had joined a gang that committed fifty-two robberies in a six-week crime spree. His last crime was in the early hours of Sunday, March 12, 1961, when he and two other men entered the East Harlem bar. Mays, a slight man of five feet seven, fired two shots into the floor and immediately got the attention of the bartender, the crowd at the bar, and those sitting in its eight booths.

He then grabbed a wad of cash from the bartender and ordered the customers to put their wallets and purses on the bar, speeding up the process by

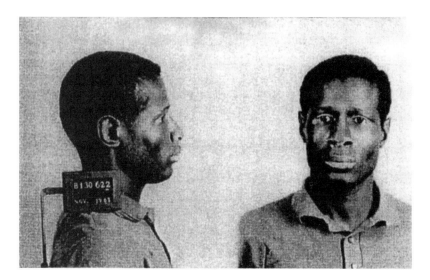

Fig. 46. The last inmate Hover electrocuted, in 1963, Eddie Lee Mays, who killed a woman during a robbery. (New York State Archives)

shouting, "I'm going to kill someone! I mean it! I'll show you!"[7] Before Maria Marini, who was in one of the booths, could hand her purse to him, he grabbed it from her. And when he found no money in it, he put his gun to her head and fired, killing her instantly. He made a quick exit with his two accomplices and $275. There was, of course, no shortage of witnesses and the police arrested him sixteen days later.

Although prosecutors offered to accept a plea of second-degree murder and a sentence of life imprisonment, Mays insisted on a trial, telling his lawyers that he would "rather" fry than go to prison. And although they thought he was crazy and twice requested a psychiatric exam, the court denied them.

The evidence was convincing. The bullet taken from his victim's skull matched one fired from Mays's gun. Several customers identified him. And there was a transcript account of his admission of guilt, although he denied that he had made it, saying at the trial that the killing was an accident.

After ninety minutes, his jury, which included Robert Sour the composer of "Body and Soul," found him guilty, and Judge Irwin Davidson sentenced him to death. One anonymous juror said that he felt sympathy for Mays because he was a poor man from a poor neighborhood. Sour said that there were two black people on the jury, both of whom thought he should be executed.

Attorney Edward Bloustein, opposed to the death penalty, undertook the appeal pro bono as he believed that Mays was criminally insane. And he argued passionately before Judge Charles S. Desmond that "a society which kills even though the killing is sanctified by law, is a less kind society, a less just society and a less merciful one." Mays was unexpectedly philosophical about his fate, writing to Bloustein, "I have resigned myself to accept what follows. I am a human being."[8]

He refused a last meal, but asked for a pack of Pall Mall cigarettes. Accompanied to the chair by a chaplain and Warden Denno, he had no last words for the witnesses and died at 10:04 PM on August 15, 1953. Mays left behind an estranged wife, Ruth, in Baltimore, two children, a sister, and three brothers. No one claimed his body, so he was buried by the state.

The two men who had entered the bar with him had admitted their guilt and were sentenced to life. One was paroled in 1976 and became the manager of a plant in the Bronx. The other was paroled in 1977, only to die of brain cancer the following year. The young lookout had been sent to a reformatory.

Of the last fourteen men electrocuted at Sing Sing, one was white, one was Puerto Rican, and twelve, including Mays, were black.

By 2000 anyone interested in an insider's view of Sing Sing's past contacted guard George McGrath, the prison's unofficial historian. From his second-floor office in what used to be the warden's house, he had a clear view down the hill to the old death house. Frequently called upon to answer questions from the press, officials, and the public, he had access to four ledgers in the New York State Archives in Albany that listed the history of the death house inmates from their arrival to violent departure, details on how to run death row, and how to handle an execution. He could tell them that no warden had lasted as long as Lewis Lawes or had such a positive impact.

The list went as follows: John T. Deegan took over from Denno in January 1967, and lasted two years. James L. Casscles followed, and left after three years. His successor, Theodore Schubin, stayed the same length of time. Acting Warden Joseph Higgins then filled in for three months until Harold Butler was appointed in 1975, but he quit after only two months. The new warden, William G. Gard, served for two years. In August 1977 Walter Fogg did a one-month stint as acting warden until Stephen Dalsheim agreed to become Sing Sing's chief. Three years later, Wilson E. J. Walters was in charge for the customary three years. The warden who followed, James E. Sullivan, broke recent records by making it to five years. John P. Keane outdid him by lasting nine, handing the reins to Charles Greiner in March 1997. Three years later on May 4, 2000, the present warden, Brian S. Fischer, took charge.

Fig. 47. Pipe-smoking executioner Robert Elliott, who wrote a book about his work. (New York State Archives)

Unless they, like Lewis E. Lawes, wrote of their experiences, little is known about these wardens.

Sing Sing's executioners, with the exception of Robert Elliott, were secretive men, anxious to avoid publicity. Elliott wrote a book about his experiences as an executioner, and someone blew up his house. No one was hurt, and it was rebuilt by the state. Understandably, Sing Sing's last executioner, from 1953 to 1962, Deputy Sheriff Dow B. Hover, went to great lengths to hide his identity. He even changed his car's license plate, before he drove from his home in Germantown to the prison to carry out an execution. His name first came to light when Sing Sing's missing archives were recovered. But that was all, until an article about him by Jennifer Gonnerman, titled "The Last Executioner," and his photograph appeared in New York's *Village Voice* on January 24, 2005.

His daughter, Gladys Bohnsack, and son, Dow, have very different views of him. Dow says that his father felt bad about his work, and went to his minister for reassurance. Gladys says that he was a cold man who never held her hand or told her that he loved her. "He was also a perfectionist," she told me. "All the

Fig. 48. Sing Sing's last executioner, Deputy Sheriff Dow B. Hover, who went to great lengths to hide his identity. (Courtesy of Gladys Bohnsack)

clocks in our home had to be set perfectly on time."[9] Hover suffered from chronic, crippling migraine headaches, and died in 1990 at eighty-nine, of what was officially described as undetermined causes, although he had been found in a parked car full of exhaust fumes.

Not much is known about most death-house inmates, except those who made the front pages of the newspapers because of their bizarre, sensational, or horrendous crimes. And, apart from their letters, the archive reveals only a brief record of their existence. Along with their full-face and profile mug shots are their minibiographies or obituaries. These include their fingerprints, names, inmate numbers, birthdate, ages, education (mostly very little), occupations (waiter, messenger boy, truck driver, counterman, laborer, stamper, handyman, laundry worker, transient, unemployed), crimes, accomplices (if any), names of the judges who sentenced them, dates of the sentences, when they arrived at Sing Sing, and dates of their executions.

Life and a shocking death in sixty words or less.

Fig. 49. A rare photo of an unidentified man being electrocuted in Sing Sing. (New York State Archives)

Chapter Twelve

SING SING IN THE TWENTY-FIRST CENTURY

If Ted Conover had any hesitation about exposure to the horrors of prison, it was trumped by his curiosity. Evidently interested in the world's dispossessed, and in those defending or defying the system—his previous book, *Coyotes*, explored the lives of illegal Mexican immigrants—he now set his sights on Sing Sing, especially the prison guards or correction officers as they are officially known. But he was rebuffed by the authorities, who declined his request to observe guards in action. So he went undercover, as a Sing Sing prison guard himself, and, after ten months on the job, from April 1997 to January 1998, wrote a compelling account of an ordeal that gave him nightmares and put a strain on his marriage.

During seven weeks in Albany training to be a Sing Sing guard, Conover was supposed to learn the dozens of prison rules by heart, which included:

1. Pictures, photographs, newspaper clippings, and one small national flag (10" × 12") are to be taped or fastened to the top only of the cell wall in the designated 2' × 4' area. Other symbols not authorized will be confiscated.
2. Display of pictures or photographs of nudes will only be placed where they cannot be seen from outside the cell or cubicle (above cell door, or inside locker).
3. Visibility into the cell must not be obstructed by furniture, clotheslines, clothes, bedding, or towels.

But when the recruits began on-the-job-training at the prison, they found convicts blatantly breaking the rules, with music blaring from their radios, hard-porn girlie photos clearly visible from outside the cells, and sheets hanging from the cell bars to hide whatever they were up to. Conover and fellow trainees reported this to their training officer, who agreed that everything wasn't as it should be, but insisted that it was their job to strictly enforce the rules. He also advised them to discuss with their families the possibility of being taken hostage by the inmates during a riot. Not wanting to frighten her, Conover chose not to warn his wife.

On first arriving at the prison, Conover noticed that most inmates were in great shape from weight lifting, and was surprised at the number who were scarred from what seemed to be gunshots or stabbing. In fact, at least half seemed to have been shot or stabbed. Recent scars were a clue as to those who had been involved in recent fights in the prison itself. And telling inmates to take their shirts off was one of the first methods of finding the culprits. A tip from Sherlock Holmes?

During his time at Sing Sing, Conover worked in the huge B-Block of the prison, in the psychiatric ward, and—his most dangerous assignment—in the Box, a two-story solitary-confinement building. The thirty convicts on its top floor were under protective custody, in danger, if left to mingle with the general population, of being killed or injured. On the ground floor were inmates who had attacked guards. In comparative safety, a guard on each floor sat in a cagelike structure from which he operated levers that opened and closed the inmates' cell doors.

Despite attempts to deprive dangerous inmates of anything resembling a weapon that could maim or kill, one had fashioned out of many rolls of toilet paper a noose as strong as rope, with which, if it hadn't been discovered, he might have hanged himself. Another had escaped from a shower stall through a door left ajar, grabbed a mop handle, and used it to smash fifty-eight windows. When guards overpowered him, they found a glass shard hidden in his waistband.

Forewarned, the warden ordered teams of guards, including Conover, to search the cells in the Box and strip-search the inmates. Looking like a swat team, protected with helmets, Plexiglass visors, stab-proof vests, knee and elbow pads, and thick latex gloves, they began their task while another guard followed with a video camera, to record the action in anticipation of potential lawsuits.

Conover entered the first cell, wished its occupant a polite "Good morning," then calmly announced his intentions. Appearing somewhat confused, the inmate stripped, handed over all his clothes, then bent over to show nothing was hidden in his anus. No problem. After he had dressed, Conover's partner handcuffed the compliant inmate, who then stepped out of the cell.

The cell search revealed a glimpse of hell, with roaches crawling over the bedsheets, garbage littering the floor, and gang graffiti scrawled on the walls. Conover was surprised to find, by contrast, a chess set made of toothpaste caps, and beautifully handwritten entries in Spanish in the inmate's several notebooks. Nothing found was forbidden—not even the garbage—and the inmate was uncuffed and returned to his cell.

In the second cell they confiscated an unauthorized extra pillow. But before they'd completed the search they heard a team of cell-extraction guards about to force an unwilling inmate to cooperate. Conover watched them go through this man's cell like a human battering ram, shouting, "Stop resisting! Stop resisting!"—a legal requirement in anticipation of undue-force lawsuits. They brought out a still-resisting short black man despite handcuffs and leg restraints. Other inmates began yelling that the guards were "bitch-ass faggot motherfuckers" who were getting off on seeing them naked. Others threatened lawsuits. Some called the black guards in the cell-extraction team "house niggers," chanting, "Kill all the house niggers!"

Conover and his partner were now on their third cell occupied by a young black man, who said that he was not going to show them his asshole, and demanded to speak to a sergeant, who met the same resistance. Conover thought it had been stupid to resist, especially after the extraction team went into action and forced him to comply—and found no contraband in his cell or in his body. He was returned to his cell, looking, it seemed to Conover, thrilled and defiant.

Afterward, when the guards had hugged and slapped each other on the back like a victorious football team, and the glow of victory and rush of adrenalin had subsided, Conover rethought the situation. Now the young man's stupidity in resisting began to look principled. "He was renouncing his imprisonment, our authority, the entire system that had placed him there," Conover concluded, and "if enough people did that together, the corrections system would come tumbling down."[1]

What seemed to him a waste of time was the way Sing Sing treated the mentally disturbed, which included a lot of inmates. A decade-old study, he noted, stated that of the state's seventy thousand inmates, 5 percent or thirty-five hundred were seriously and persistently mentally ill. And if they hadn't been in prison, they'd have been confined to psychiatric hospitals. Another 10 percent, or seven thousand inmates, were supervised by prison psychiatrists and taking drugs for their mental illnesses. Called "bugs" by guards and inmates, unless violent, they mostly stayed in the general population.

Conover's experience confirmed the statistics. Many of his charges were either mildly mentally ill, talking to themselves and failing to take showers; or severely disturbed, not aware that they were in prison, trashing or setting fire to their own cells, trying to hang themselves or to slash their wrists or throats. And he agreed with the official who said that prison made crazy people worse, and drove sane people crazy.

He encountered some of them in Sing Sing's Psychiatric Satellite Unit (PSU) on the second floor of the hospital. The PSU was one of his favorite assignments, because the place was quiet and clean, and the patients were subdued by drugs and under careful supervision. It was obviously not a very demanding job, because the guard in charge spent much of his time reading religious tracts or doing crossword puzzles.

On first arriving there, Conover recognized a small Dominican who, when in B-Block, had torched his cell. Now he appeared perfectly at home in his high-security cell in the psychiatric unit. He had even decorated it to

Fig. 50. Investigative reporter Ted Conover in his uniform as a Sing Sing guard. He wrote a lively and moving account of his experiences titled *Newjack*, prison slang for a new recruit. (Courtesy Ted Conover, photo Jennifer Klein)

his taste, festooning each metal bar with toilet paper, with more swatches of toilet paper stuck to the walls with toothpaste.

That first morning, Conover escorted several mental patient-prisoners, one at a time, into a conference hall, to talk with a panel of five, including a psychiatrist, a social worker, and a nurse. One white inmate told the group that he was upset because two demon prison guards were secretly communicating with a Space Being on A-Block roof. When the psychiatrist prescribed Haldol, an antipsychotic medicine, the inmate shook his head, muttering, "Once you start takin' that shit . . . ," implying that it was worse than nothing. He also rejected the offer of a milder drug. But after the psychiatrist got him to agree that he would take antibiotics if he had a cold, adding, "Well, this is an infection in your head," the inmate agreed to take it.

A Latino admitted to the group that while in Sing Sing he had taken marijuana, crack, heroin, and Valium, but that he now knew it was important to stop drugs, so that he might be paroled and take care of his family. Conover suspected that his confession, and implicit promise to give up drugs, were just a ploy for early parole.

The next in line, a white man, spoke somewhat incoherently about threatening letters and people out to get him. A woman on the panel asked if he knew what to avoid, and he responded, "Homosexuals, drugs, dice." Then he paused, and she prompted him: "Gangs, gambling, gays and drugs." "Right," he said, apparently reassured by this litany of the forbidden.

The morning's last patient behaved like a recalcitrant zombie, and refused to return to his cell. It took Conover and two other guards to force him back into it. Afterward, the head guard discouraged Conover from writing up the use-of-force incident in his logbook as a waste of time, saying: "Won't no punishment come of it for him because he's a bug. Forget it." Conover took his advice, thinking that the force they had used on the man was like a lot what happened in prison, "brutal, but reasonable under the circumstances."[2]

Conover's book, *Newjack: Guarding Sing Sing*, was published in 2000 to great acclaim, and guards, former guards, and relatives of guards wrote to tell him that he'd got it right. His picture of hell on the Hudson rang true.

The following year Human Rights Watch released a report by attorney Joanne Mariner, titled *No Escape: Male Rape in U.S. Prisons*, which included dozens of victims' firsthand accounts. Mariner maintained that "rape occurs in U.S. prisons because corrections officials, to a surprising extent, do little to stop it from occurring." And that prisoners' complaints of rape are not taken seriously, and their avenues of redress are typically blocked. "Rape," she concluded, "is not an inevitable consequence of prison life, but it certainly is a predictable one if little is done to prevent and punish it."[3]

Since the report's publication, Human Rights Watch has teamed up with Stop Prison Rape (SPR), a national organization devoted to stopping sexual violence in prisons. Their work inspired congressional hearings and the introduction of a bill, the Prison Rape Reduction Act. It would authorize a study of the problem and suggest ways for guards to detect and prevent prisoner rape.

According to Conover, rape didn't seem to be a significant problem at Sing Sing, although sexual activity was not unknown. A front-page *New York Daily News* story in the late 1980s headlined "Sing Sing Sexcapades" told of "a clique of rogue Correction officers" and "trysts between male inmates and female guards."[4]

After eight months in Sing Sing, Conover concluded that the most common type of sex among inmates, after autoeroticism, was consensual. A guard who had trained with him once pulled down a sheet hung—against the rules—across cell bars, and caught two men having sex. And several times at lineup, Conover heard Sing Sing's only female sergeant warn female guards not to wear makeup or engage in flirtatious behavior with inmates. "Obviously there was a reason for that," wrote Conover. "Sex was in the air."

A young woman who had trained with Conover to be a guard was fired for having sex with an inmate in a bathroom, while another inmate had acted as lookout at the bathroom door. Afterward, the lookout had "demanded his own piece of the action, and blabbed when she turned him down." And then, writes Conover, shortly "after I left Sing Sing, another female officer was apparently fired for having sex with one of my most macho and obnoxious keeplocks [dangerous prisoners kept in their cells twenty-three hours a day] on R-gallery."[5] Although, Conover continued, "the rape of the white middle-class inmate is a staple of contemporary prison movies from *American Me* to *Midnight Express* to *The Shawshank Redemption* . . . it is such a fixture of how middle-class America thinks about prison, [that] people who hear I worked in Sing Sing always bring it up; within a few minutes—if they dare bring it up at all. . . . Certainly prison rape still occurs [but] several longtime inmates I spoke with thought it was almost a thing of the past. . . . One [reason] is the willingness of the courts to hear inmates' lawsuits against states. This has forced states to take the protection of vulnerable prisoners as a high priority. Protective custody [PC] is now a big deal. Inmates who ask for protection but fail to get it can make expensive claims."[6]

Conover was prophetic. Not long before his arrival at Sing Sing, an inmate had razor-slashed another as he walked to his cell. According to the victim, himself serving twenty years to life for attempted murder, he nearly bled to death, and had to be treated in the hospital for deep cuts on his face and back. After he had recovered, and was moved to the Elmira Correctional Facility, he sued Commissioner Glenn Goord of the State Department of Correctional Services, and a Sing Sing official, William Connolly, for not protecting him from the near-fatal attack. He claimed that they had ignored his requests to be segregated from the general prison population. He had needed protection, he explained, because he had been an informant against a street gang leader in an attempted murder case.

His attorney, Paul Kerson, said that, because the thirty-one-year-old plaintiff was still in danger, having received death threats, his identity was being kept secret.

Testifying for the defense, Connolly suggested that after almost every prison fight, the injured inmate blamed a gang member, adding, "In most cases, it is an inmate involved in criminal activity against another inmate, and it has nothing to do with the Bloods or the Latin Kings." Goord reported that there was no problem with gangs in New York State's seventy prisons, including Sing Sing. And that the number of attacks that result in hospitalization "consistently goes down."

In closing remarks, State Attorney Susan Odessky asserted that the plaintiff "did nothing to seek protection at Sing Sing."

Kerson, however, urged the jury to award his client $7.5 million because of "negligence beyond negligence," and that such an award would send a message that would force the state to change a policy that allows for no real monitoring of gangs in prison. After a week's trial, in May 2004, the Manhattan jury did just that: it awarded the mystery man exactly $7.65 million.

Jim Flateau, a Sing Sing spokesman, said that the potentially wealthy plaintiff had been in prison for a brutal attack that left his victim with a serious face wound, a collapsed lung, and damage to other organs. And that if the large award survived the inevitable appeals, it would go to the inmate victim under the Son of Sam law. This was passed after "Son of Sam" serial killer David Berkowitz had been offered a small fortune to tell his story. Kerson said he will argue that his client deserves the jury award as a crime victim. Kerson's client was naturally overjoyed with the verdict.[7]

Overjoyed inmates are in very short supply. After his stint at Sing Sing as a volunteer teacher, John Cheever wrote, "If prison were constructed to make any living thing happy it might have been the cats."[8] He had noticed that a large colony of wild cats lived on the prison ground, and he saw them in the spring and summer, sunning themselves on the grass, awaiting food that the inmates would leave for them. Two decades later, their offspring's offspring were still there.

Cheever should have added "birds" to the happy creatures.

Although inmates were forbidden pets, they went to ingenious efforts to break the rules. On returning from meals, they stuffed bread in the chain-link fence along the gallery and sparrows flew to eat it, watched by inmates back in their cells. A Pakistani prisoner, who had become a bird expert, told Conover that the female bird he could see from his cell was feeding her second lot of offspring that year. His friend in a nearby cell had fashioned a birdcage for his pet sparrow from a cardboard box in a mesh laundry bag, which he hung from the cell ceiling. One day, Conover was walking past some cells when he spotted a baby owl in his path with a string tied to its leg. As he approached, the string was rapidly disappearing into a cell—the owl being pulled along with it. Conover quickly stepped on the string, and cut it with his pocketknife, saying, "No bird torture." But the cell's Spanish-speaking inmate yelled anxiously, *"No, C. O., he can't fly!* He fell down from the nest. I feed him, else he die!"[9]

Conover picked up the bird, which perched on his finger and didn't attempt to escape. So he handed it back.

A muscular Italian American inmate from Bensonhurst, Brooklyn, had secreted a kitten in his cell, which he had furnished with gifts from a friend that would have thrilled Martha Stewart—matching bedsheets, pillowcase, and bedside mat, all burgundy colored. To complete the picture, he had fixed a burgundy-colored handkerchief over his washbasin, giving the cell a warm burgundy glow. When Conover asked him about his pet, which often escaped from the cell, the inmate quipped, "Only pussy I'll ever get." Which, wrote Conover, "made me nervous for the cat."[10]

Another pet-owning inmate had fashioned a transparent pyramid out of plastic wrap, masking tape, and sticks. He kept a spider in the structure, which had built its web there, and fed it cockroaches hidden in a box under his bed.

Although guards were discouraged from chatting with prisoners, Conover enjoyed frequent conversations with an intelligent, charismatic prisoner, who pointed out that new prisons were already under construction for future felons who were now only four or five years old—an augury of the swelling prison population.

One of his favorite "chat buddies" among the inmates was a flamboyant black transvestite with huge sagging breasts, pot belly, and yellow teeth who had been found guilty because, he said, he was "poor, black and gay." Known to fellow cons as "Grandma" and as "Janice" to friends on the outside, he had often been imprisoned for prostitution, and was now in for from four to twelve years, for the second-degree murder of his ex-lover. He claimed that "They didn't have my prints on the knife or anything." In a "place where macho was the rule," Conover found him "a refreshing sort of female presence," recalling that when "Grandma" was confused, he placed his hand on his cheek "like a befuddled belle." Ridiculed and ostracized by most other inmates who treated him as an untouchable, he was unfailingly polite and even charming to Conover, who felt sympathy for him as a fellow "outsider."[11]

Equipped with latex gloves and a tongue depressor, Conover also took part in the twenty-four-hour suicide and drug-overdose watch of prisoners in six psych-unit cells. Those suspected of having swallowed a drug in a packet to avoid detection were held in cells for seventy-two hours without access to water, and wore only paper gowns and no underwear as guards waited for them to have a bowel movement in order to grab "the prize packet." It was not his favorite assignment.[12]

Suicide watch was more restful, especially as the bearded and mustached Puerto Rican inmate he was watching remained asleep for hours at a time, waking only to ask for a cigarette. Conover saw from previous logbook entries that he was at times very active, singing "White Christmas" while dragging around on a string a plastic paper cup he called his cat, prying loose floor tiles to swallow pieces of them, then using what was left to make deep cuts in his leg, wrist, chest, and near his jugular.

Conover played chess with him through the cell bars, and told him that Princess Diana had died the previous night. The inmate said that prison gangs had pressured him into undertaking risky, illegal assignments, on the grounds that, if caught, the mentally ill were usually excused. And their pressure had driven him to try to kill himself. He admitted that, "fucked-up" on drugs and alcohol, he had killed a man who beat up women. Now, however, he believed that the Alcohol and Substance Abuse course he'd taken would help him to stay clean.

He told Conover how he looked forward to being sent to a gang-free state mental hospital at Marcy, where he could see a movie every day, four men shared a room, the doors were unlocked in the daytime, and the only punishments were being put in restraints or tranquilized when they "stick you in the ass."

Their conversations were frequently interrupted by a black man in an adjoining cell who greeted each passing guard or nurse with "Top of the morning to you, sir!" and then resumed singing his favorite songs from

Broadway musicals, especially *New York, New York*. He also annoyed the Puerto Rican prisoner with his "bullshit" talk about Jesus Christ being black.[13]

In his no-holds-barred book, Conover tried to enhance the generally low public image of prison guards as sadists or simpletons: "Every single story about guards seems to reinforce the brutal stereotype. When I see accused officers on television read the remarks of union reps in the papers, what disappoints me is the universal denial that the events ever took place as alleged, or any admission of the obvious, that among the many good officers there are a few bad ones. Guards don't dare admit that all of us at times feel like strangling an inmate, that inmates taunt us, strike us, humiliate us in ways civilians could never imagine, and that through it all the guard is supposed to do nothing but stand there and take it. This information wouldn't excuse the crimes, but it might chip away at the stereotype by making a few of the incidents more *understandable*. Instead, guards adopt a siege mentality—a shutting up, a closing of ranks—that is law enforcement at its stupidest."[14]

He had mixed feelings about the inmates. He would willingly have whacked some, enjoyed conversations with others, liked a few, despised some, and felt sympathy for others. He learned early on that a guard never helps an inmate carry a heavy load. That was one of the first rules he broke. He also learned that deadly physical force against a prisoner was justified in three situations: to prevent an escape, in self-defense, and to prevent arson. While he was there no one, apparently, had to kill an inmate, though he saw quite a few bruised and bleeding after various confrontations.

Conover recalled how, "At the beginning of a graveyard shift [a lieutenant] warned us COs [guards], 'Remember if they're dead and hard you're gone.' Meaning that if an inmate has rigor mortis by the time you get to him you're fired."[15]

He had only to look around in the prison with its preponderance of black men to realize that the system was unfair, which was confirmed by an article he read stating that in the 1990s when Wall Street was booming, one out of three black men between the ages of twenty and twenty-nine were either behind bars, on probation, or on parole.

Sing Sing at first added Conover's *Newjack* to the "contraband" list, then a couple of months later allowed inmates to buy it, after six pages had been ripped out (39–40, 49–52, 81–82, 277–80).

But the Albany censors sometimes took as long as six months to remove the pages, and, at other times, did not return the book to the inmate.

Conover responded on his Web site: "Were these legitimate security concerns? I don't believe so. Riots have almost always been the result of poor prison administration or operation, not knowledge of our top-secret aikido grips. I had thought carefully about whether anything in *Newjack* could conceivably endanger my fellow officers before I included it in the book, and no officer has yet complained to me about those revelations."

But when, in early February 2004, seven people, among them a Sing Sing guard and two inmates, were accused of planning an elaborate escape, Westchester County prosecuting attorney Jeanine Pirro speculated that the book was used as a primer for the group: to get a handle on the layout of the prison, how and when guards signed in and out, and how they identified themselves, and so forth.

As a guard, Conover had sometimes felt trapped and wondered how he would escape if, as an inmate, he was dressed in the green garb of the inmates instead of his own gray uniform. Eventually, he told a reporter, he came up with what he thought "was a pretty good plan. But I didn't put it in [my] book."[16] Apparently the escape planners read his mind. According to Pirro, "It is alleged that on April 24, 2003, Jatanya Belnavis and a male accomplice, entered Sing Sing wearing phony correction officers' uniforms and wigs. The pair carried a bag containing fake badges and identification cards for the inmates they intended to break out of the facility. In addition they possessed loaded 9 mm and .38 caliber handguns. But the attempt was aborted, when Belvanis suffered a panic attack and had to exit the facility before the escape plan could be carried out."[17]

Belvanis allegedly returned on May 6, with Barry Alexander aka Sidiq and possibly others, hoping to escape detection in the confusion of the shift change when some three hundred guards left or entered Sing Sing. But the team arrived too late, after the shift change had occurred.

The third escape attempt, according to DA Pirro, went into effect the next morning, when Barry Alexander and Tony Dubose purportedly parked a motorcycle near Sing Sing prison to help two inmates make a quick getaway.

Dubose—offered a $15,000 bribe by the planning committee—dressed in a fake uniform, tried to enter Sing Sing as a "new transfer" guard from another prison. But he didn't make it. When officials asked for his credentials, he made a hurried exit, saying that he'd get them from his car, and disappeared, leaving behind a bag of fake uniform items and a canister of pepper spray—illegal in the prison.

In early February 2004, New York police arrested seven people including two inmates and a Sing Sing guard, and accused them of planning the failed prison escape. The case was solved largely thanks to the Ossining cop who had questioned the two who were leaving a motorcycle near the prison and was able to identify them. Quangtrice Wilson, a former Sing Sing guard, pleaded guilty to receiving a several-thousand-dollar bribe to give the escape-planning team information on the prison layout, its operation and security procedures, a description of guards' uniforms, and employee identification cards. She also gave cell phones to the two long-term inmates.

When the plot was uncovered, the prison was immediately locked down. Nobody was allowed in or out, except for two drivers and escorts—who then transferred the inmates who had tried to escape, to two different prisons.

Since Conover's time, another attempt to explore this still largely secret prison-world has been undertaken by Rhonda Moskowitz, who's making a film documentary about Sing Sing's Jewish inmates. The idea came to her after reading a *New York Times* article about Jewish prisoners celebrating Hanukkah in the prison.

Had she been plugging her idea to Hollywood producers demanding the plot in a nutshell, it might have been: "Men who committed unspeakable crimes, but still feel connected to their Jewish values." The title? "*American Prison: The Forgotten Jews.*" Her goal? "To humanize the prisoners and show their connection with religion." The budget? "About $700,000."[18]

She had phoned Sing Sing and asked if she could film about two dozen Jewish inmates, most serving long sentences for murder or manslaughter. She explained her project and soon after was making monthly visits to the prison with homemade cookies and a camera. At first she was astonished to be shaking hands with killers, but not for long. On Simchas Torah holiday, which celebrates the reading of the Torah, she was dancing with them in the chapel. On Hanukkah, she joined them for chicken soup and latkes made by the inmates. And she interviewed and filmed them for hours.

A *Boston Globe* reporter interviewed her in 2002, for a story headlined "Jewish Faith Behind Bars: Novice Filmmaker Documents Religion at Sing Sing Prison." She spoke of one man studying the Torah in his cell and another who had prevented fellow inmates from committing suicide. And she explained that what most interested her about the inmates was their capacity for redemption. She and the reporter then watched a roughly shot video on the TV screen showing Jewish prisoners celebrating Passover and singing Hebrew songs of freedom. She pointed out William Tager, a stout, bearded man, serving time for manslaughter. A paranoid schizophrenic, Tager had been obsessed with the idea that the television networks were tormenting him by bugging his home. That was his motive, he said, for fatally shooting Theron Montgomery, an NBC stagehand, outside the *Today* show studio, at Manhattan's Rockefeller Center in 1994.

Tager's arrest eventually helped to solve a mystery about the CBS news anchor Dan Rather. One night in October 1986, a well-dressed man had chased, punched, and kicked Rather on a Manhattan sidewalk, as he kept asking him, "Kenneth, what is the frequency?" Not getting an answer, he took off and disappeared. The attack baffled Rather and everyone else who heard of it for years. It inspired a hit song, the punch line to jokes, and any number of wisecracks. Rumors suggested that the attacker had been a KGB agent, or a jealous husband who simply got Rather's first name wrong.

Rather's emotion recollected in tranquility, was: "I got mugged. Who understands these things? I don't. . . . I didn't make a lot of it at the time and I don't now. I wish I knew who did it and why, but I have no idea."[19]

The mystery attack inspired a hit song, "What's the Frequency, Kenneth?" and Dan Rather accompanied the band R.E.M. in singing it when they appeared on David Letterman's *Late Show*. In 1997, while interviewing Tager in Sing Sing, where he was serving a sentence for killing Theron Montgomery, a psychiatrist identified him as Rather's mystery mugger. Tager also admitted that Rather was one of several media personalities he had blamed for beaming signals into his head, and believed that if he could find out the correct frequency, he could block the tormenting signals. When the *New York Daily News* sent Dan Rather photos of Tager, he identified him as his mugger. So the decades-old mystery was solved. "Everybody's had their guess about what happened, and some have had fun with it," he told the newspaper. "Now the facts are out. My biggest regret is he wasn't caught before he killed someone."[20]

Should anyone be in doubt, New York district attorney Robert M. Morgenthau officially confirmed the account, writing to the *New York Times* in November 2004: "In the course of our prosecution, Mr. Tager made detailed statements admitting the earlier assault on Mr. Rather. . . . Mr. Tager's knowledge of nonpublic details of the attack on Mr. Rather, along with other facts and circumstances, left no doubt about his guilt. A prosecution for assault was precluded by the statute of limitations, but Mr. Tager, now 56, was sentenced to 12½ to 25 years on manslaughter and weapons charges."[21]

Rhonda Moskowitz, who calls Tager "Manny," concluded: "People are not all good or all bad; but mixed. We're shocked when good people do bad things, but what about bad people doing good things?"[22]

Many might consider Anthony Papa, the twenty-nine-year-old owner of a radio repair business in the Bronx, a bad person. Desperate for money, with a wife and small daughter to support, and with his business failing, Papa agreed to a bowling partner's proposition—to deliver an envelope containing 4½ ounces of cocaine for $500. The bowling partner happened to be a part of a police sting operation. As Papa recalled: "Twenty undercover cops came out of nowhere and put me under arrest. The individual who put me up actually had three sealed indictments and worked for the police. The more people he drew into the operation the less time he got. This is standard procedure in New York City. Rapists and murderers get away with less." But the judge couldn't give him less, because the Rockefeller Drug Laws mandate a fifteen-year-to-life sentence for selling two ounces or possessing more than four ounces of cocaine.

In prison Papa found some relief from his loneliness, grief, and boredom by acquiring two college degrees and attending a graduate New York Theological Seminary course. An education supervisor recalled: "He was lost; he didn't know what was going on. Then he discovered art and it just grabbed him."[23] Despite the restrictions on most painting materials such as metal, wood, and flammable material, he improvised: he cleaned his brushes with cooking oil, and used toilet paper cardboard as a palette knife. Guards confiscated as contraband some of his political paintings that protested the system.

After several years his wife divorced him. In 1994 his self-portrait, titled *15 Years to Life,* was chosen for exhibition in the Whitney Museum of American Art—and it brought public attention to his case.

Two years later, on December 23, 1996, a guard ordered Papa to leave the yard and go to the office of the deputy of security. Papa anticipated that some of his political paintings were going to be confiscated as contraband—as they had been previously. Expecting at best a disciplinary ticket, at worst, time in solitary, he was surprised to find the deputy of security smiling, "I just got off the phone with the governor [Pataki], he said." And when Papa heard the "magic word—clemency—he fell against the wall and cried." In 2004, he wrote of his experiences in *15 Years to Life: How I Painted My Way to Freedom,* in which he exposed "the vice that went on there, that female correction officers sell their bodies, prostitution, selling drugs."[24] He also sold the film rights.

Papa told *Nation* reporter Rebecca Tuhus-Dubron that in prison, "besides my gift in art, I also discovered my potential awareness. Prison is a very spiritual place. That's something very mystical about spending time in a cage for [twelve] years, you discover who you are."[25]

He became an outspoken advocate against the war on drugs, and was the keynote speaker at a large drug-law reform rally in Albany, New York. He cofounded Mother's of the N.Y. Disappeared to spotlight the unfairness of the Rockefeller Drug Laws. Papa also visited Spofford Correctional Facility for Youth where he was distressed to see ten-to-fifteen-year-old boys and girls incarcerated, many for substance-abuse offenses. He realized that, unless something was done, the boys were destined for Sing Sing.

During the week of December 6, 2004, the New York Legislature agreed to reduce the penalty for first-time drug offenses and to increase the amount of narcotics in the possession of a suspect to qualify as a serious felony. It also let prisoners, serving time for drug offenses, apply for a reduced sentence.

Papa's view of Sing Sing as a former inmate is of a much grimmer hellhole than was portrayed by Ted Conover. In Papa's Sing Sing, the inmates rule and almost everything's up for sale.

As Papa told *Counterpunch* interviewer Lucy Herschel, "Sing Sing was a cesspool. Parts of the prison were like the old Times Square—you could buy any type of weapon, TV sets, any form of contraband, drugs. There were more drugs in Sing Sing than on the streets. The point I like to make is, if you can't control drugs in a maximum-security prison how can you control drugs in a free society?"[26]

Ted Conover responded to my questions about Papa's stay at Sing Sing: "Papa was a prisoner during one of Sing Sing's dark periods—a time in the 60s and 70s when corruption was rife and there were many scandals. And not only at Sing Sing—this was a low point for other infamous prisons, such as Massachusetts' Walpole. I wouldn't say that Sing Sing has gone from being like the old Times Square to the new Times Square—a prisoner can still procure drugs there (as in almost every prison)—but it's much, much different. I never saw a contraband TV or heard of an actual contraband gun, and things are done much more according to the book. The big contraband concern today in many prisons is cell phones."

The warden's character seems vital to the prison environment. When Conover was there, Greiner was in charge and, according to Conover, "he had a reputation as tough and firm—a guard's guard. He struck me as measured and even-tempered, and I think that was the impression other officers had of him, as well."[27]

AFTERWORD

SING SING TODAY AND TOMORROW

Brian Fischer followed Greiner as warden (superintendent) on May 4, 2000, and has since found that real estate agents have got it right: location is everything. Sing Sing's location largely explains its security problems.

Sing Sing is surrounded by a security nightmare—being close to high-traffic areas, private housing, public roads, a river, a county sewage treatment plant, a public park, and has railroad tracks running right through it.

That railroad divides the fifty-five-acre prison in two. Today, the western area between the railroad tracks and the Hudson River, called Tappan, is surrounded by a sixteen-foot-high fence, and houses up to 482 medium-security prisoners. All have been categorized as nonviolent and medium-security risks and are in for three years or less. The area also contains athletic, education, and storage buildings.

The main maximum-security prison is designed to hold 1,757 inmates and is enclosed on the east, northeast, and southeast by a twenty-four-foot-high concrete wall. The west, northwest, and southwest edges have a sixteen-foot-high fence topped with razor wire. Eighteen guard towers have been built at intervals around the perimeter, occupied around the clock by armed guards. Other armed guards in vehicles patrol the prison grounds and buildings outside the walls. The entire fenced perimeter is lit at night, and electronic sensors have been installed near the railroad tracks.

Minorities, especially poorly educated young African American males, have increasingly ended up in prison, some having chosen a life of crime

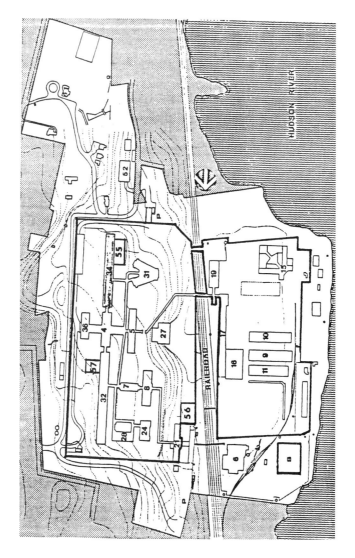

Fig. 51. An Overview. Buildings on Sing Sing's fifty-five acres: Housing, 5, 7, 8, 9, 10, 11, 32, (A-Block Housing) 33, A-Block Recreation, 57; (B-Block Housing), 34; B-Block Recreation, 55; B-Block Visiting, 56; A-Block Food Service, 4, 36; Recreation, 15, 16, 31; Visitors, 19, 21; Registry, 17; Administration, 21, 41; Powerhouse, 6, 52; Parking, P; Parking garage, 27; Laundry, 24; Education, 19; County Sewage Plant, 8. The western section of the prison on the Hudson River and divided from the main prison by a railroad houses medium-security prisoners and is known as Tappan. (New York State Archives)

rather than having taken the miserable, poverty-level jobs available to them. Some suggest it would be cheaper and much safer to send them all to Harvard, which is probably true. (The per capita cost for Sing Sing inmates in fiscal year 2003–2004 was $29,906.) Most are handicapped from the start by America's unfair education system, in which, as children, they go to underfunded, underequipped schools where even the best teachers are hamstrung by discipline problems.

In America today there are 685 prisoners per 100,000 people. The countries of the European Union have 87 prisoners for every 100,000 people. Sing Sing inmates today are overwhelming the poor; the sick, mentally and physically; the drug-addicted; the uneducated; and, of course, the career criminals. What more can be done for those in prison than to reward those who play by the rules, treat the sick, educate the illiterate, and train the willing for work that may await them when they're set free?

While in prison, all able inmates must either work or attend treatment or educational programs twice a day. And they work almost everywhere: the kitchen, the infirmary, the commissary, and on maintenance, including the lawns and grounds. Each program period lasts three hours—one in the morning and one after lunch. The employed inmates are paid from ten cents to $2.58 an hour, and work for six hours a day, five days a week.

Because federal and state funds for college education in Sing Sing were cut in 1995, three years later a group of volunteers in conjunction with Mercy College, of Dobbs Ferry, New York, established the nonprofit Hudson Link for Higher Education in Prison, to prepare its students for constructive and meaningful lives when they leave prison.

To the stirring strains of "Pomp and Circumstance" played on a flute, its first graduates, twenty men serving long sentences for murder, manslaughter, robbery, and criminal possession, marched in academic caps and gowns to hear opening remarks by Warden Fischer and a commencement address by the esteemed African American actor-writer-director Ossie Davis.

The sixteen graduating bachelors of science, and four associates of science, had worked during the day and studied at nights up until 11 PM, when the lights went out. One had spoken only Chinese until he went to prison; another, a fourth-grade dropout, had been unable to read or write.

Some professors had been anxious about teaching in Sing Sing, but, one of them, Rosemarie Murray, said that, because the inmates were so eager to learn, most came away inspired by the experience.

During the graduation ceremony, Warden Fischer said: "No college is like the college at Sing Sing. It offers hope to anyone who is willing to change. These men have changed and become role models for the prison."[1] Seventy-five more inmates have since signed up for the program.

In his commencement address, Ossie Davis said, "You are on the verge of seeing an old man cry. . . . In order to change the world, you must change yourself." He explained that Malcolm X was one of his personal heroes because, "He started on the negative side of society and through incarceration found his way to clarity and change. Using his mind he became a leader of men, as you are. . . . I thank you for the gift you give me by enriching the end of my life. God bless you. Now go and do good works."[2] (Ossie Davis died at age eighty-seven, on February 4, 2005, in his Miami Beach hotel room, while making a movie titled *Retirement.*)

Shelley Alkin, dean of academic advisory at Mercy College, told a reporter that a few of the graduates may never be paroled from prison, "but their children will go to college and they will follow in the footsteps of college graduates, not prison inmates."[3]

The impact on children of having relatives in prison was the subject of the novel *Visiting Day*, by Jacqueline Woodson, who based the story on her own moving memories of trips to see her uncle Rober Leon Irby, a Sing Sing inmate. The Osborne Association, named after Thomas Mott Osborne, decided to sponsor a movie based on her book. Warden Fischer welcomed the film crew and actors into his prison to enhance its authenticity. (Woodson's *Visiting Day* was shown on TV's PBS-Channel 13 on December 15, 2004, and again on January 17, 2005.) Some guards were filmed at their routine assignments and the man who was the focus of the film was, in fact, a Sing Sing inmate.

When I asked Woodson about her Sing Sing visits as a child, she replied:

I remember the feeling of the gates shutting behind me when we visited my uncle [with relatives]. I think that feeling never went away. My uncle was in and out of jail from the time he was about 19. We were never told [what crimes he was in for]. So I truly don't know. The people who would know— my grandmother and my uncle—have died. He was the youngest boy, spoiled, I'd say, and very, very good looking. A hustler, I know now— flashy dresser, beautiful women always around him. He danced like James Brown, and was as smooth as anything. I absolutely adored him.

I remember the long bus rides up to Sing Sing—I wrote one of my first pieces at the age of seven on a bus traveling to Ossining. I don't know if my mom and grandma referred to it as Sing Sing—NO ONE in our neighborhood EVER admitted they had a relative in prison. But just about everyone had a relative who had "decided to move upstate." In my book, *Locomotion*, the character's foster brother moves upstate—at first it was going to be that he was in prison—admitted in the text. But then I decided to write it the way "I" remember it—"the need to be upstate for a while."

Prisons didn't rehabilitate my uncle—it finally broke his spirit. He came home—at the age of 40 and never went back again. But then he was diabetic and had high blood pressure. He died at 47 from complications of the diabetes, from never taking his medication. I say he committed suicide, gave up.[4]

More recently there have been attempts in Sing Sing to further encourage and rehabilitate the inmates, for example, under the auspices of Rehabilitation Through the Arts (RTA), a theater program for inmates founded by Katherine Vockins. In January 2003 Warden Fischer and his deputy went backstage to pray with inmates for the success of a play, *Stratford's Decision*, a comedy written, codirected, and performed by inmates in Elizabethan costumes. The integrated cast gave three performances for fellow inmates and one for an invited audience of several hundred civilians. Apparently the prayers were answered, with laughter throughout—especially when the queen's jester followed a sedate minuet by courtiers with a break dance.

That December, Warden Fischer was presented with a silver plaque to honor Sing Sing employees. They had donated $5,000 to support the North East Knights basketball team at the Special Olympics New York Summer Games for the mentally retarded, held at Long Island's Hofstra University.

Among the welcome visitors to the prison today is Kobutsu Shindo, a Buddhist priest who lives across the river in Ramsey, New Jersey, and teaches inmates how to practice Zen contemplation. His published newsletter is received by over six hundred inmates.

Sing Sing continues to be a magnet for movie and TV companies in search of authentic location scenes. Jesse L. Martin and Dennis Farina were there in 2004, filming an episode of *Law and Order*. Billy Crystal and Robert De Niro went in 2002, and again in 2004, to film scenes for *Analyze This* and its sequel, *Analyze That*, about a mob boss and his psychiatrist.

There are moves afoot to let the public into the still largely secret world of Sing Sing. Both County Executive Andrew Spano and Warden Brian Fischer have backed a plan to create a Sing Sing museum, encouraged by the news that more than fifty prison museums around the world, including Alcatraz on the west coast, are great tourist attractions.

There already is a small private Sing Sing Prison Museum in the nearby town of Ossining in which visitors can examine a replica of the electric chair made by inmates in the Building Maintenance Vocation Class of 1991, two prison cells, and several homemade weapons confiscated from inmates. The proposed more comprehensive Sing Sing museum would probably be in the prison's former power plant. But "the heart of the plan," writes Michael Hill, "calls for opening up a portion of the original cell block, which housed inmates until the 1940s. Today, the five-story structure is a stone shell of itself after damage from a fire in the 1980s. Its walls are crumbling slightly at the top and weeds sprout from its blacktop floor."[5] Tourists would reach it through a tunnel.

The National Trust for Historic Preservation and Historic Hudson Valley enthusiastically support the plan.

No one has yet suggested resurrecting Chapin's flower gardens.

"Sing Sing has a history to it," Warden Fischer said. "Why deny that history to the public?"[6]

NOTES

CHAPTER ONE: RIDING THE TIGER (1821-1839)

1. Gustave de Beaumont and Alexis de Tocqueville, *On the Penitentiary System of the United States*, trans. Francis Lieber (New York: Augustus M. Kelley, 1970).

2. Carl Sifakis, *Encyclopedia of American Crime* (New York: Facts on File, 1982), p. 450.

3. Thomas A. Bailey, *The American Pageant: A History of the Republic* (Boston: A. C. Heath, 1956), p. 257.

4. According to Herbert Asbury in his 1927 book, *The Gangs of New York.*

5. Dr. Fosgate, *New York Times,* February 18, 1852.

6. Ted Conover, *Newjack: Guarding Sing Sing* (New York: Random House, 2000), p. 175.

7. De Tocqueville letter to Abbe Lesueur, Beinecke Rare Book and Manuscript Library, Yale University.

8. George Wilson Pierson, *Tocqueville and Beaumont in America* (New York: Oxford University Press, 1938), p. 102.

9. Ibid., p. 101.

10. De Beaumont and de Tocqueville, *On the Penitentiary System of the United States*, p. 209.

11. Ibid., p. 211.

12. Sifakis, *Encyclopedia of American Crime*, p. 451.

13. Pierson, *Tocqueville in America*, pp. 102–103.

14. W. David Lewis, "From Newgate to Dannemora: The Female Criminal and the Prisons of New York," *New York History* 42 (October 1961), and Ithaca, NY: Cornell University Press, 1965).

15. Sifakis, *Encyclopedia of American Crime*, p. 451.
16. Conover, *Newjack*, pp. 180–81.

CHAPTER TWO: ANOTHER REIGN OF TERROR (1840-1859)

1. John Luckey, *Life in Sing Sing State Prison, as Seen in a Twelve Years' Chaplaincy* (New York: N. Tibbals, 1860), pp. 244–45.
2. Ibid., p. 245.
3. Ibid.

CHAPTER THREE: ABRAHAM LINCOLN PASSES THROUGH (1860-1887)

1. Lewis E. Lawes, *Twenty Thousand Years in Sing Sing* (New York: R. Long and R. R. Smith, 1932), p. 97.
2. Ibid., p. 87.
3. Ibid., p. 96.
4. Ibid., pp. 89–91.
5. Ibid., p. 92.
6. Ibid., p. 98.

CHAPTER FOUR: THOMAS EDISON PROMOTES HIS RIVAL'S ELECTRIC CHAIR (1887-1904)

1. Lewis E. Lawes, *Twenty Thousand Years in Sing Sing* (New York: R. Long and R. R. Smith, 1932), p. 98.
2. *New York Herald*, July 31, 1888, p. 1.
3. *New York Times*, July 31, 1888, p. 1.
4. Craig Brandon, *The Electric Chair, An Unnatural American History* (Jefferson, NC: McFarland, 1999), p. 174.
5. Ibid., p. 173.
6. "A Roasting of Human Flesh in Prison—Strong Men Sickened and Turned from the Sight," *New York World*, August 7, 1890, p. 1.
7. *New York Times*, August 7, 1890, p. 2.
8. Lewis E. Lawes, *Meet the Murderer* (New York: Harper & Bros., 1940), p. 13.
9. The source for this account is *Then, Now and Tomorrow: The History of Sing Sing*, published by the warden, John P. Keane, assisted by Sing Sing employees and inmates, 1996.

10. Lawes, *Meet the Murderer*, pp. 13, 14.

11. Amos O. Squire, MD, *Sing Sing Doctor* (Garden City, NY: Garden City Publishing, 1937), pp. 2–4.

12. Lawes, *Twenty Thousand Years*, p. 10.

CHAPTER FIVE: THE CONVICT WHO TRAPPED HIMSELF AND THE GREAT RIVER DISASTER (1904-1914)

1. *New York Times*, December 21, 1906, p. 3.

2. Ibid., July 18, 1907, p. 14.

3. Ibid., July 19, 1907, p. 4.

4. Ibid., October 8, 1910.

5. Ibid., p. 2.

6. Ibid., January 27, 1911, p. 1.

7. Amos O. Squire, MD, *Sing Sing Doctor* (Garden City, NY: Garden City Publishing, 1937), p. 141.

8. Ibid.

9. Ibid.

10. Ibid., p. 147.

11. *New York Times*, May 13, 1913, p. 7.

12. Grand Jury Report, Westchester County, June 19, 1913.

13. Lewis E. Lawes, *Twenty Thousand Years in Sing Sing* (New York: R. Long and R. R. Smith, 1932), p. 103.

14. *New York Times* editorial, November 18, 1913, p. 10.

15. "Sir Arthur Conan Doyle Visits and Criticizes Sing Sing Prison," *New York Times*, May 31, 1914, p. 1.

16. Arthur Conan Doyle, *Memories and Adventures* (Boston: Little, Brown & Co., 1924), p. 289.

17. *New York Times*, July 7, 1914, p. 4.

18. Ibid., July 10, 1914.

19. Ibid., October 5, 1914, p. 10.

20. Frank Tannenbaum, *Osborne of Sing Sing* (Chapel Hill: University of North Carolina Press, 1933), pp. 66–67.

CHAPTER SIX: WARDEN OSBORNE— THE VOLUNTARY PRISONER (1913-1920)

1. Thomas Mott Osborne, *Within Prison Walls: Being a Narrative of Personal Experience During a Week of Voluntary Confinement in the State Prison at Auburn, New York* (Rome, NY: Spruce Gulch Press, 1914), pp. 16, 17, 18.

2. Ibid., p. 18n.

3. Ibid., p. 153.

4. Frank Tannenbaum, *Osborne of Sing Sing* (Chapel Hill: University of North Carolina Press, 1933), pp. 67, 68.

5. Ibid., pp. 66–67.

6. Ibid., p. 68.

7. Thomas Mott Osborne, *Prisons and Common Sense* (New York: J. B. Lippincott, 1924), pp. 8, 9.

8. Tannenbaum, *Osborne of Sing Sing*, p. 35.

9. Ibid.

10. Ted Conover, *Newjack: Guarding Sing Sing* (New York: Random House, 2000), pp. 197, 198.

11. Francis Hackett, "Are Convicts Human?" *New Republic*, January 15, 1916, p. 274.

12. Ibid.

13. Tannenbaum, *Osborne of Sing Sing*, p. 69.

14. August Heckscher, interviewed by Paul Cummings for the Smithsonian Archives of Art, May 1970.

15. Osborne, *Prisons and Common Sense*, p. 89.

16. Rudolph W. Chamberlain, *There Is No Truce: A Life of Thomas Mott Osborne* (New York: Macmillan, 1935), p. 293.

17. Ibid., p. 294.

18. Osborne, *Prisons and Common Sense*, p. 75.

19. Thomas Mott Osborne, *Society and Prisons* (New Haven, CT: Yale University Press, 1916), p. 192.

20. Scott Christianson, *With Liberty for Some: 500 Years of Imprisonment in America* (Boston: Northeastern University Press, 1998), pp. 210, 211.

21. Ibid., p. 211.

22. Chamberlain, *There Is No Truce*, p. 300.

23. Osborne, *Prisons and Common Sense*, pp. 86–87.

24. Chamberlain, *There Is No Truce*, p. 306.

25. Tannenbaum, *Osborne of Sing Sing*, p. 110.

26. Chamberlain, *There Is No Truce*, pp. 313–14.

27. Ibid., p. 314.

28. Ibid., p. 319.

29. Ibid., p. 330.

30. Ibid., p. 329.

31. Ibid., pp. 349–50.

32. Ibid., p. 349.

33. Ibid., p. 347.

34. "Whitman Forced Osborne Out," *New York Times*, December 31, 1915, p. 4.

35. Hackett, "Are Convicts Human?" p. 273.

36. Amos O. Squire, MD, *Sing Sing Doctor* (Garden City, NY: Garden City Publishing, 1937), pp. 157, 58.

37. Ibid., p. 160.

38. Ibid., pp. 165, 166.

39. Ibid., p. 167.

40. "Bryan at Peekskill Praises Soldiers," *New York Times*, July 5, 1916, p. 18.

41. "Convicts' Carnival Welcome Osborne: Prisoners in Costume and Wild with Joy," *New York Times*, July 17, 1916, p. 1.

42. Michael L. Radelet, Hugo Adam Bedau, and Constance E. Putnam, *In Spite of Innocence* (Boston: Northeastern University Press, 1992), p. 284.

43. Tannenbaum, *Osborne of Sing Sing*, p. 359.

44. Ibid.

45. Lewis E. Lawes, *Twenty Thousand Years in Sing Sing* (New York: R. Long and R. R. Smith, 1932), pp. 106, 107.

CHAPTER SEVEN: WARDEN LAWES AND THE ROSE MAN OF SING SING (1920-1929)

1. The quotes attributed to Lewis Lawes and not specifically sourced are from his books *Twenty Thousand Years in Sing Sing* (New York: R. Long and R. R. Smith, 1932), *Invisible Stripes* (New York: Farrar and Rinehart, 1938), and *Life and Death in Sing Sing* (New York: Doubleday, 1928).

2. Ibid.

3. Ibid.

4. Lewis E. Lawes, *Meet the Murderer* (New York: Harper & Bros., 1940), pp. 133, 134–37.

5. Lawes, *Twenty Thousand Years*, pp. 301–303.

6. Steve Weinberg, *Armand Hammer: The Untold Story* (Boston: Little, Brown, 1989), p. 31.

7. Lawes, *Twenty Thousand Years*, pp. 121, 122.

8. Ibid.

9. Harold Kellock and Beatrice Houdini, *Houdini: His Life Story from the Recollections and Documents of Beatrice Houdini* (New York: Blue Ribbon Books, 1931), p. 344.

10. Charles Chaplin, *My Autobiography* (New York: Simon and Schuster, 1964).

11. Lawes, *Twenty Thousand Years*, pp. 227, 228.

12. Ibid., p. 230.

13. Ibid.

14. Ibid., p. 231.

15. James McGrath Morris, *The Rose Man of Sing Sing: A True Tale of Life, Murder, and Redemption in the Age of Yellow Journalism* (New York: Fordham University Press, 2003), p. 7.

16. "Makes Prison Yards a Thing of Beauty," *New York Times*, October 19, 1934, p. 27.

17. Peter Maas, *The Valachi Papers* (New York: Putnam's, 1958), p. 77.

18. Ralph Blumenthal, *Miracle at Sing Sing: How One Man Transformed the Lives of America's Most Dangerous Prisoners* (New York: St. Martin's, 2004), pp. 128–29.

19. Ibid., pp. 136–37.

20. Amos O. Squire, MD, *Sing Sing Doctor* (Garden City, NY: Garden City Publishing, 1937), pp. 199, 200.

21. Ibid., p. 200.

22. Blumenthal, *Miracle at Sing Sing*, p. 100.

23. Ibid., pp. 185–86.

24. James Cagney, *Cagney by Cagney* (New York: Doubleday, 1976), pp. 24, 25.

25. Ibid., p. 25.

26. Ibid.

27. Damon Runyon, *Trials and Other Tribulations* (New York: Lippincott, 1946), pp. 139, 140, 141, 142, 152.

28. Ibid., p. 144.

29. Denis Brian, *Murderers Die* (New York: St. Martin's, 1986), pp. 31–36.

30. Morris, *Rose Man of Sing Sing*, MS p. 418.

31. Lawes, *Twenty Thousand Years*, pp. 234, 235.

32. Ibid., pp. 139–40.

CHAPTER EIGHT: MURDER INCORPORATED AND THE MOVIES (1930-1949)

1. Denis Brian, *Murderers Die* (New York: St. Martin's, 1986), p. 50.

2. Ibid., p. 68.

3. Ibid., pp. 68, 69.

4. Ibid., p. 69.

5. Wenzell Brown, *Women Who Went to the Chair* (New York: Collier Books, 1963), p. 113.

6. Michael L. Radelet, Hugo Adam Bedan, and Constance E. Putnam, *In Spite of Innocence: The Ordeal of 400 Americans Wrongly Convicted of Crimes Punishable by Death* (Boston: Northeastern University Press, 1992), p. 344.

7. Harold Mehling, "The Two Faces of Richard Whitney," in *Scoundrels and Scalawags* (New York: Reader's Digest, 1968), p. 253.

8. Ibid.

9. Lewis E. Lawes, *Twenty Thousand Years in Sing Sing* (New York: R. Long and R. R. Smith, 1932), p. 17.

10. Ralph Blumenthal, *Miracle at Sing Sing* (New York: St. Martin's, 2004), p. 262.

11. Quentin Reynolds, *Courtroom: The Story of Samuel S. Leibowitz* (New York: Farrar Straus and Giroux, 1950), p. 191.

12. Ibid., pp. 304–305.

13. Brian, *Murderers Die*, p. 226.

CHAPTER NINE: THE LONELY HEARTS KILLERS AND THE ROSENBERGS (1950-1982)

1. New York State Archives.

2. Ibid.

3. Camillo Weston Leyra with Richard Gehman, "My Five Years in Sing Sing's Death House," *American Weekly*, October 14, 1956, p. 24.

4. Denis Brian, *Murderers Die* (New York: St. Martin's, 1986), pp. 102–105.

5. Curt Gentry, *J. Edgar Hoover: The Man and the Secrets* (New York: Norton, 1991), p. 424.

6. Louis Nizer, *The Implosion Conspiracy* (New York: Doubleday, 1973), p. 413.

7. Jack V. Fox, "Sing Sing Boss Ends 40 Years at Prison Job," *New York Times*, January 11, 1967, p. C–20.

8. The Rosenberg Letters, New York State Archives.

9. Robert and Michael Meeropol, *We Are Your Sons: The Legacy of Ethel and Julius Rosenberg* (New York: Ballantine, 1976), p. 133.

10. Gentry, *J. Edgar Hoover*, p. 428.

11. Leyra and Gehman, *My Five Years*, p. 24.

12. Ibid.

13. Brian, *Murderers Die*, p. 132.

14. Michael L. Radelet, Hugo Adam Bedan, and Constance E. Putnam, *In Spite of Innocence: The Ordeal of 400 Americans Wrongly Convicted of Crimes Punishable by Death* (Boston: Northeastern University Press, 1992), pp. 331, 332.

15. Craig Brandon, *The Electric Chair: An Unnatural American History* (Jefferson, NC: McFarland & Co., 1999), p. 240.

16. Radelet, Bedan, and Putnam, *In Spite of Innocence*, p. 354.

17. *New York Times*, January 11, 1967, p. C–20.

18. Ben Cheever, ed., *The Letters of John Cheever* (New York: Simon & Schuster, 1988), Letters: May 9, 1971, and end of May 1971.

19. Susan Cheever, "A Duel of Cheevers," *Newsweek*, March 14, 1977, pp. 69, 70.

20. Susan Sheehan, *A Prison and a Prisoner* (Boston: Houghton Mifflin, 1978), pp. 14–19.

21. Ibid.

22. James Lardner, *Crusader: The Hell-Raising Career of Detective David Durk* (New York: Random House, 1996), p. 204.

23. Official report by Scott Christianson for Gov. Mario Cuomo.

24. Ibid.

CHAPTER TEN: RIOTS AND REFORMS (1980s AND 1990s)

1. Steve Lerner, "Rule of the Cruel," *New Republic*, October 15, 1984, pp. 18, 19.

2. Ibid., p. 19.

3. *New York Times*, January 10 and 11, 1983, p. 1.

4. *New York Times*, January 12, 1983.

5. Mario M. Cuomo, *Diaries of Mario M. Cuomo: The Campaign for Governor* (New York: Random House, 1984), p. 14.

6. Ibid., p. 39n.

7. Ibid., pp. 259, 260.

8. *New York Times*, January 12, 1983, p. 1.

9. Almost all quotes concerning the 1983 Sing Sing riot are from Scott Christianson's official report for Gov. Mario Cuomo.

10. Ibid.

11. Ronald Sullivan, "New York State Prisoners Work or Else," *New York Times*, January 27, 1992, p. B12.

12. Douglas Martin, "Field Trip! Destination Sing Sing," *New York Times*, May 25, 1991.

13. Ibid.

14. "The Rabbi at Sing Sing Tends an Isolated Flock," *New York Times*, April 22, 1992, p. B5.

15. Jonathan Mark, *The Jewish Week*, September 17, 1999, p. 4.

16. Press Release, New York State, Gov. Pataki's Press Office, March 7, 1995.

17. Alison S. Lebwohl, "Up the River," *AFSCME Public Employee Magazine*, July/August 1998, http://www.geocities.com/MotorCity/Downs/3548/facility/luther.html.

CHAPTER ELEVEN: RECOVERING THE PRISON'S MISSING ARCHIVES

1. Bob Keeler, "Is New York Ready to Kill Again?" *Newsday Magazine*, September 19, 1982, p. 36.

2. Isidore Zimmerman with Francis Bond, *Punishment without Crime: The True Story of a Man Who Spent Twenty-four Years in Prison for a Crime He Did Not Commit* (New York: American Weekly, 1964), p. 153.

3. This and all subsequent letters in this chapter are from the Sing Sing archives in Albany, New York.

4. Francis Moss, *The Rosenberg Espionage Case* (San Diego, CA: Lascent Books, 2000), pp. 93–94.

5. Michael Meeropol, July 17, 1995, Rosenberg Fund for Children.

6. Sing Sing archives.

7. Russ Tarby, "Riding the Lightning," *Syracuse New Times*, December 2, 2004, http://newtimes.rway.com/1998/081298/cover.htm.

8. Ibid.

9. Interview with Gladys Bohnsack, January 28, 2005.

CHAPTER TWELVE: SING SING IN THE TWENTY-FIRST CENTURY

1. Ted Conover, *Newjack: Guarding Sing Sing* (New York: Random House, 2000), pp. 132–35.

2. Ibid., pp. 138–44.

3. Joanne Mariner, *No Escape: Male Rape in U.S. Prisons* (New York: Human Rights Watch, April 2001).

4. "Sing Sing Sexcapades," *NewYork Daily News*, January 30, 1988, pp. 1–2.

5. Conover, *Newjack*, p. 263.

6. Ibid., pp. 262, 263.

7. Associated Press, May 7, 2004.

8. Conover, *Newjack*, p. 242.

9. Ibid., p. 270.

10. Ibid., p. 271.

11. Ibid., pp. 259–61.

12. Ibid., pp. 144, 145.

13. Ibid., pp. 148–51.

14. Ibid., pp. 282–83.

15. Ted Conover e-mail to author, December 24, 2004.

16. Bob Minzesheimer, "Escape into Reading Takes a Literal Turn," *USA Today*, February 12, 2004, http://www.usatoday.com/life/books/news/2004-02-11-newjack _x.htm.

17. Jeanine Pirro, DA, Westchester County, Press Release, September 9, 2004.

18. "Jewish Faith Behind Bars: Novice Filmmaker Documents Religion at Sing Sing Prison," *Boston Globe*, July 14, 2002, http://www.shininglightproductions.com/ _wsn/page3.html.

19. Yahoo! June 19, 2001, http://ask.yahoo.com/ask/20010619.html.

20. Marcus Errico, "Now Rather Knows 'the Frequency,'" *E! Online News*, January 29, 1997, http://www.eonline.com/News/Items/0,1,613,00.html.

21. Robert M. Morgenthau, *New York Times*, November 5, 2004, Letter to the editor.

22. "Jewish Faith Behind Bars."

23. Anthony Papa interviewed by Amy Goodman and Ellis Henican, Democracy Now, December 18, 2004, http://www.democracynow.org.

24. Ibid.

25. Rebecca Tuhus-Dubrow, "Talking with Anthony Papa," *Nation*, December 9, 2004, http://www.thenation.com/doc.mhtml%3Fi=20041227&s=tuhusdubrow.

26. Lucy Herschel, "An Interview with Artist Anthony Papa," *Counterpunch*, December 4/6, 2004, http://www.counterpunch.org/herschel12042004.html.

27. Ted Conover e-mail to author, January 10, 2005.

AFTERWORD: SING SING TODAY AND TOMORROW

1. Betsy Guest, "Commencement at Sing Sing," Hudson Link for Higher Education.

2. Ibid., and Marcela Rojas, "A Day of Pride at Sing Sing," *New York Journal News*, June 6, 2004, p. 1A.

3. Carin Rubenstein, "A Bachelor's Redemption: At Sing Sing Prison, Inmates Broaden Horizons Through Education," Hudson Link for Higher Education.

4. Jacqueline Woodson e-mail to author, February 4, 2005.

5. Michael Hill, *Associated Press*, August 8, 2001.

6. Ibid.

SELECT BIBLIOGRAPHY

Allen, Barry E., and Clifford E. Simonsen. *Corrections in America.* New York: Macmillan, 1986.

Asbury, Herbert. *The Gangs of New York.* 1927. Reprint, New York: Thunder's Mouth Press, 2003.

Bedam, Hugo Adam, ed. *The Death Penalty in America.* New York: Anchor, 1964.

Bernstein, Iver. *The New York City Draft Riots.* New York: Oxford University Press, 1990.

Blumenthal, Ralph. *Miracle at Sing Sing.* New York: St. Martin's Press, 2004.

Brian, Denis. *Murderers Die.* New York: St. Martin's, 1986.

Brown, Wenzell. *Women Who Died in the Chair.* New York: Collier Books, 1958.

Cagney, James. *Cagney by Cagney.* New York: Doubleday, 1976.

Chamberlain, Rudolph W. *There Is No Truce: The Life of Thomas Mott Osborne.* New York: Macmillan, 1935.

Chaplin, Charles. *My Autobiography.* New York: Simon and Schuster, 1964.

Cheever, Benjamin, ed. *The Letters of John Cheever.* New York: Simon and Schuster, 1988.

Cheli, Guy. *Sing Sing Prison, Images of America.* Mount Pleasant, NC: Arcadia Publishing, 2003.

Christianson, Scott. *With Liberty for Some: 500 Years of Imprisonment in America.* Boston: Northeastern University Press, 1998.

———. *Condemned: Inside the Sing Sing Death House.* New York: New York University Press, 2000.

Conan Doyle, Arthur. *Memories and Adventures.* Boston: Little, Brown, 1924.

Conover, Ted. *Newjack: Guarding Sing Sing.* New York: Random House, 2000.

Danforth, Harold R., and James D. Horan. *The D.A.'s Man.* New York: Crown, 1957.

De Beaumont, Gustave, and Alexis de Tocqueville. *On the Penitentiary System in the United States and Its Application in France.* New York: Augustus Kelley, 1970.

Dewey, Thomas E. *Twenty Against the Underworld.* New York: Doubleday, 1974.

Douglas, Warren, with James Cagney. *Cagney.* New York: St. Martin's Press, 1983.

Elliott, Robert G., with Albert R. Beatty. *Agent of Death.* New York: Dutton, 1940.

Fowler, Gene. *The Great Mouthpiece: A Life of William J. Fallon.* New York: Bantam, 1962.

Frank, Judge Jerome, and Barbara Frank with Harold M. Hoffman. *Not Guilty.* New York: Doubleday, 1957.

Furneaux, Rupert. *Courtroom U.S.A.2.* Baltimore, MD: Penguin, 1963.

Gaddis, Thomas E., and James O. Long. *Killer: A Journey of Murder.* New York: Macmillan, 1970.

Glueck, Bernard. *Studies in Forensic Medicine.* Boston: Little, Brown, 1916.

Gosch, Martin A., and Richard Hammer. *The Last Testament of Lucky Luciano.* Boston: Little, Brown, 1975.

Graham, David, and Ted Robert Gurr. *The History of Violence in America.* New York: Bantam, 1969.

Hughes, Rupert. *The Complete Detective.* New York: Sheridan House, 1950.

Ives, George. *A History of Penal Methods: Criminals, Witches, Lunatics.* Montclair, NJ: Patterson Smith, 1970.

Joyce, James Avery. *Capital Punishment: A World View.* New York: Grove Press, 1961.

Kellock, Harold. *Houdini: His Life-Story.* New York: Blue Ribbon Books, 1931.

Kessner, Thomas. *Fiorello H. La Guardia and the Making of Modern New York.* New York: McGraw-Hill, 1989.

Lawes, Lewis E. *Life and Death in Sing Sing.* New York: Doubleday, 1928.

———. *Twenty Thousand Years in Sing Sing.* New York: R. Long and R. R. Smith, 1932.

———. *Cell 202—Sing Sing.* New York: Farrar and Rinehart, 1935.

———. *Meet the Murderer.* New York: Harper & Bros., 1940.

Lewis, W. David. "The Female Criminal and the Prisons of New York." *New York History* 42 (October 1961).

Longstreet, Stephen. *City on Two Rivers.* New York: Hawthorn, 1975.

Luckey, John. *Life in Sing Sing State Prison, as Seen in a Twelve Years' Chaplaincy.* New York: N. Tibbals, 1860.

Maas, Peter. *The Valachi Papers.* New York: Putnam's, 1968.

McKelway, St. Clair. *Gossip: The Life and Times of Walter Winchell.* New York: Viking, 1940.

Meeropol, Robert, and Michael Meeropol. *We Are Your Sons: The Legacy of Ethel and Julius Rosenberg.* New York: Ballantine, 1976.

Morris, James McGrath. *The Rose Man of Sing Sing: A True Tale of Life, Murder, and Redemption in the Age of Yellow Journalism.* New York: Fordham University Press, 2003.

Nash, Jay Robert. *Bloodletters and Bad Men.* New York: Warner, 1975.

Nizer, Louis. *The Implosion Conspiracy.* New York: Doubleday, 1973.

Osborne, Thomas Mott. *Within Prison Walls: Being a Narrative of Personal Experiences During a Week of Voluntary Confinement in the State Prison at Auburn.* New York: Spruce Gulch Press, 1914.

———. *Society and Prisons.* New Haven, CT: Yale University Press, 1916.

———. *Prisons and Common Sense.* New York: J. B. Lippincott, 1924.

Persico, Joseph E. *The Imperial Rockefeller.* New York: Simon and Schuster, 1982.

Pierson, George Wilson. *Tocqueville in America.* Baltimore: Johns Hopkins, 1996.

Powers, Richard. *The Life of J. Edgar Hoover.* New York: Macmillan, 1987.

Radelet, Michael L., Hugo Adam Bedan, and Constance E. Putnam. *In Spite of Innocence: The Ordeal of 400 Americans Wrongly Convicted of Crimes Punishable by Death.* Boston: Northeastern University Press, 1992.

Radosh, Ronald, and Joyce Milton. *The Rosenberg File: A Search for the Truth.* New York: Holt, Rinehart & Winston, 1983.

Reynolds, Quentin. *Courtroom: The Story of Samuel Leibowitz.* New York: Farrar, Straus, 1950.

Ricky, Jay. *Learned Pigs and Fireproof Women.* New York: Villard, 1986.

Ross, Ishbel. *Ladies of the Press.* New York: Harper & Brothers, 1936.

Sann, Paul. *The Lawless Decade.* New York: Fawcett, 1971.

Schneir, Miriam, and Walter Schneir. *Invitation to an Inquest.* New York: Pantheon, 1983.

Seedman, Albert A., and Peter Hellman. *Chief!* New York: Arthur Fields, 1974.

Sheehan, Susan. *A Prison and a Prisoner.* Boston: Houghton Mifflin, 1978.

Sifakis, Carl. *Encyclopedia of American Crime.* New York: Facts on File, 1982.

Silberman, Charles E. *Criminal Violence, Criminal Justice.* New York: Random House, 1978.

Silverman, Kenneth. *Houdini!!! The Career of Ehrich Weiss.* New York: HarperCollins, 1996.

Squire, Dr. Amos O. *Sing Sing Doctor.* Garden City, NY: Garden City Publishing Co., 1937.

Swanberg, W. A. *Dreiser.* New York: Bantam, 1967.

Tannenbaum, Frank. *Osborne of Sing Sing.* Chapel Hill: University of North Carolina Press, 1933.

Thomas, Bob. *The Man and the Myth: Walter Winchell.* New York: Berkley, 1971.

Walker, Stanley. *City Editor.* New York: Frederick Stokes, 1934.

Weinberg, Steve. *Armand Hammer: The Untold Story.* Boston: Little, Brown, 1989.

Wellman, Francis L. *The Art of Cross Examination.* New York: Collier, 1962.

Wertham, Frederic. *A Sign of Cain: An Exploration of Human Violence.* New York: Macmillan, 1966.

INDEX

Adam, John Quincy, 11
Agron, Salvatore, "The Cape Man," escaped execution, 209
Allen, Woody (actor), 13
Appel, Chuck, "Baked Appel," executed, 153
Applegate, Everett, executed, 156
Attica Prison, 113, (riots) 194, 198
Auburn Prison, 12, 15, 16, 18, 25, 52, 54, 55, 78, 83, 85, 89, 98, 113

Baez, Joan (singer), 13
Barrett, Garrick (chaplain), 23, 24
Batterman, C. A. (chaplain), 37, 38
Beardsley, William (warden), 38
Beaumont, Charles de, 25, 26
Beck, Martha, "Lonely Hearts Killer," 168–70, 170–75
Becker, Charles (police inspector), executed, 95–98
Black Sheep (prison football team), 145
Bloch, Emmanuel (Rosenbergs' attorney), 115, 177, 178, 179, 210
Blumenthal, Ralph (author), 133, 135, 161

Bly, Nellie (reporter), 13, 117, 118
Bohnsack, Gladys (last executioner's daughter), 220
Boy, Louis, gives blood for sick child, 164
Braverman, Rabbi S. (prison chaplain), 65
Brennan, Justice William J., 190
British House of Commons, 28
Bronson, Charles (actor), 13
Brophy, Edward, V. (warden), 112
Brown, W. R. (warden), 47, 52, 54, 55
Brush, Augustus A. (warden), 49, 50
Bryan, William Jennings, 13, 107
Buchalter, Louis (aka Louis Lepke), "Czar of the Rackets," 157–59, 166
Bulletin, later *Sing Sing Bulletin* (prison paper), 122
Burger, Chief Justice Warren, 191
Butler, Harold (warden), 192, 219

Cagney, Jimmy (actor), 13, 135, 146
Capote, Truman, 12, 152, 173
Carey, Hugh (New York governor), 208
Carnegie, Dale, 167

Cashin, William J. (chaplain), 124, 129, 130

Casscles, James L. (warden), 192, 219

Chapin, Charles, "Rose Man of Sing Sing," 121, 122, 124–30, 142, 143, 193, 244

Chaplin, Charles (actor-director), 13, 123, 124

Cheever, John (author), 13, 188–90, 229–30

Cheever, Mary (John's wife), 190

Clancy, James (warden), 78–82

Clark, B. S. W. (warden), 44

Conan-Doyle, Arthur, 12, 78, 80

Connaughton (head guard), 56, 60

Conover, Ted (guard and author *Newjack*), 13, 206, 223–28, 230–34, 237

Cooke, Cardinal, 13

Cosa Nostra (Mafia), 129, 151

Crater, Joseph (judge), 183, 184

Crowley, Frank, inmate, 148, 149

Crystal, Billy (actor), 243

Cuomo, Mario (New York governor), 13, 195–96, 197, 199, 201

Curry (chaplain), 96

Dalsheim, Stephen (warden), 192, 219

Dannnemora (Clinton) Prison, 92, 101, 113, 120, 207

Danza, Tony (actor), 13

Davis, Bette (actor), 146

Davis, Edwin (executioner), 58, 59, 139

Davis, Ossie (actor-writer), 13, 241, 242

Deegan, John T. (warden), 187, 192, 219

Dempsey, Jack (boxer), 136

De Niro, Robert (actor), 243

Denno, Wilfred (warden), 166–68, 177, 180, 184, 187, 210, 215–16, 219

Derrick, Calvin (warden), 112

Dewey, Thomas (DA), 150, 151, 157–58, 164–65, 187

Diana, Princess of Wales, 231

Donovan, Thomas J. (Catholic prison chaplain), 171, 173, 174

Dorner, Frederick (head guard), 102, 104, 108

Dreiser, Theodore (author), 13

drug traffic, 81, 83, 89, 94, 116, 151, 192, 193, 231, 235–37

Durston, Charles (warden), 52, 54, 58

Edison, Thomas, 11, 48, 50, 52, 54

Edmonds, John (prison inspector), 30, 31, 34

Eisenhower, Dwight D., 178

electric chair, 48–51, (first execution) 52–54, (later executions) 55–56, 58–59, (first woman victim) 60, 63–64, 66, 94–97, 104, 107, 110, 116–17, 120–21, 130, 133, 136, 139–42, 150, 152, 155, 157–59, 162, 164, 166, 168, 170, 173, 180–81, 185–87, 207, 209–11, 214–16, (last execution) 217–19

Elliott, Robert (executioner), 139–42, 152, 156, 166, 220

Elmira Prison, 113

Falk, Peter (actor), 13

Fallon, William Joseph (Assistant DA), 103

Farina, Dennis (actor), 243

Feklisov, Alexander (KGB), 211

Fernandez, Raymond, "Lonely Hearts Killer," 170–74

Fischer, Brian (warden), 207, 219, 239, 241–44

Fish, Albert (cannibal), 154–56

Fogg, Walter (warden), 219

Ford, Henry, 107

Fowler, Gene (reporter), 142

Foxx, Red (comedian), 13

Francel, Joseph (Rosenbergs' executioner), 180–210

Frost, Jesse (warden), 64, 66, 67, 69–71

Gallo, "Crazy" Joe, 187, 188
Gamblers Anonymous, 167
Gard, William (warden), 192, 219
Garfield, John (actor), 146
Gigli, Benjamini (opera singer), 13, 123
Golden Rule Brotherhood, 80, 83, 90–92
Goord, Glenn (Commissioner State Department of Correctional Services), 229
Grant, David, J. (warden), 112
Grant, Ulysses S., 46
Gray, Judd, executed, 136–39, 141, 142
Great Meadow Prison, 98, 99
Greer, Bishop, 95
Greiner, Charles (warden), 206, 219, 237, 239

Haight, Edward (youngest person executed), 164
Hamby, George (inmate Nellie Bly watched executed), 117
Hammer, Julius (inmate father of Armand Hammer), 112, 121
Hawn, Goldie (actor), 13
Higgins, Joseph (warden), 192, 219
Hoover, Edgar, 158, 174, 178
Houdini, Beatrice (Harry's wife), 122, 142, 143
Houdini, Harry (escape artist), 12, 122, 123, 143, 205
Hover, Dow B. (executioner), 166, 216, 220, 221
Howard, Thomas (secretly photographed execution of Ruth Snyder), 140, 141
Hubbell, Gaylord (warden), 44
Hudson Link for Higher Education in Prison, 241
Hulbert, John (executioner), 116, 139
Human Rights Watch, 227, 228
Hunt, Washington (New York governor), 35

Javits, Jacob (US senator), 13
Johnson, Addison (warden), 61, 63, 64, 66

Kaufman, Judge (sentenced the Rosenbergs), 178, 179
Keane, John P. (warden), 202, 219
Kelley, L. J. (head guard), 216
Kelly, I. J. (warden), 209
Kemmler, William (first electrocution victim), 52–55, 58, 139
Kennedy, John (warden), 71, 72, 74, 75, 77, 78
Kirchwey, George (warden), 101, 103, 105, 107–109, 142
Koslowe, Rabbi Irving (prison chaplain), 176, 178, 180, 203–205

La Guardia, Fiorello (New York mayor), 123, 150, 151
Lawes, Joan Marie (Cherie) (warden's daughter), 119, 144
Lawes, Katherine (warden's wife), 114, 142, 156
Lawes, Lewis (warden), 12, 38, 56, 111–19, 121–24, 128–30, 133–35, 138–41, 145, 146–50, 152, 156, 158–62, 165, 177, 192, 193, 219, 220
Lehman, Herbert (New York governor), 150, 155, 156, 164
Leyra, Camilo Weston, 170–72, 174, 180–83
Liebowitz, Sam, 143, 158, 165, 182
Lincoln, Abraham, 11, 41, 175
Lipton, Thomas, 13, 132
Lockstep abolished, 61
Lockwood, Munson J. (warden), 36
Luciano, Charles "Lucky," 151, 164
Luckey, John (chaplain), 33–35, 41
Lunacy Commission, 52, 212, 217
Lynds, Elam (Sing Sing's first warden), 12, 13, 15–20, 23–25, 28–32, 45, 89

Mays, Eddie (last executed inmate), 186, 217–19
McCaffrey, John (chaplain), 130, 149
McCormick, Thomas (warden), 80, 82
Morgan, J. Pierpont, 66
Morgenthau, Robert (New York DA), 235
Morris, James McGrath (author, *Rose Man of Sing Sing*), 128
Moyer, William H. (warden), 112
Murder Incorporated, 11, 150, 157, 158
Mutual Welfare League, 93, 94, 98, 101, 107, 108, 121, 130, 135

Newgate Prison, 16–20, 25
New York gangs, 17, 42, 110
Nizer, Louis (attorney-author), 175

O'Brien, Pat (actor), 146
Osborne, Thomas Mott (warden), 12, 83, 85–116, 118, 242

Papa, Anthony, 235–37
parole, 61, 64, 116, 219, 227
Pataki, George E. (New York governor), 205, 207, 236
Pauley, Jane (TV reporter), 13
Pets in Prison, 117, 119, 149, 176, 230
Pirro, Janine (DA), 233
Plaza Hotel, 126
prison escapes and attempts, 31, 36, 37, 39, 50, 57, 63, 66–71, 74, 78, 93, 105, 106, 110, 115, 137, 161, 192, 205, 208, 216, 217, 233, 234
prison riots, 43, 78, 83, 189–201
Psychiatric Satellite Unit, 226
Pulitzer, Joseph, 50

Rattigan, C. F. (warden), 85
Riley, John B. (prison superintendent), 81, 101
River, Geraldo (TV reporter), 13
Rockefeller, Nelson (New York governor), 185, 186, 189, 209, 212, 236

Roosevelt, Franklin Delano, 89, 150, 186
Roosevelt, Theodore, 60
Rosenberg, Ethel, 11, 174–76, 178–82, 203, 210–12
Rosenberg, Julius, 11, 174–78, 180, 181, 210–12
Rosenberg (Meeropol), Michael, 178, 179, 211
Rosenberg (Meeropol), Robert, 178, 179, 182, 211
Runyon, Damon, 137
Russell, E. M. (warden), 43
Ruth, Babe, 13, 129

Sage, Omar V. (warden), 60
Schubin, Theodore (warden), 192–219
Seward, William Henry (New York governor), 204
Sing Sing archives, 207–21
Smith, Al (New York governor), 113, 117, 124, 133, 139, 150
Snyder, Ruth, 136–42
Snyder, William E. (warden), 166
Squire, Amos O. (prison doctor), 60, 61, 71–74, 104–106, 116, 124, 131, 132, 162
Star of Hope (inmate magazine), 82
Stop Prison Rape (SPR) (national organization), 228
Sullivan, James (warden), 200, 202, 219
Sunday, Billy (evangelist), 13, 95
Surratt, Mary, 175
Sutton, Willie, 150
Sweet, Charles (prison doctor), 132, 141, 142, 162, 164

Teresa, Mother, 13, 201, 202
Tierney (warden), 45
Tocqueville, Alexis de, 13, 15, 25, 28
tortures, 22, 34, 36, 38, 41
Tracy, Spencer (actor), 13, 146, 177
Tweed, Boss, 11

Valachi, Joseph, 129
Vanderbilt, Commodore, 12, 48

Walker, Jimmy (New York mayor), 150, 151
Wallace, Mike (TV reporter), 13
Walpole Prison, 237
Walters, Wilson (warden), 192, 195, 199, 200, 219
Ward, Ferdinand, 46
Warner Brothers, 146
Weed, George S. (warden), 82, 83
Wertham, Frederick (psychiatrist), 153–55, 169, 170, 173
Westinghouse, George, 11, 48–50, 52
White, Justice Byron, 190

Whitman, Charles (New York governor), 90, 96, 99, 101, 102, 110, 111
Whitney, Richard (former head of New York Stock Exchange), 12, 159–61
Willis, Bruce (actor), 13
Winchell, Walter (gossip columnist), 158
Wise, Rabbi Stephen, 13
women reporters who visited Sing Sing, 117
women's prison, 30, 31
Woodson, Jacqueline (author), 242

Yates (chaplain), 52

Zelig, Big Jack (hit man), 96